Political Theory and Praxis: New Perspectives

The University of Minnesota Press
gratefully acknowledges the support for its program
of the Andrew W. Mellon Foundation.
This book is one of those in whose financing
the Foundation's grant played a part.

POLITICAL THEORY

AND PRAXIS

NEW PERSPECTIVES

Edited by TERENCE BALL

UNIVERSITY OF MINNESOTA PRESS □ MINNEAPOLIS

Copyright © 1977
by the University of Minnesota.
All rights reserved.
Printed in the United States of America.
Published by the University of Minnesota Press,
2037 University Avenue Southeast,
Minneapolis, Minnesota 55455,
and published in Canada
by Burns & MacEachern Limited,
Don Mills, Ontario

Library of Congress Catalog Card Number 77-073320

ISBN 0-8166-0816-4

Dedication

To the Memory of Hannah Arendt

This collection of essays was to have been presented to Hannah Arendt on the occasion of her seventieth birthday. Now, sadly, we must instead dedicate it to her memory. With her death we lost one whose life exemplified the bios theoretikos. Her words are her deeds. They will be remembered.

> Grau, teuer Freund, ist alle Theorie
> Und grün des Lebens goldner Baum.

> —Goethe, *Faust*, 2038-39.

Preface

The nine essays presented here were commissioned and written especially for this volume. We had hoped to present our collective work to Dr. Hannah Arendt on her seventieth birthday. Her death in 1975, at age sixty-nine, dashed the hope. Although none of us was ever her student in a formal sense, we all learned from her, even—or perhaps especially—when we disagreed with her. And this is as it should be, for philosophy thrives on disagreement. But if we disagreed in our conclusions and differed in our methods, we agreed that the questions she posed were the right ones. Some of these questions are raised anew in the following essays.

In commissioning and assembling these essays, I incurred many debts, not the least of which is owed to the contributors. It is a tribute to their patience, perseverence, and good humor that none withdrew from our collective enterprise, despite the delays and disappointments that seem always to beset such efforts.

The publishing of scholarly works is nowadays a risky venture. For daring to take the risk I am grateful to the University of Minnesota Press. I am no less grateful to my colleagues for having fashioned an environment in which scholarly endeavor is not only possible but also pleasurable and to my students for making it more pleasurable still. It remains only to thank my son Jonathan for his help in preparing the index.

Terence Ball
Minneapolis, 12 April 1977

Contents

Political Theory and Praxis: New Perspectives

Editor's Introduction

Terence Ball

> *All theory is autobiography.*
>
> —Nietzsche

The aphorism is apt: a theory is a "structure of intentions"[1] which cannot be separated from an intender, a thinker whose creation the theory is. What is always intended is that we view the world in a new way and from a different perspective. After all, to theorize meant originally to see—literally at first and later metaphorically (as in Plato's "seeing with the mind's eye").[2] Theorizing, then, is the relationship between an observing subject and the object of scrutiny. This relationship has itself been viewed in various ways and from different perspectives. Conceptions of theory, of practice, and of their conceptual and practical interrelations have been and continue to be diverse and often divergent. The essays collected in this volume reflect this diversity even as they reflect upon it. Horkheimer's classic essay[3] notwithstanding, there are more than two ways of thinking about theory and its relation to practice.[4] His distinction between traditional and critical theory, valuable as it is, is but one way among many of approaching what Habermas calls "the theory-practice problematic."[5] Some of the other ways and byways are explored by the contributors to this volume.

Although this is a book by many hands, each is joined with the others in a common enterprise. In one sense we are interested in the same thing: the relationship between theory and practice. Yet in another, and perhaps profounder, sense we are not interested in the same thing at all—for the mean-

3

ings of the concepts theory and practice have themselves changed over time. If our individual essays are devoted to conceptual analysis (though not in the attenuated Anglo-American sense), our collective enterprise is devoted to conceptual history.[6] Taken together, our essays attest to the truth of Kierkegaard's remark that "concepts, like individuals, have their histories, and are just as incapable of withstanding the ravages of time as are individuals."[7]

I

This Kierkegaardian theme is sounded and explored in Nicholas Lobkowicz's essay in Part I. The theory-practice problematic today, he argues, is "radically different than in antiquity."[8] In his essay Lobkowicz explicates the classical concepts of theoria and praxis and traces their subsequent transmission and transmutation into the modern scientized concepts with which we are most familiar. Originally the theorist's way of life (the bios theoretikos) was contrasted with that of the active citizen (the bios politikos), each being distinct from the other and in its own way self-sufficient. This is *not* to say, however, that theoria and praxis are separate and distinct, for the activities of theorizing and political participation were, each in its own way, forms of praxis. And praxis was any activity that was self-contained, i.e., complete in itself and not directed as a means to an end. Thus praxis (doing) was contrasted with poiesis (making or producing), the latter being any activity directed toward achieving a separately identifiable end; poiesis is, in a word, instrumental (that we are tempted to say "practical" is itself an indication of our distance from the Greeks), or, in Weber's term, "Zweckrational."[9] Modern conceptions of theory and practice—including most notably the Marxist—tend to conflate the distinction between doing and making. In its scientized version, the relationship between theory and practice is viewed as an instrumental one; theory is related to practice as plan is to product(ion). Theories in the natural and social sciences are nowadays judged by their "yield," "pay-off," or "fruitfulness." A theory is said to be good—true, even—only to the extent that it produces results.[10] And since traditional or normative political theories have produced few, if any, results, they are of course deemed deficient or at any rate inferior to modern explanatory and instrumental theories of social and political behavior.[11] Lobkowicz concludes his essay—as Fay in his own way concludes this book—with a critique of the presuppositions and implications of this instrumentalist conception of theory and practice.

Whereas Lobkowicz treats the differences between classical and modern conceptions of theory and practice, the essays by J. Peter Euben and myself are concerned with ambiguities and tensions within the classical tradition. Euben sees Thucydides as the pivotal figure in the transition from the pre-philosophical pre-Socratic tradition of "thought and deed" to the reflexive or philosophical Socratic conception of "theory and practice." In the former a deed or an action acquires its full meaning and significance in talking about and reflecting upon it. On one level Thucydides's *History* is a telling about and reflection upon great deeds and misdeeds. But on another level it is a detached theoretical explanation of human folly and error, described as though the historian had a god's-eye view of events. Thucydides is both a storyteller and a theorist; or, rather, he is neither the one nor the other. For in the transition between the two traditions Thucydides, Euben says, "stands largely free of the older tradition but [is] not yet part of the philosophical reconstruction" that is the legacy of Socrates.[12]

In my own contribution to this volume I emphasize a different tension: that between the Platonic and Aristotelian conceptions of political theory. I begin with the widely accepted (but misleading) modern view that Plato is the "pure" and Aristotle the "practical" theorist. The essential distortedness of this view can best be revealed by attending to their different conceptions of theoria and praxis, along with their divergent views of the theorist's proper role. I agree with Lobkowicz that neither Plato nor Aristotle regarded theory and practice as wholly separate and distinct; indeed, theorizing is a special kind of praxis. There are in effect two kinds of praxis: theoretical and political. And I agree with Lobkowicz that, for Aristotle at least, theoretical praxis and political praxis are two quite different and distinct ways of life. They are not, however, of equal value, since, in Aristotle's view, political praxis is not a wholly self-contained and self-sufficient activity. Political praxis is therefore, by Aristotle's reckoning, an inferior kind of praxis—if indeed it is praxis at all. For political praxis begins already in Aristotle to become political poiesis: the seeds of later confusions are sown by Aristotle himself. In any event Aristotle concludes that theory and (political) praxis are autonomous spheres of activity and that, further, since theorizing is the more detached, active, and self-sufficient activity, the bios theoretikos is the superior way of life. For Aristotle the theorist qua theorist must be a stranger to political problems and concerns. The theorist's detachment from political life is an ideal to be sought if not always achieved. For Plato it is quite otherwise: the bios theoretikos can be lived to its fullest only within and through the polis, or more precisely, the well-ordered city-state depicted in the *Republic*. The structure of the polis must correspond to the structure of the theorist's soul (psyche).

Plato does not say that the philosopher ought to be king; he says instead that the philosopher *must* be king if he is to *be* a philosopher in the fullest sense of the term. Unlike Aristotle, Plato holds that the bios theoretikos cannot be lived alone, in splendid isolation; it must be lived in and through the well-ordered polis. It is in this sense that Aristotle must be accounted the "purer" and Plato the more "practical" theorist.

II

The essays in Part II turn our gaze from Greece to Germany. It is with Kant, especially, that the theory-practice problematic is reopened and regarded in a new way. Kant's ontological distinction between noumena and phenomena gives rise to his distinction between "practical" and "theoretical" philosophy. Practical philosophy is concerned with the free (acausal) noumenal realm, theoretical philosophy with the deterministic phenomenal realm; to the former belong political theory and ethics, to the latter, the natural sciences. As the gulf between noumena and phenomena is an unbridgeable ontological one, so too, it appears, is the gulf between theory and practice. And since man is both a "practical" and a "theoretical" being, he is divided within and from himself. Kant, his critics said, had found man whole but left him an inwardly shattered being. To put man back together again, to restore him to wholeness, was taken by Hegel as his primary philosophical labor.[13] It was left to Marx to argue that the task was not a philosophical one but a practical one (practical in a distinctly non-Kantian sense). Against Kant's critics Carl Raschke argues that Kant's critical philosophy leaves no unbridgeable chasm between theory and practice. That Kant himself does not construct such a bridge does not mean that he believed it a priori impossible to do so. How he could have done so—and in a way compatible with Marx's own dialectical conception of the unity of theory and practice—is suggested in Raschke's reconstruction (and, one might say, rehabilitation) of Kant.

If in the history of the theory-practice problematic Kant marks a watershed, Hegel and Marx represent The Great Divide. Despite their other deep and genuine differences, Hegel and Marx are at one in repudiating what they take to be the undialectical and ahistorical formalism of Kant. The nexus between theory and practice must, they maintain, be viewed dialectically and developmentally; that is, theory and practice are not abstract concepts but rather stand in relation to each other as poles in a dialectical unity. True, Marx charged Hegel with having reconciled theory and practice only abstractly and not actually.[14] But Marx's criticisms, fundamental and important though they are, should not be allowed to obscure his indebtedness to Hegel, and particularly — as Peter Fuss argues — to Hegel's concept of human emancipation. Neither Marx nor Hegel, however, was correct in inferring that human emancipation was to be achieved through the activities of a "universal class" — for Hegel the Civil Service, for Marx the proletariat. Marx's investing the proletariat with full responsibility for revolutionary action, Fuss maintains, merely remystifies the relation between theory and practice. But by now the damage has been done; all is a moral and political muddle. Fuss concludes his rather pessimistic essay with a call to begin again. In his own way Fuss contributes to the completion of the dialogue between Hegel and Marx, "a dialogue . . . which to this day remains radically unfinished."[15]

A dialogue between Marx and Nietzsche, by contrast, could hardly be begun, much less finished. For what common ground could possibly exist between the rationalist, revolutionary, egalitarian Marx and the irrationalist, reactionary, elitist Nietzsche? Just this: both, Edward Andrew argues, subscribed to an instrumentalist or scientist view of theory and practice. A theory, according to this view, is neither true nor false simpliciter; rather, it is useful or useless, efficient or inefficient, well or ill adapted to achieving practical ends. As the proof of the pudding is in the eating, so the proof of the theory is in the practice. Social and political praxis serves to test — and thus to verify or confute — the theory. What is being tested, however, is not the truth of the theory but its practicability — and the nerve or "will" of the practitioner who would remold and remake political reality. To say that Marx and Nietzsche shared this instrumentalist conception of theory and practice is not to deny that their differences are genuine and deep; it is merely to emphasize the pervasiveness of the instrumentalist view of theory and practice. Andrew's essay thus underscores and provides additional evidence for Lobkowicz's claim that the modern conception of theory and practice is a scientist one. And in this respect the Germany of Marx and Nietzsche is light years away from the Greece of Thucydides, Plato, and Aristotle.

III

Might not this vast distance yet be bridged? Or, to speak in the Hegelian idiom, might these disagreements be simultaneously preserved and transcended? The essays in Part III are critical examinations of recent attempts to bring some order out of an apparent moral, political, and conceptual chaos. Our confusion stems in large measure from what Lobkowicz calls the scientizing of theory and practice, which is perhaps best exemplified in the social and behavioral sciences.

Hannah Arendt, to whose memory this volume is dedicated, attempted to bring some order out of this chaos. Richard Bernstein's essay is both a tribute to and a critique of her attempt. Arendt begins by reverting to, and recovering, the forgotten meaning of a concept such as action (praxis) and then goes on to distinguish it from other concepts, e.g., labor and work.[16] Our modern confusions are conceptual ones in that they stem in part from our failure to make crucial distinctions. As our vocabulary is impoverished so too is our world. And yet our impoverished vocabulary, Arendt suggests, is an instrument well suited to describing a world diminished by the near-absence of action, or praxis. In a sense the life of action is for Arendt what the bios theoretikos was for Aristotle—self-moved, self-sufficient, and self-justifying. Her prephilosophical, pre-Socratic conception of the primacy of action relegates theory to a secondary role. The theorist's task is a hermeneutic one; it is to interpret, to illuminate and discern the meaning of, action. For since action is by its very nature open-ended, its meaning may not be known to the actor himself. Arendt's theorist—like Hegel's philosopher—reflects upon and finds meaning in action only retrospectively: "Action reveals itself fully only to the story-teller, that is, to the backward glance of the historian . . ."[17] For Arendt, as for Thucydides (see Euben's essay), the theorist's task is a historical one; it is to recall, recover, round out, and give meaning to human deeds.

But since, on Arendt's reckoning, the realm of action has virtually disappeared from the modern world, the theorist becomes of necessity an archaeologist, reconstructing the distant past to remind the present of the extent of its loss. Most important, we have all but lost the capacity to act freely, that is, politically.[18] One of Arendt's persistent themes, as Bernstein notes, is that action has given way to behavior, that is, the sort of regular, routinized activity that is amenable to social-scientific analysis precisely because it exhibits "behavioral regularities." Action, being free and essentially unpredictable, is best studied by the political theorist; but behavior, being unfree and predictable, is best studied by the social scientist. If political theory be dead, that is because politics is dead. Political theory thrives only in a world in which action —political praxis—is possible. The revival and recovery of the one depends upon the revival and recovery of the other. Political praxis may be in eclipse, or decline, but we can never say with certainty that political praxis has disappeared forever. For, given Arendt's understanding of action as involving new beginnings, one can never rule out the possibility of praxis arising in novel forms. Even in modern mass society — the antithesis of political community — the possibility of acting politically is not entirely absent. Such was the case, for example, in the resistance movements in the Second World War, in the early civil rights movement in the American South, and in the initial stages of resistance to the Vietnam War.[19] Still these are, in Arendt's view, brilliant exceptions to the dismal rule. Whether exception will become rule, and rule exception, we cannot say: the future is open-ended and cannot be foretold.

Raymond Nichols, like Arendt, conceives of "politics as action"; but, like Bernstein, he criticizes Arendt for having drawn some distinctions too sharply (as when she categorically distinguishes action from labor and work) and others not at all. Arendt's view of action as unpredictable and open-ended, says Nichols, bears a discomfiting resemblance to the degraded and counterfeit forms of action advocated by modern Hippies, Yippies, and assorted countercultists. If action is to have meaning it must, he argues, have limits; and limits are set by traditions which supply a contextual and conceptual setting, a stage upon which to act. To act without a stage, without the limits defined by a common language and tradition, is not to *act* at all; it is to play the part of a buffoon. The modern "rebel" whose "action" is all sound and fury signifying nothing has his prototype in the buffoon. The genuine rebel might well have his prototype in the harlequin, the fool or jester of courtly times. Whereas buffoonery is simply misbehavior, harlequinade is action of a profoundly political sort. Indeed it is harlequinade, Nichols argues, which in our day "emerges as a model for rebellion: a form of innovating activity (action), directed at and occurring in a public, touching on public authority."[20] To the extent that la condition humaine is la comédie humaine, it requires comedic illumination of its darker recesses.

In the final essay in this volume Brian Fay asks — if I may translate his question into Arendtian terms — how might unfree and self-destructive behavior be displaced by free action? Fay rejects the behaviorist answer that men may be forced to be free. Instrumentalist theories of social change and behavioral modification, being the property of "experts," tend to be put to manipulative and coercive use (as in — to cite an extreme case — *A Clockwork Orange*). To be forced to be free by an expert is very nearly a contradiction in terms. How then, Fay asks, might people change themselves? Against the instrumentalist conception of theory and practice Fay outlines his own "educative" model.[21] This model, which is rooted in critical theory, "is predicated on the notion that changing people's basic understanding of themselves and their world is a first step in *their* (my italics) radically altering the self-destructive patterns of interaction that characterize their social relationships."[22] But this task is all the more difficult because systematic self-misunderstanding is embedded in concrete social structures and practices (e.g., advertising) which some people, at least, have an interest in maintaining. How, Fay asks, are changes in people's self-understanding to come about, except by changing these structures? And since these changes will be resisted even by those whom the theory is meant to liberate, can their resistance be overcome in ways consistent with the educative model—i.e., in ways that are themselves educative rather than coercive and manipulative? Fay rejects the instrumentalist contention that the noncoercive and nonviolent society must be achieved by violent and coercive means. But he also rejects the idealist claim that social structures and practices are caused by ideas (but not vice versa) and can be changed simply by changing men's ideas. For the idealist there is no problem of *structural* resistance, because the idealist has no appreciation of structural determinism to begin with. Fay accepts the fact of structural determination without, however, opting for the instrumentalist's solution to the problem of resistance. In looking for a via media between these extremes Fay—like the other contributors to this volume—shows how theory and the theorist may shed some light in these dark times.

PART I
Origins

I

On the History of Theory and Praxis

Nicholas Lobkowicz
(Translated by Jere Paul Surber)

Let me begin with a brief explanation of the structure of my essay. In the first section I sketch the two most important contexts in which theory and praxis were discussed in antiquity. In the second section I take up two problems that were discussed in antiquity in both these contexts: the primacy of theory over praxis and the impossibility of scientizing praxis. In further remarks I attempt to show how it has come about that the nature of the problem today is radically different than in antiquity. In a short final section I present a few thoughts concerning what are, in my opinion, the problems that presently require further discussion.

I

The first context in which theory and praxis were treated in antiquity is in the discussion of the bioi, the human ways of life, which allegedly goes back to Pythagoras but which probably first arose in the Platonic academy. It originates in the typically Greek manner of posing the question concerning who is the happiest, the wisest, or the best (a question often asked of the Delphic oracle). Cicero reports that Pythagoras answered the question about what he understood the neologism *philosophos* to mean by comparing the three different types of men who attend festive games:[1] some come to peddle their wares for a profit, others to achieve honor with their bodily strength, and still

13

others only to gaze at the statues, the athletic accomplishments, and to hear the official speeches. This is true of men in general: some desire money and sensual gratification, others power and the authority of command, but others —the philosophers—choose to contemplate the most beautiful things, tōn kallistōn theorian. Pythagoras thinks the philosophers have chosen the best way; they are fettered by no passions and devote themselves to the divine.

Whether Pythagoras actually answered in this way or whether the story is a legend of the Platonic academy, it is based upon two plays on words which are untranslatable in English. The origin of the word theory is usually explained by indicating that theoria literally means "watching" and is related to theoros, the designation for the spectator at festival performances. However, the Greek listener also knew that theoros was originally the title of the emissary of a polis who was supposed to consult the oracle and that the official delegation that a Greek polis sent to a neighboring city-state was designated theoria, whether it was to take part in the sacred rituals of the cult of the city-state or, on its own initiative, to honor the divinity of the neighboring polis. *Theoria* had so much to do with witnessing festival performances that it was self-evident to the Greeks that one witnessed a sacred performance. This sacred connotation of theoria was further reinforced by the fact that this expression reminded the Greeks of the word theos, or god. Not only Plutarch but also the Greek ·Fathers of the Church like Gregory of Nyssa, Basil the Great, and Pseudo-Dionysius would later call attention to this connection: that theoria is already on the basis of its etymology not simply secular witnessing but observation of god and the divine.

The complex of ideas about the types of men or the human ways of life is taken up by numerous Greek authors, complicated to the point of obscurity by Plato, and finally terminologically fixed by Aristotle with his characteristic knack for drawing pregnant distinctions. According to his account, there are three basic ways of life: the life devoted to theoria, which is that of the philosopher or, what expresses the same thing for the Greeks, the scientist; the life of the enfranchised citizen of the polis devoted to political praxis; and the life of desire of the rich man of leisure. As Aristotle states at the beginning of the *Eudemian Ethics*, however, this is not a division of *all* human ways of life. For the three ways of life that have been mentioned are each in its own way perfect: they presuppose a certain material independence and are thereby styles of life in which the free (in contrast to the slaves) and relatively well-to-do (in contrast to the daily wage earners, artisans, and impoverished farmers) members of the polis can pursue their eudaimonia, their objective fulfillment, which is, at the same time, their subjective happiness. Of course the life of desire is immediately judged to be of lesser value in accordance with the prevalent Greek conceptions. As Aristotle ironically remarks, the saying of the legendary Assyrian king Sardanapalus, "I possess only what I have eaten and the desires which I have received through passion," could just as well have been written on the grave of a bull.[2] Thus, only two genuine alternatives finally remain: the bios theoretikos, the philosopher's way of life which is devoted to the eternal and divine and, for this reason, is a bios xenikos, a life almost unavoidably estranged from the polis; and the bios praktikos or politikos, the politician's way of life, which is directed to the destiny and daily problems of the polis.

Three observations seem appropriate regarding this first context. The first is that, on the one hand, the opposition between the theoretical life of the philosopher and the practical life of the politician was in no way viewed in antiquity — at least up to the Neoplatonists — as irreconcilable. Socrates and Plato characterize the philosopher as the true politician and Plato sets forth the ideal of the Philosopher-king in the *Republic*. Aristotle concedes that even the philosopher cannot wholly avoid participating in the life of the polis.[3] Later, the Stoics will also prefer a "mixed way of life" and the philosopher will attempt to be, if not a ruler like Marcus Aurelius, then a counselor to the rulers like Seneca or at least an influential politician like Cicero. However, this opposition is viewed as fundamental: it is the biographical expression of the opposition between the eternal and divine on the one hand and the transitory and human on the other. It is no accident that Aristotle based his demand that the philosopher not withhold himself from political life upon the statement that the philosopher is also a man. Basically, theorein is already understood in antiquity, as it is later in Christian mysticism, as an acting of the divine in man, whereas everyday political activity constitutes the typically human.

My second remark concerns the fact that, upon closer examination, this discussion has an ideological component. It serves to justify the way of life of the philosopher who pursues interests which, at first glance, have nothing to do with the problems of society.[4] Aristotle uses two types of arguments. On the one hand, he points out that the theoretical life concerns itself with the divine, that it is an actualization of noûs and thereby of the divine in man, and that it is pleasing to the gods. On the other hand, he tries to prove that all the advantages that distinguish the life of the enfranchised citizen are present in an exceptional degree in the philosophical life. The activity of the philosopher is less tiring and can be pursued with less interruption than that of the politician; the philosopher is freer from the exigencies of daily life than is the politician; he is more independent than the politician; and so on. This discussion serves as a self-justification of the philosopher — a point which one should not lose sight of even in contemporary discussions concerning the primacy of theory or praxis.

Third, this discussion obviously has very little to do with what we today call theory and praxis. Basically, it is not at all about an opposition between theory and praxis but about two forms of praxis: the praxis and life-style of the theoretician and the praxis and life-style of the practician. For this reason the problem never arises for the Greeks in the sense of a contrast of theory as inactivity to praxis as activity; both are activities that presuppose a high degree of leisure in the sense of being independent of those activities that serve only to sustain life.

In the second context in which theory and praxis were treated in antiquity, the discussion likewise did not fundamentally concern a relationship of something like thought and action. The second context deals with the theory of "scientific" knowledge; strictly interpreted, it concerns the various forms of theory. Already in Plato the discussion of the ways of life leads to considerations about the ways of knowing that correspond to them. If the philosopher, on the one hand, contemplates the eternal and divine and, on the other, speaks about man, his praxis, and the polis, he obviously deals with entirely different domains of objects to which must also correspond different ways of knowing. Again it is Aristotle who fixes the terms of this discussion. There is a knowledge of the eternal and unchanging which one can only observe: the unchanging structures of the sublunar world, the regularities and objects of mathematics to which the order of the heavenly bodies corresponds in reality, and finally the movers of the heavenly bodies, including, above all, the Unmoved Mover. It is with these objects that theoretical knowledge is concerned. At the same time there is knowledge of those things that are finite, changing, and fashioned by man. Practical knowledge deals with human action and its orientation toward the good, poetic knowledge with the production and orientation of man toward a work.

This tripartite division of the modes of knowledge is neither a classification of science in the strict sense of the word nor a division of cognition in the comprehensive sense in which, for example, perception could also count as being cognitive. Rather, it is concerned with a classification of the sphere of cognition that can be articulated in language and within which one can argue pro or con. This is important inasmuch as Aristotle apparently thought that only theoretical knowledge is science in the authentic sense of the word, whereas practical and, even more clearly, poetic knowledge are relegated to the border area between science and experience. This is because only the objects of theoretical knowledge are things that cannot be other than they actually are and—what constitutes for the Greeks the essence of science—regarding which it can be seen, on the basis of a knowledge of the respective aitiai, that their factic being "thus and not otherwise" is necessary. In contrast to this, practical knowledge, as Aristotle presents it, e.g., in the *Nichomachean Ethics*, is an understanding of relationships that are essentially contingent.

This already suggests why there is indeed an ongoing discussion throughout antiquity about theory and praxis but almost never one about their relation to one another. For the ancients this relation does not basically obtain, since theory fundamentally deals only with the necessary (and, to that extent, divine) whereas human praxis is contingent. This is, in fact, the ultimate meaning of Aristotle's famous assertion that only the uneducated could expect the same sort and degree of precision (akribeia) in political science as in the theoretical sciences.[5] Aristotle understands akribeia to mean two things: the precision with which a state of affairs can be confirmed, and the degree to which the aitiai can be comprehended. *Aitiai* here means the grounds that determine the "cannot-be-otherwise" of this state of affairs and that, so far as it is known, provides the basis for the possibility of the precision of knowledge. As Aristotle again and again states, it is neither possible nor necessary in the sphere of human behavior and human action to establish more than a mere "so it is" (oti). There is no explanation proving the necessity of the facts on the basis of a deduction from axioms in which essential relationships are grasped, i.e., no knowledge (dioti).[6]

This conception has three consequences. First, practical knowledge cannot be an end in itself. Regarding the eternal and unchanging things, it is meaningful to strive to attain knowledge for its own sake, considering its divine nature. For the knowledge of the divine is, as is every instance of knowledge, an assimilation into its object. He who concerns himself with the divine imitates it. Nonetheless, this imitation is never the application of a theory to praxis but resembles the relationship that the religious man believes holds between prayer and daily life. He who dwells with God in prayer acts rightly—though he cannot say that prayer gives him practicable insights. In contrast to this, a sort of knowledge which may, on principle, arrive at nothing that can be viewed as necessary, as with practical knowledge, can only be meaningful if it serves some other end. Certainly practical knowledge also aims at truth, but this truth is itself of a practical sort and is pursued only for the sake of good action.

Second, the practical knowledge dealt with by the philosopher does not suffice when deciding how one should conduct oneself in a particular situation. On the one hand, right action is something entirely concrete and no knowledge, not even the practical, can comprehend the particular; it always concerns the universal. On the other hand, practical knowledge is imprecise. To employ one of Plato's examples, ethical laws and norms as well as civil laws are not a work of precision like that of the turner but are more comparable to the game rules in athletic contests. They merely state in a general way what applies in most cases. For this reason the ethics of antiquity assigns a tremendous significance to experience and prudence. Whatever significance a practical knowledge about ethical and political relationships may have, when it deals with concrete action it is far surpassed by the significance of experience or, strictly speaking, "experiencedness" and that specific ability, which can be developed only through practice, to decide rightly in a particular situation.

Third and last, this conception of praxis as lacking in precision is carried over without much reflection to poiesis. The distinction between praxis and poiesis can be best rendered in English by our much less precise distinction between doing and making. Praxis, or doing, is that human mode of conduct that contains its meaning in itself and whose completion therefore consists of its satisfactory accomplishment. The constantly recurring Greek example is flute playing, but all ethical and political actions are interpreted according to this model. Poiesis, or making, by contrast, is production: its completion and meaning subsist in the work that it leaves behind. He who builds a ship or attempts to cure a sick man has ultimately achieved nothing as long as the ship is not finished or health is not restored. By contrast, he who acts as a responsible member of the polis never finishes, because every political action entails others, but he can at each instant be at his goal, which is to act as a good man. The authentic political action, as the Greeks understand it, is not something like a path or step *to* completion but a part of the completion itself.

What most concerns me here is the claim that, in relation to theoria, the Greek thinks of poiesis in very much the same way as he does of praxis. Poiesis, too, deals with contingencies, on account of which there is no theoretical knowledge of production but only a poetic knowledge which is oriented almost totally toward experience and a facility analogous to prudence. Thus there are, to be sure, many discussions in Greek medicine concerning whether the physician must acquaint himself with the theoretical disciplines; but this is, almost without exception, an academic discussion which concerns only the education (paideia) of the physician, not his art of healing. In deciding whether he should dispense a certain medicine for a particular disease, the theoretical sciences are hardly useful to the Greek or Roman physician. Of much greater significance is the ability of the physician. Thus, even into the late Middle Ages, medicine is not designated as a scientia but as an ars, just as we also speak nowadays of the art, not of the science, of healing.

So much for the two contexts in which the discussion about theory and praxis arose in antiquity. Within them, theory and praxis are never discussed in the modern sense of a theory that is applicable in practice. There are several reasons for this. First, theory and science are never conceived as a system of propositions but as an activity. This view, which was self-evident in the Middle Ages even into the fourteenth century, has been rehabilitated for the first time in modernity by Heidegger.[7] Second, praxis is not identical with human action which can be contrasted to knowing. The discussion always concerns three types of activity, theoria, praxis, and poiesis. Third, theory fundamentally concerns contexts in which both doing and making are impossible. As it is suggestively stated by Aristotle, "We are all agreed that an object of science cannot be otherwise than it is; the object of science exists necessarily."[8] Fourth and last, for the Greeks it is contingency that specifically characterizes the human sphere: in the realm of praxis and poiesis no necessity prevails and it is therefore impossible for science to establish relevant aitiai.

II

If one surveys the history of the pair of concepts theory-praxis from the Greeks to the present, one soon sees that, in spite of the numerous detours and even attempts to reverse this development, two things happened. First, the primacy of theory over praxis gradually became more questionable to the philosopher, until today it appears almost impossible still to maintain this position seriously. Second, though it occurred largely because of a misunderstanding, the attempt was made to an ever greater extent and obviously with an increasing degree of success to falsify the Greek concept of the impossibility of scientizing praxis.

The first development mentioned above in no way first begins—as one might think — with Marxism. Rather, the Christianity of the first centuries seems to have produced the decisive impetus. The Greek Fathers of the Church already felt themselves compelled, on the basis of the Christian doctrine of charity, to attribute to the practical life an essentially greater significance than antiquity would have considered defensible. This concerns not merely the message of Christ, in which very little is said of theory in either the ancient or modern senses, but a lot of human actions and ways of relating to God and to one another. Also relevant is the fact that in the first centuries of Christianity, Neoplatonism had developed a new understanding of both theoria and the practical life. For classical antiquity, theory in the sense of a genuine contemplation of the divine and theory in the sense of a scientific analysis were not sharply distinguished — and this in spite of the clear insight of, for example, Aristotle that God can only be inferred as the primary cause and cannot be experienced as an immediate given. For the Neoplatonists, however, the concept of a mystical union with the divine One leads to a sharp separation between a discursive science and theoria in the sense of contemplation. With Gregory of Nyssa Christian theology also takes over this distinction. In his homily on the Song of Songs Gregory distinguishes between two sorts of theoria: one which corresponds to the Platonic dialectic and thus to science which works with many concepts and another which is a "seeing of God in the darkness," that is, contemplation.[9] This Neoplatonic exaltation of theoria as an ultimate mystical contemplation which was taken over by the Christian authors results in the blurring of that sharp distinction, which was still evident in the Roman Stoics, between the practical life as a political life of fulfillment and all other life-styles. The vita activa becomes transformed from a bios politikos to, on the one hand, a life of Christian charity and, on the other, to a collective concept of all life-styles and vocations that have to do with the necessitas praesentis vitae. As for the life of Christian charity, it becomes a vita which, as the complement to contemplation, has incomparably more importance than antiquity was prepared to ascribe to the bios politikos.

After Origen it then becomes customary to carry on the discussion about the vita activa and the vita contemplativa by means of the Gospel's account of Mary and Martha.[10] How far removed is the Christian view from that of classical antiquity becomes quite clear in the sermons of Augustine. Augustine cites Christ's suggestion that Mary has chosen the best way which will not be taken from her, while Martha would dedicate herself only to the corporeal and thereby transient needs of the Lord. Yet he suggests that Martha's activity is the task of the Christian in this world: Quod agebat Martha, ibi sumus, quod agebat Maria, hoc speramus (While that which Mary did is what we hope for, Martha's doing is where we are now). The theoretical life can attain its fulfillment only in the afterlife. Though it continually remains the ultimate goal, it becomes, as it were, a reward for at least partially offering up the vita contemplativa in this world for the vita activa.[11]

After the end of the fifteenth century this view is gradually repressed again because the distinction between the two generae vitae becomes the schema for the discussion of the various aspects of the life of the religious orders and later of the advantages of the various orders. The Christian laity plays an increasingly lesser role in this discussion, and, for this reason, the problematic of the bioi or vitae perishes with the disappearance of the social relevance of the religious orders at the beginning of modernity, or else it becomes a mere academically discussed subdivision of practical theology and the theology of the orders.

Furthermore, a similar fate befalls the Greek discussion of the modes of knowledge. For the long time it remains a subdivision of Christian theology — as in the discussions in the High Middle Ages about whether theology is or is not a theoretical discipline (that it is, had been self-evident to the ancient authors) or whether it contains dimensions of practical science within it (as the Franciscan order especially and Duns Scotus obviously thought). With Descartes's radical concept that there is only one science, namely that constructed on the model of mathematics, this disucssion comes to a sudden halt. As he says in the *Regulae ad directionem ingenii*, there is only a single sort of human wisdom, which is just as little differentiated by the distinctness of its objects as light is when it falls on various things.[12]

In this development the High Middle Ages plays a somewhat different role than one might think, given the usual conceptions about scholasticism. For scholasticism is in no way only a high point of systematic Christian theology; it is also a point at which certain insights of older Christian authors are covered over and forgotten and in which later errors have their origin. I would like to illustrate this with three brief examples.[13]

First. The self-assured manner in which Thomas Aquinas, for example, defends the primacy of the theoretical over the practical is a return — even in its Christian modification — to the ancient conception which, if one may so express it, reverts to a viewpoint older than the evangelical conception of someone like Augustine. In the various discussions about the nature of theology or even about the characteristics of the visio beatifica, like that which occurs in the thirteenth and fourteenth centuries between the Dominicans and Franciscans, it is as if Aristotle and Augustine struggle with one another. In this dialogue, which continues through two centuries, St. Thomas is the exponent of the ancient conception and Bonaventure and Duns Scotus the exponents of the Christian conception.

Second. The encyclopedists of the twelfth and early thirteenth centuries (notably Hugo and Richard of St. Victor and, later, Dominicus Gundissalvi) had developed an interest in poetic disciplines which accorded with a realistic observation of the technology that had been advancing since the beginning of the second century. Thus Hugo of St. Victor also recognized, in addition to a propadeutic logica and the traditionally understood theorica and practica, a mechanica. He explicitly describes this as the group of those disciplines and arts that, as an omnium rerum fabrica, direct those activities without which we cannot live but with the aid of which we can live better. As far as I can establish, the same thoughts go back to the Arabs; but although the rediscovery of the Greeks, above all of Aristotle, occurs through the mediation of the Arabs, the influence of the theoretical knowledge of the Greeks, which had been forgotten in the meantime, is so great that in high scholasticism the interest in what we would today call the disciplines of production almost totally disappears. Of course St. Thomas also recognizes a scientia factiva which corresponds to the poetic knowledge of the Greeks, but the examples that he employs are so sporadic and abstract that one clearly sees that it interests him solely for the sake of the completeness of the classification of science. As for the rest, the forerunners of modern natural science in the thirteenth and fourteenth centuries (e.g., Grosseteste, Dietrich of Freiberg, Roger Bacon, and Nicholas of Oresme) conduct their investigations exclusively from speculative and sometimes religious interest (as when optics is studied in connection with the metaphysics of light). The fact that their research might be of significance for the fabrica rerum is indeed occasionally mentioned by these authors but only as an aside.

Third. In the High Middle Ages the fateful confusion between doing and making begins to make itself felt, a confusion from which the theory-praxis discussion will suffer for centuries. Certainly St. Thomas, as a good Aristotelian, is obviously familiar with the distinction between praxis and poiesis as actio and factio. But when he is not commenting on Aristotle and speaks in general about human actions, he continually illustrates actio, the medieval counterpart to praxis, by activities of production. This is more than a conceptual sloppiness, of which St. Thomas can hardly be accused. It is a consequence of, among other things, the idea, which is foreign to the Greeks, that God has created the world and, to that extent, can be understood mutatis mutandis as producer. In spite of the lack of interest in the details of the activities of production, this leads to an immense increase in the value of poiesis and eventually to a disappearance of the distinction between praxis and poiesis. An indication of this is the title of the first major surgical treatise of the West: the *Practica chirurgica* of Roger of Salermo. Where one would have expected "mechanica" or "poietica," it reads "practica"—just as we today also speak of a medical practice.

It is now often asserted that the "revolutionary" change from medieval to modern science was due to a practical or, to speak more precisely, poetic interest. Marxist authors in particular have tried to prove that the emergence of modern science has its origin in the novel needs of production or even in an interest in goal-oriented action and in possible technical utility.[14] Even if one would have to deduce the type of modern empirical theories transcendentally from the same interests (which appears in no way convincing to me), this idea is *historically* false. However fundamentally different the concept of science of a Descartes, Galileo, or Newton may be from that of someone like St. Thomas Aquinas, they are agreed in one respect: viz., theory requires no justification for its existence through praxis or poiesis. In fact, one can go even further: the Cartesian concept of science excludes such a justification on principle because in it theory and cognition become identical. The essential difference between the medieval and modern concept of science lies precisely in the following two facts. First, the new type of theory claims to be the sole legitimate form not only of science but of sound knowledge in general. Second, the view arises that, with this new type of theory, a scientizing of human action is possible which, however, is first brought to bear not in the area of production at all but in that of action. Long before the view that the modern natural-scientific theory is relevant to production begins to make its advance, it is regarded as self-evident that the classical practical disciplines, i.e., ethics and politics, can be scientized with the help of the new theory. Not only for Descartes and Hobbes but even for Malebranche, Leibniz, and Wolff it goes without saying that the Aristotelian thesis of the impossibility of scientizing praxis or of the ultimately unscientific nature of practical knowledge is baŝed simply on the inadequacy of ancient and medieval theory. Locke proves that this is in no way merely a mistake of the rationalists. Though he denies that physics possesses genuine certainty, he thinks that it could be shown that moral and political ideas are "as incontestible as those in mathematics" and that they could be demonstrated with the same degree of precision "as that a triangle has three angles equal to two right ones."[15] If one tries to summarize this characteristic development in a nutshell, one must perhaps say: not only has the classical view that there are various types of knowledge that are irreducible to one another disappeared, but, even more, the discovery of the potential deducibility of directions for production from theory is as unreflectively transferred to action as antiquity had transferred its thesis of the nondeducibility of practical directions to production. The ancient-medieval and the modern mistakes mutually complement one another. However, whereas the ancient error rests, at least in part, on the idea that a theory that is relevant to production is of no use, the modern error arises from the fact that the difference between doing and making is forgotten and all human action is gradually conceived according to the model of production. The concept of an ability to totally scientize human action that results from this has, at the same time, the consequence that the thesis of the primacy of theory finally becomes untenable. For if every direction for action ultimately can be deduced from a theory and all theory can be translated into directions for production, there is nothing left as autonomous in either knowledge or action which could be contrasted to the other as superior. For this reason it is no accident that in the epoch from Descartes to Kant the theory-praxis problematic is almost completely silenced or, in any case, is almost never explicitly and systematically discussed.

III

It would be too great a task for a brief presentation to treat the very complex rediscovery of the difference between doing and making in Kant and its later confusion in German idealism. Nevertheless, two remarks about Marxism seem to be called for and can also serve as a transition to my concluding comments. There is certainly no philosophical tradition in which so much was and is said about theory and praxis as in the Marxist—and in which, at the same time, it remains so radically unclear what theory and praxis actually are. Rüdiger Bubner, in his sensible booklet on theory and praxis as post-Hegelian abstractions, has ironically but rightly pointed out that in this tradition praxis is simply everything that cannot be identified as theory.[16] But conversely, the same could be said of theory. If one follows the development from the Left Hegelians up to the New Left or Soviet philosophy, theory is first of all an abridged version of the philosophy of Hegel, then the critique of Hegelian philosophy, then the critique of the existing order from ultimately Hegelian premises, then Marxism which has become ossified into a palliative doctrine, and finally everything that is advocated by the professional at any given time—whether this be the party or the intellectual, who, according to Horkheimer's famous statement about traditional and critical theory, should bear in mind that true theory constantly must be reformulated in accordance with new conditions. Parallel to this, praxis is first a critique of the existing order derived from theory, then the history of laboring humanity, then a history of the workers' movement, and finally everything that the progressive theoretician does, to which Engels (who is thoughtlessly parroted in this and in many other respects by Soviet philosophy) adds industry and experimentation. Only one thing is common to these variants of praxis: they have almost nothing at all to do with praxis in the original sense but represent an enormous reduction of all human action to poiesis. Even at those points where praxis is understood as political action, it is always the production of a state of affairs.

This is even true when it is recognized, e.g., by Habermas and the Yugoslavian Praxis group, that the reduction of all essential human activities to labor and production, which is especially characteristic of the "hard-line" Marxists, is an untenable simplification.[17] For even emancipatory action must finally be interpreted according to the model of poiesis: it is the production of a situation that does not contain its justification in itself but derives it from its results.

The conclusion that I want to draw from these observations is that, contrary to all appearances, when taken in the strict sense there never was an account of theory and praxis, in any event not of their relation to one another. There were discussions of various types of praxis and various sorts of theory; there were discussions of the relation between theory and production, between theory and history, and between theory and experience. But the real problem, which the famous passage in the *Nichomachean Ethics* poses, has never really been genuinely discussed: namely, is it possible to develop a theory relevant to praxis which actually is a theory and which is actually relevant just to praxis and not to every other possible thing?

If one wanted to discuss this question today, one would have to begin by saying something more precise about praxis and then, in addition, about theory. Basically, the philosophers have made it rather easy for themselves: instead of looking around and carefully recording what man does, they developed rubrics and induced generations to think within them. This reproach applies less to the philosophers of antiquity than to those who think in the categories developed by them, that is, to their successors and ourselves. For the original context in antiquity of the theory-praxis discussion, the question of the ways of life did not lay claim to being an adequate presentation of all sorts of human conduct. It concerned the question of the good life which, moreover, was not accessible to most. And regarding the discussion of the sorts of knowledge, it corresponded to the three fundamental interests that the aristocratic Greek recognized: science, politics, and the multitude of activities that were carried out by slaves and artisans, as well as by the physicians and those who occasionally wrote plays and poetry. By contrast, if we today ask ourselves whether it is sufficient to divide the human modes of conduct into theory, praxis, and poiesis or simply into theory and praxis, the former comprising knowing and thinking, the latter acting, we must have serious doubts. If it is obvious that rose gardeners and municipal politicians have something in common, what serves to contrast their activities to scholarly activities? Is there any reason to act, as is readily done today, as if there are two essential activities, science and politics, or thinking and working — and everything that we do and that appears relevant to us could be subsumed under such categories? Is the dialogue that occurs at a meeting theory or praxis? Is the activity of an administrative official, whose task consists of sorting documents, praxis or poiesis? And what of the thousands upon thousands of activities that men perform daily: driving to work, reading the newspaper, preparing for a holiday trip, delivering a lecture, conferring with other men, making way for another on the street, opening cans, and shooting films?

Naturally, one can comprehend all of this as praxis and contrast it to theory, whether in the sense of a bios theoretikos of an individual scientist or in the sense of that which is set down in scientific works. And naturally one can then immediately add that all of this is socially mediated. But nothing is ultimately accomplished with such coarsely meshed concepts. What is required is a realistic survey of what man does and then an attempt to order this complex profusion according to types of activities, of which there are certainly more than three or only two.

The next step would consist of asking what and how we know and can know about each type of activity. Thereby, for almost every type of activity there would correspond a profusion of theories. Take, for example, research and teaching. The mass of specific activities of which this type of activity consists can be investigated by psychologists, sociologists, historians, linguists, theologians, and by physiologists, chemists, and physicists. Each approaches this type of activity with his own type of theory — and each undoubtedly has something meaningful to contribute. But is this sufficient to enable us to say that we would have succeeded in scientizing human praxis, whether it is in the sense that contingent praxis becomes accessible to science or in the sense that we have or can only meaningfully strive for a science concerning how one can and should conduct research and teach?

The answer will not be a simple "yes" or "no" but will be extremely varied. Yet it will not be the answer to an idle question, especially not for the representatives of that vague group of disciplines that are, in a rather high-flown manner, designated as social sciences. When one sees what effort certain disciplines apply to constructing models of human action or to developing decision- and systems-theories, one cannot help but ask himself whether and how they are actually in a position to bring us closer to human action in a manner that could be characterized to even some extent as scientific.

In this manner, perhaps, the classical discussion about the merits of the various bioi could be unraveled in a new way. For the question, for example, of whether the bios theoretikos is intrinsically meaningful without reference to other actions is in no way one that can be answered merely in an arbitrary manner or in a way that can be decided individually. It also involves the question concerning whether, as the Greeks thought, there are theories which both tell us something essential and cannot on principle be translated into directions for action. And it also involves the question about whether there are modes of action or aspects of modes of action that are on principle inaccessible to theoretical penetration and whose accomplishment, for that very reason, must be left to the experience and prudence of the individual. For a bios theoretikos that might arrive only at insights which are to be translated into directions for action cannot be an end in itself, since its goal by its very nature points beyond itself. But likewise, a praxis that can be totally scientized cannot be a culmination of human life, that is, the goal to which all others are subordinate. For, as Aristotle writes at the beginning of the *Metaphysics*, man by nature desires to know; this is no less true today than it was more than two thousand years ago. If practice can be scientized, it is not practice but theoria which is the goal.

It seems to me that at least to this extent the original concept of antiquity is still valid: knowledge as well as action can only meaningfully be final ends if there is a sort of knowledge that does not refer beyond itself to action and a sort of action that remains inaccessible to knowledge, or at any rate to scientific knowledge.

II

Creatures of a Day:
Thought and Action in Thucydides

J. Peter Euben

I

The proper relation between theory and practice has become almost as prominent a concern outside the academy as in it. The contrasts between what is said
(or promised) and what is done (or fulfilled), between what is "in theory" (or
ideally or formally so) and what is "in practice" (really and actually the case),
are familiar to all. They were already present in the revolutionary period, when
the promise of America as a land of political liberty and virtue was defined
in contrast to the corruption that had overtaken the English Constitution. It
was then the hope that such contrasts would no longer have meaning in the
United States. With a similar hope but altered definition of what might be realized, the framers of the Constitution, themselves men of theory and practice,
looked forward to the institutional embodiment and theoretical sanction of
their new science of politics. That the contrasts they hoped to silence remain,
is, perhaps, a testament to their failure; though the fact that such contrasts
quickly became politically circumscribed is also a testimony to their success.
In any event American political history reveals a sporadic but persistent outrage
on the part of movements, parties, groups, and individuals at the discrepancy
between American ideals and reality, promise and actuality, theories and prac-

Note. For their kind criticism I thank Gary Miles, John Schaar, Ann Lane, Olga Euben,
Allyn McAuley, Tom Zeman, and Warren Lane.

tices.[1] In these terms the political activism of the past decade and a half appears as a recapitulation of traditional patterns of American protest.

There is surely something to this view. But emphasis on historical continuity may underestimate the sense of disorientation that attends the growing belief that much in the world and our thought about it is fragmented and disjunctive in ways it need not be and ought not be. As the faith that America was a force for liberation faded into the bitter consciousness that it was simply one force in the struggle for power (and a force, moreover, with a penchant for choosing the wrong political friends and enemies), the suspicion grew among many Americans that our theory as well as our practice is flawed; that it is no mere accident of history or mere failure to live up to ideals that our institutions are in such disarray. For these men and women our theories appear at best naive, at worst rationalizations which, intentionally or in effect, sustain a technocratic elite, an exploitative economic system, and an untenable international position.

Complementing this political unease with theory and practice is an intellectual critique of those categorical oppositions that have characterized modern thought and life: dichotomies such as fact and value, subject and object, mind and matter, science and art, objectivity and subjectivity, reason (or Reason) and passion, intellect and fantasy, reality and appearance, the individual and the state, the private and the public, the inner and outer life. More and more such dualities are seen as alienating, rigid and misconceived, capable of being mediated or integrated by a proper understanding of Being, God, forms of life, authenticity, revolutionary praxis, "deep structure," language, or science. Though the separation of theory and practice is still defended as necessary to maintain the integrity of each, increasingly it is unity of integral plurality that is sought.

One such attempt is that tradition of thought which draws on Hegel and Marx. Though susceptible to jargon and convoluted ideological abstractions, the tradition has definite notions about how the separation of theory and practice is maintained, why its unity is desirable, and, at least until recently, what forces could be relied on to bring such unity into being. It claims for itself a philosophical and political self-consciousness lacking in other theories[2] and offers a relatively coherent picture of what it means to act in the context of the modern nation-state.

Given the tone and arguments of its founders, it is not suprising that discussion of theory and practice in this tradition should be philosophical and global. This is clearly its great strength and power. But there is another view which complements and emends this tradition in political and theoretical ways, one that is prephilosophical and local in its approach to history and politics. For obvious reasons this way of thinking and doing politics cannot simply be reincorporated into a historical context as different from its point of origin as our own (though such differences are often exaggerated). But it can serve to reopen issues deemed settled and remind us of what is forgotten by the translation of historical and political experience into world historical processes and generalizations about human nature.

It is this complementary view I want to delineate in this essay. To do so, I will be primarily concerned not with the problem of theory and practice but of thought or speech (logos) and action or deed (ergon).[3] The two problems are related but not identical. For one thing, the former emerges from the latter, appearing only with the birth of political philosophy in Plato and Aristotle. For another, the extent of separation between theory and practice is more substantial than that between speech and deed. Theory-practice questions are abstract and universal (even when the explicit aim is "practical"), less immediately drawn from, or located in, concrete historical and political situations.

An analogy will make the point clearer. If we visualize two circles with a common center but of differing size, it is obvious that the larger circle is farther from the center and that, as it becomes larger and its area increases, its visible (though not geometrical) relation to any center becomes difficult to see. To the human eye it loses its shape as a circle. Now speech and deed is the smaller circle, one step removed from the center of a concrete political and historical culture but still in close proximity to it in thought and action. Its distance from the center (its roots and origins) is not such that it destroys the balance of senses and mind, particularity and generality. Theory and practice is the remote circle. Because its discourse and focus are less clearly tied to a particular center, it is more general, abstract, and conceptual. Let me expand the analogy and the significance of the circle image. By so doing, what is at stake politically in the distinction between theory-practice and speech-deed will be clarified and the focus and historical location of the essay will be justified.

Now a circle is a boundary or limit, enclosing and thus marking off what is inside from what is outside. But more than that, what is inside shares a bond of location and proximity, whereas what is outside lacks such definition. In these terms it is both boundless and bondless. The political import of this can be discerned as early as Homer for whom the circle or ring was the proper way for men to assemble. To break up an assembly was literally to "loosen the circle."[4] We retain a sense of this in our phrase "a circle of friends," a finite group of people united by acquaintance, common sentiments and interests—

in short, an association. And that of course is the heart of Aristotle's definition of a polis. Indeed the word polis itself connoted a ringed wall (though not every polis had one).

What is at stake in loosening the circle is developed in two pre-Socratic fragments. The first, by Heraclitus, states that "the people should fight for the Law (nomos) as if for their city walls." It is not simply that the walls and laws are related but that each is essential to the life of the polis, and in analogous ways. The walls exist not only to protect physical life but to protect the distinctive shared culture embodied in the laws. And it is only the laws that insure that the walls can indeed protect men, since if they fail, as in a civil war, the walls become a prison. Furthermore, the laws protect men from their own ceaseless passions which, if left uneducated, destroy the polis as completely as any military disaster. Finally, as the walls differentiate the human community within from the strangeness of outside nature, the laws differentiate citizens from permanent strangers (like foreigners) or temporary ones (like the young) until they are educated to citizenship, that is, until they come to live among a circle of friends.

The second fragment is from a somewhat later writer, Alcmaeon of Croton, who wrote, "men perish because they cannot join the arche (beginning, first principle) with the telos (end, or governing aim)."[5] Now this implies that the wider the circle, the more difficult the union; the more difficult the union, the more men act randomly; the more men act randomly, the more likely they are to perish physically and culturally. For what men need, and what the walls and laws provide, is sufficient serenity, regularity, and boundedness to make visible the connection of an initiating principle of action and its guiding end. Without these men will lack confidence in the continuity of the world and refuse to assume responsibility for what they do.[6]

In these terms a large circle, lacking easily visible boundaries, leaves men unable to assemble as human beings, unprotected physically and culturally, strangers rather than friends, acting randomly without a common central point of reference. And this applies not only to the relations among citizens but to the relation between theory and practice. It is obviously no accident that the movement from polis to isopolity, cosmopolis, and empire is paralleled by both the development of the circle into a geometric figure describing the heavens (and soul) and a change from historical political theory to political philosophy.

Because of these concerns, Thucydides is a pivotal figure. It is true that his survey is bounded. But the sharpness of his focus intensifies a field of experience such that one is able to isolate some enduring aspects of political life and reflection, forgotten, or absorbed into abstraction, by the philosophical tradition. One can see in Thucydides's *History* (as in Euripides's plays) that differentiation and corruption of political life which was both preface to and context for political philosophy and the discovery of the soul. Thucydides traces this movement in terms of the relation between speech and deed. But he not only traces it, he is part of it. Thus my concern is with both the relation of speech and deed in Thucydides and Thucydides's speech and deed; with his attitude toward Pericles and Athens and the place of that attitude in what Jaeger has called the organic unity of Greek thought.[7] Indeed, despite different accent marks and varying assessments of Greek culture, almost all the best cultural histories of the period share Jaeger's sense that this unity dissipates over time, particularly during the fifth century B.C. Whether in celebration or disappointment, all trace a movement from myth, symbol, common sense, and poetry to rationalization, analysis, logic, concept, intellect, system, philosophy, naturalism, and prose; from heroic morality, shame-culture, and community to ethics, individual responsibility, guilt-culture, skepticism, and relativism. In this movement Thucydides (and Pericles) stands largely free of the older tradition but not yet part of the philosophical reconstruction.

II

The self-conscious articulation of the opposition between theory and practice, which began with the emergence of political philosophy and solidified in the Neoplatonism and Pythagoreanism of later centuries, rested on the assumption that theory and philosophy, at their Ionian origins and by their nature, were opposed to practice and the life of action. But the doxographical tradition which embodied this assumption is suspect, listing as it does the opinions of earlier thinkers as if they were all answers to the same questions asked in the same way.[8] Nor is the tradition that made the earliest philosophers/scientists prototypes for philosophical men in all ages, any more reliable.[9] Again, this seems self-serving, a later reconstruction intended to justify an emergent philosophical vocation opposed to the life of politics and practice. Indeed, no such opposition could be clearly articulated until human nature and political life became a philosophical issue and the physical cosmos a pattern and standard for polis life. Furthermore, it is unlikely that a self-conscious conception of philosophy as a distinctive form of life (such as is attributed to Pythagoras and implicit in Plato) could arise in the absence of a distinctive philosophic or scientific vocabulary. As has been suggested, pre-Socratic philosophic (and medical) principles and language derive from the experience of the increasingly democratic polis.[10]

It may even be misleading to believe that Ionian philosophers/scientists engaged in "pure theory," though it is true that they lacked the "manipulative mentality" that characterizes most modern science.[11] For though philosophy may have begun in wonder, wonder and curiosity about the world are not distinctive to philosophy but are Greek phenomena.[12] Homeric heroes face the gods with wonder and amazement, marveling at them as something familiar but beautiful and perfect beyond things in the world. But not only the gods inspire wonder. Many things in the world, especially the deeds of men, are beautiful and a wonder to behold. It is this joy in seeing that is the source of Greek philosophy, but it itself becomes philosophized. One can understand what this means and how it occurs by tracing the development of the notion of theory.

The origins of theory and theorist are found in the post-Homeric words theoria, theorein, and theoros, all having to do with seeing.[13] Initially a noun meaning to be a spectator, the word later became a verb meaning to witness, look on, or contemplate. (Both meanings can be found in subsequent Greek literature.) In its earliest appearance, it "does not reflect an attitude or emotion linked with sight, nor the viewing of a particular object [but instead] represents an intensification of the normal and essential function of the eyes."[14] Now the meaning of this intensification can be clarified by going back to Homer (remembering that he does not use the word theoria). Snell argues that for Homer the eye serves as a model for the absorption of experience so that knowing something *means* having seen it. Thus to see much, sufficiently often, is to have both intensive and extensive knowledge.[15] This might be taken to imply that an intensification of even the normal function of the eyes involves a different degree of absorbing experience and thus knowing; that even in its beginnings, looking or seeing could involve unique sorts of knowledge and relations to reality.

Originally, a theoros was either an ambassador sent by a polis to the sacred festivals of another state, or more likely, an envoy sent to consult the Delphic oracle, the arbiter of sacred law, religious ritual, and rites of purification (especially for those guilty of murder). The theoros, then, went to the source of truth to bring back the words of the god to the political authorities of his polis. As an intermediary between the polis and the priestess, he was expected to render a full account of what he had heard and seen. Theognis (who may himself have been a theoros) insists that adding or taking away from what the god says, is a serious offense. The theoros needs that intellectual precision, honesty, and moral virtue appropriate for one who deals with the Delphic god.[16] Gradu-

ally the meaning of theoros became more general and included going to witness religious and athletic festivals (spectacles) abroad. Thus theory came to
mean what a spectator at games does, i.e., inspecting, watching, witnessing,
taking account of things that catch the eye. As the role of theoros broadened,
such spectating became less passive. Even more than in Theognis it demanded
the capacity to explain and understand what one sees, distinguish what is essential to a performance or ritual from what is incidental, and transmit such knowledge to the polis in honest, useful form.

Because theory entailed undertaking a journey abroad to see, a theorist and
theory came to be associated with traveling, particularly over vast distances to
non-Greek cultures.[17] (The ships that carried the theoros were called theoridos.)
Thus theory came to mean seeing with an eye toward learning about different
lands and institutions, alien practices and experiences, distilling and comparing
the pattern of things seen while engaged in travel.[18]

As we have seen, the theoros originally had an official public position and
might even be charged with insuring that certain public matters were carried
out with due regard for religious practices, such as oaths for peace treaties,
purification rites, or payment of penalties. What he did then was done for the
polis, not for himself. There is no sense of theory as a distinct activity or vocation unrelated to public life, no notion that such activity alienates men from
their fellow citizens. Yet at some point this sense and notion did develop, as
another and extended meaning of theory grew up alongside the older ones. As
this happens there is a gradual separation of theory from its public office and
roots, a turning inward and outward, away from the polis. It is not clear when
or how this happened—whether it can usefully be said to be nascent in Homer,
or present when Solon leaves Athens for the sake of theory,[19] or constitutive
of Ionian or Pythagorean philosophy. But one can, with hindsight, see the potential for these developments within the earlier notion of theory itself.

For one thing, on his travels abroad the theorist was expected to report
back what he had witnessed. But except when sent to bring back a verbatim
rendering from Delphi, such reportage inevitably meant that he had also to
distill, classify, and compare what he had seen. Now for a Greek this did not
necessarily mean that he would think unpatriotically, disparaging his own
home because he had visited the homes of others. Nevertheless it is easy (for
moderns perhaps too easy) to see how this comparative understanding could
eventually issue in a critical sense toward the particularity, even arbitrariness, of
his own culture and stimulate a drive to find a higher unity or reality beneath
the particularity of appearances, whether in nature, Being, or human nature.

One can see, too, how a search for a unity beyond the multiplicity of the phenomenal world might culminate in both a repudiation of common sense and a claim for superior understanding. This growing detachment from, and analytic stance toward, the polis suggests that the theorist was coming to expand the object of his spectating from festivals, to the affairs of men in general, to the cosmos and eternity itself. It suggests, too, how theory could become a divine vocation. For from the very beginning the theorist was sent to bring back the word of a god. Though initially an emissary on behalf of his polis, the theorist began to claim for himself a special relation to the god. He insisted that because theory was a divine activity, the theorist was most akin to the gods. Thus the theorists' travels were no longer seeing the institutions, laws, and spectacles of men but a path or road to the divine in the form of contemplation of nature or intensive inward witnessing of the cosmos of the soul.

For Pythagoras, theory is a way of life, concerned with purification of the soul and escape from the cycle of birth and death. Its point is contemplation of the divine, eternal beauty of the heavens and discovery of the ultimate, secret mathematical harmony of the universe.[20] With Heraclitus, philosophy becomes a critique of the senses, which by themselves are defective instruments of knowing, because they are incapable of recognizing the commonality behind appearances and insufficiently directed by knowledge of the Logos.[21] Unless and until men know the Logos (universal law, governing order, reality, Being) and make it their guide to conduct, they will live in their own private worlds (literally idiotes), ignorant of what is common.[22] They must turn inward to the soul—the Logos in microcosm, the seat of feeling, and the entity of which moral and intellectual qualities are rightly predicated—to be reflectively aware of what they do and critical of the ignorance of others.[23] Hence the search for knowledge becomes intensive rather than extensive.[24] With Parmenides, the senses and flux of the world are repudiated in the name of a reality of Being, "far from the path trodden by mankind."[25] Logic and Reason condemn the world of men to contradiction, thought about the world to opinion. Perhaps already in Socrates, but more fully in Plato and Aristotle, philosophy and theory as contemplation emerge as distinct from thought and reasoning. It is their view which dominates "metaphysical and political thought throughout our tradition."[26]

Until Socrates and Plato brought the now philosophized theory into the polis as a stranger among the citizens, *political* theory was a contradiction. For politics concerned the affairs of men while theory was speculation about the nature, genesis, and origins of the universe. There could be no split between theory and practice until the two were seen as somehow concerned with the same subject matter. And this required disarray, confusion, disintegration in the affairs of men before theory and philosophy could make their presence felt and relevant. It is this disarray that Thucydides and his *History* illustrate and portray.

In a general way Thucydides was heir to a culture partly formed by the development of science and philosophy.[27] But he is largely uninterested in theoretical speculation about the nature of the universe, searching for an immutable logos in the soul, or ascendance to true Being. What matters to him is foresight and intelligence (gnome), not the philosophic noûs of Anaxagoras and Plato. His concern with knowledge is political in inspiration and purpose. It is the actions of men and cities that are the focus of the *History*. He portrays a human power so magnificent that its achievements are a monument for all time, while displaying the physical decay and spiritual erosion of that power until, beaten at all points and altogether, "the Athenians were destroyed, as the saying is, with total destruction."[28] He leaves us too with his own immortal monument— a *History* which partakes of the brilliance it describes and whose limitations are those of his Athenian compatriots. It is a book with no resting place in cosmology, philosophy, or religion; like his fellow Athenians, it is born into the world to take no rest itself and give none to others.[29]

III

Thucydides's *History* is a tragedy in the largest sense.[30] Its first impression is of an exuberant confidence in the capacity of men to so master the world by uniting power and intelligence, action and thought, that they rival the immortal gods. Thus the unsurpassed greatness of Athens transforms her from a historical entity into an "imperishable monument" for all men who love action.

You must realise the power of Athens, and feed your eyes upon her from day to day, till love of her fills your hearts; and then when all her greatness shall break upon you, you must reflect that it was by courage, sense of duty, and a keen feeling of honor in action that men were enabled to win all this and that no personal failure in an enterprise could make them consent to deprive their country of their valor, but laid it at her feet as the most glorious contribution that they could offer. For this offering of their lives made in common by them all they each of them individually received that renown which nevers grows old, and for a sepulchre, not so much that in which their bones have been deposited, but that noblest of shrines wherein their glory is laid up to be eternally remembered upon every occasion on which deed or story shall fall for its commemoration. For heroes have the whole earth for their tomb; and in lands far from their own, where the column with its epitaph declares it, there is enshrined in every breast a record unwritten with no tablet to preserve it, except that of the heart. (107-108)

But the lasting impression is more complex. For the very qualities that made for greatness—daring, innovation, great power, energy, restlessness, even intelligence—are self-destructive. The greatest achievement warps the political and moral personality which made it possible, until at last Athens becomes Corcyrea. Words change their meaning—honor becomes success, patriotism and loyalty, selfishness—sentiments of decency, moderation, and justice are obliterated. Then the realism and tyranny of empire turns inward to intensify domestic factionalism. Finally speechless and impotent, Athens becomes a victim of necessity, unable "to fix the exact point at which our empire shall stop."[31] But the tragedy is mankind's as well as Athens's. For in the end human intelligence, for all its brilliance and power, is unable to contain the forces it expresses and makes possible. The greatness of historical events is as much their power to destroy as to create. This is rooted in a tragic dialectic of all civilizations, whose transformation of intellectual and moral conceptions into reality eventually issues in a war which overpowers men, thereby reducing them to a brutality worse than their original situation. Finally, the *History* is a tragedy of the separation of speech and deed, thought and action. "The death of Pericles and the Peloponnesian War," Cronford writes in *The Unwritten Philosophy*, "mark the moment when men of thought and men of action began to take different paths, destined to diverge more and more widely till the Stoic sage ceased to be a citizen of his own country and became a citizen of the world."[32]

All I shall do in the following sections is portray that tragedy in a number of ways, each iteration adding dimension, it is hoped, to our understanding of how, why, and with what consequences political thought and action divided and in their separation became tranformed. I shall do this first through a contrast between the harmony of thought and action, speech and deed in Pericles and Periclean Athens, with its absence in the Athens and character of his successors; second, through an analysis of the incident at Melos; and lastly, by looking at the fate of speech itself. I choose example and iteration as a mode of exposition, for it seems to be truer to Thucydides's conception of political knowledge and to the way he embeds his teachings in the architecture of his work. Propositional argument runs the danger of ignoring the elusiveness of the *History*, misunderstanding what Thucydides expects men to learn about political things, and misconstruing the contingent nature of politics.

One further introductory comment. Because there are political costs to the separation of speech and deed it does not follow either that their mere unity is sufficient or that such unity must always take the same form.[33] In one sense Alcibiades may be said to unite speech and deed as completely as Pericles, yet it is clear that Thucydides regards him as inferior to Pericles. In what way is this inferiority linked to the unity or separation of speech and deed, thought and action?

The unity of speech and deed is not simply a matter of congruence between what is said and what is done. It involves the ability of intelligence, speech, and concept to give the world human impress by having deeds, actuality, and reality embody what is conceived of by men. It requires the continuous fulfillment of initiatives without which the efficacy of intelligence could not be sustained. But there are limits to how much human power can transform conception into reality. When Pericles, in his first speech, urges the Athenians to think of themselves as islanders (which they are not), he intends this self-conception to be a premise for action. He could not ask them to conceive of themselves as a land power, not only because Athens lacked Sparta's army but primarily because she lacked the material and cultural realities for that to become true. If the unity of speech and deed includes both the transforming of word into deed within the necessary limitations of time, place, and culture and the insuring that this be maintained continuously, then Pericles, not his successors, truly unites speech and deed: Thus Thucydides is doing more than holding up Pericles's unity of speech and action as an ideal from which later Athenian leaders fall short. He is making the stronger claim that they did not politically unite them at all.

A

It is Themistocles not Pericles who most fully unites thought and action. The architect of Athenian navel power, he is a man who "exhibited indubitable signs of genius" and has therefore a "claim on our admiration quite extraordinary and unparalleled." Unlike Pericles, Themistocles was not philosophically well educated. It was "by his own native capacity, alike unformed and unsupplemented by study" that he was the most able to judge what to do in a crisis and the most penetrating prophet of the distant future. To Thucydides's amazement, Themistocles was not only a fine "theoretical expositor of all that came within the sphere of his practice," but he could also render intelligent judgments about things about which he had no experience.[34] In Themistocles's mind, feeling, opinion, purpose, and action are one; thought seems an immediate representation of reality.

With Pericles, thought or speech and action or deed are not an unselfconscious unity but a harmony integrated and balanced in his mind, character, and person. There is a reflective element to his intellect and speech, which grows as the war progresses. Though Thucydides has the most unambiguous praise for Themistocles as the founding architect of Athenian power, it is Pericles and Periclean Athens that he sees as the culmination of the growth of human power depicted in the "Archeology." As Athens is the culmination of that growth, Pericles is the supreme interpreter and visionary of that power. It is the harmony he sustains and the Athens he leads that are the standards by which all other political leaders and the decay of Athens are judged. In his speech and deed, and those of his fellow citizens, there is expressed, in thought and action, the greatest possibilities of human freedom and power.

It is by contrast with Pericles that other Athenian leaders — Cleon, Alcibiades, Nicias — are found wanting. None of them combined the capacity to see what was called for in policy and vision, expound it clearly with what Aristophanes terms an "Olympian eloquence" and the comic writer Eupolis calls a "spell" that could "prick men's hearts and leave behind the sting,"[35] and do so while remaining steadfastly devoted to their city and incorruptible by money or flattery. All the others — because they lack some political ability, some trait of character or mind — debase, twist, or weaken the fabric of Periclean leadership and Athens. Cleon, Pericles's conscious follower who pursues a similar strategy, has, as Gomme bluntly puts it, "a vulgar mind, acute in a second-rate manner, without intelligence or humanity."[36] As "the most violent man at Athens" (164), he has no understanding of Pericles's visionary imperialism and is responsible for the near massacre at Mytilene, the actual one at Scione, and the rejection of peace after Pylos. Reducing politics to force, he manages to keep the war going to cover his evil doings. His inability to distinguish friends from enemies, his imputing dishonesty and self-interest to his opponents, his attack on speech itself and the faith in reason and education upon which it rests does not recall Pericles but anticipates Corcyrea, where

Words had to change their ordinary meaning and to take that which was now given them. Reckless audacity came to be considered the courage of a loyal ally; prudent hesitation, spacious cowardice; moderation was held to be a cloak for unmanliness; ability to see all sides of a question, inaptness to act on any. Frantic violence became the attribute of manliness; cautious plotting a justifiable means of self-defense. The advocate of extreme measures was always trustworthy; his opponent a man to be suspected. (189)

Unlike the soldiers Pericles eulogizes and whose courage he unfolds into the greatness of Athens, Cleon dies running away like a coward.

Alcibiades is a more complex figure and a more difficult case. A conscious follower of Pericles and a member of his clan, his ward and thus almost a son, he appears to be Pericles's most likely political heir.[37] And in many ways he is. Alcibiades has a vision of Athenian greatness and an eloquence appropriate for its articulation and translation into policy. He claims to be supremely patriotic and is in fact incorruptible in any petty sense. But he is not Pericles.[38] There is some flaw of character, judgment, or sensibility that makes him different; some lack in his leadership (or those he leads) such that this ardent "patriot" becomes a cause of his country's defeat.

Though Alcibiades has an understanding of Athens's grandeur, it is warped by his self-interested ambition. Prone to boasting and extravagance about himself and Athens, perpetually desiring more for himself and his city, he lacks Pericles's sense of moderation and limits and is thus unable to follow the latter's practical strategy.[39] Pericles understood and used the animating principles of his political culture without permitting them to go unchecked and dictate policy and action. If moderation is lost, the strengths contained in those principles become weaknesses. Thus if the dynamic of Athens or the ossification of Sparta[40] continues, each would be destroyed by its own particular brand of excess. This means that political leadership is a most demanding vocation, involving enunciation and embodiment of cultural principles, yet containing their most destructive tendencies. Lacking either capacity, political leaders will fail, men will be carried away in thought and deed, and the connection between intelligence and the world will be severed. It is this vocation that Alcibiades does not fully understand, and this connection he fails to realize.

For all his ability to captivate his fellow citizens, Alcibiades is not trusted by them and his initiatives remain uncompleted. And for all his protestations of patriotism, he is unrooted in the polis, for the honor he seeks is primarily his own. Yet in one sense he is the most Athenian of Athenians, the one who embodies most completely an Athenian culture bereft of traditional morality and incapable of sustaining the political intelligence of a Pericles. Without either, the tyranny of empire turns back upon the Athenians themselves, and Alcibiades is its product. "Scratch Thrasymachus," writes Arthur W. H. Adkins "and you find Agamemnon." "Give him more of a veneer," Alasdair MacIntyre adds, "and you find Alcibiades."[41]

If Alcibiades is too much the Athenian, the pious, cautious Nicias is his foil. Nicias has a deep foreboding of the impending collapse of Athens, yet is helpless to forestall it and even helps contribute to it by his speech at Athens and inaction at Syracuse. In the debate his ploy of extravagantly overstating the requirements for the expedition in hopes of dissuading his fellow citizens from undertaking it becomes a further spur to the enterprise he does not want and which he is forced to lead. Nicias's caution is not Periclean moderation; it is more characterological than political, and Nicias, for whatever reasons, is so distant from his countrymen that he lives in a different world, out of place and time, more Spartan than Athenian, or perhaps some remnant from an earlier and lost Athens.[42] If Alcibiades's actions are too purely Athenian, Nicias's are incompatible with the city's political character. Because of this, his patriotism is as egotistic as Alcibiades's, however much the two are characterological, intellectual, and political opponents. That they are, and together cause Athens's defeat at Syracuse, suggests how the aspects of political leadership united in Pericles have fallen apart.

By harmonizing thought and action, speech and deed, Pericles (as Thucydides presents him) possesses political wisdom in its fullest sense. Visible in his life, action, and speech, inhering in his mind and character, it is no more reducible to a set of rules than the teachings of Thucydides. At most, one can say a few things about parts of the whole.

Certainly foresight is an aspect of this wisdom; the ability to see what the situation demands, recognize the material and strategic bases of power, judge the animating forces that incite men to action, and then refuse to be blinded by unrestrained hope, desire, or despair. But it includes not only foresight but an awareness of the limits of foresight. Now what makes Pericles's foresight unique, what grounds it and directs it, is the vision of Athens by which Pericles unites thought and action, speech and deed in his life and in that of the city of which he is the foremost citizen.

In the Funeral Oration, where that vision is most fully presented, Pericles transforms the material and political achievements of Athens into something of such rare beauty and radiance that its life and being are no longer tied to the physical existence of Athens. That is why he speaks not just to friends and relatives of the dead, nor just to Athenians, but to all who love action. In the course of the oration the audience widens as the vision broadens, until the burden of the speech is nothing less than to put into words for future generations of mankind what is beyond speech. It is this kind of speech the deeds of the dead have called forth. It is the only act comparable to their act of bravery.

What has come into being at Athens, and is being continually recreated by the speech and deed of her citizens, is a new political form resting on principles of intelligence and choice.[43] This is what Pericles realizes and what he intends his speech to communicate to his fellow Athenians. He speaks of the fallen soldiers as released from chance. *They* are not creatures of a day, casual beings subject to moira, baffled by the unfathomable purposes of gods which they cannot affect. Because of Athens their lives have significance, their world has a human shape. He sees the polis standing between the individual citizen and the uncertainties of life, compensating men for their particular insufficiencies and protecting them against chance, while serving as both the mode and goal of that striving and acquisitiveness which non-Athenians feared as the prelude to hubris and até.[44]

Athens can do this because its great power is founded on individual will and decision to put the preservation of the whole city above self-interest. Only the *willing* unity of citizens in support of a policy decided on in common can insure respite from misfortune. Though it is Pericles who most clearly discerns the necessary decay of all human things and who is thus most alive to the potential tragedy of Athens, it is also Pericles whose vision uniquely captures the rarity of power that issues from and in freedom, action, and intelligence. Most men in most ages live their lives in fear and out of interest, victims of circumstances and subject to chance and necessity. But at certain rare moments, with sufficient power, resources, energy, devotion, and intellect, the tangible material roots blossom into flowers of awesome beauty. As this happens, the polis becomes an object of wonder and admiration no less than the gods themselves. Like them, or perhaps instead of them, its spirit, truth, and beauty will be immortal and its achievements, like those of its fallen soldiers, will not and cannot be tarnished by the defeat and disintegration of all human things. Wrote Protagoras, "Of all things the measure is man, of things that are, that they are, and of the things that are not, that they are not."[45] It is this beauty that Pericles sets before his fellow citizens. It is an ideal partly actualized in fact without the full awareness of those doing so. By making the ideal explicit and therefore visible in speech, he at once depicts Athenian greatness, the glory of the men who died in its name, and the necessity of all citizens to emulate them.

For the Athenians to see themselves as Pericles does, alters the consciousness of their power and thus the very character of their world and the possibilities of action in it. R. G. Collingwood brings out this point clearly. He argues that a human being in his capacity as a moral, political, or economic agent "lives not in a world of 'hard facts' to which 'thoughts' make no difference, but in a world of 'thoughts'; that if you change the moral, political, and economic 'theories' generally accepted by the society in which he lives, you change the character of his world; and that if you change his own 'theories' you change his relation to that world; so that in either case you change the ways in which he acts.'[46] To the degree this is so, the Funeral Oration is a call to action in the fullest sense. Its assumption and point is that the human mind can shape the world through thought and deed; that a vision of greatness, when tied to material resources, generates sufficient power for men to transform conviction into fact. Obviously the conviction is tied to, and emerges out of, the world. Yet it is not shackled to it. It is at once artificial, that is, generated by mind and speech, and given, subject to the historical experience and limitations of a particular culture.

And that suggests that Pericles's vision is not private and sui generis. At first it seems to be. He is, after all, the foremost man in Athens and holds up Athens as a work of art in a way that suggests his distance from the city and its traditions. Nevertheless his vision derives from the tradition and culture common to all Athenians. He sees more deeply and fully what his fellow citizens see and speaks eloquently of what they feel but cannot articulate. His is an ideal of what Athens has become and could become even more if she would adhere steadfastly to the finest potentialities of her culture. The people respond to the ideal and Pericles because they recognize both as somehow theirs. For Thucydides, the people freely accept Pericles's authority and his authority helps sustain their freedom.[47] This mutual respect is the true foundation of Athenian power. The people are as worthy of praise by their intelligence in choosing Pericles as Pericles is by his moderate leadership. To Pericles great power is possible only when men see themselves and are responsible actors, choosing to unite their separate wills and intentions in the interest of a larger whole. It is the task of a wise man to articulate and live a vision of the whole, thus evolving the strongest (chosen) sentiments of loyalty and patriotism. By so doing, speech and deed, harmonized in his person and vision, is also the quality that marks citizenship in general.[48]

As if to show the fragility of this harmony, remind us all how greed and fear surround even the most impressive political achievement, and test Pericles's political authority and Athenian resolve, Thucydides follows the Funeral Oration with his description of the Plague that eventually took Pericles's life. No eulogy and burial for fallen heroes now, no celebration of human intelligence. The Plague "passed all bounds (and), men, not knowing what was to become of them, became utterly careless of everything, whether sacred or profane. All the burial rites before in use were entirely upset, and they buried the bodies as best they could. Many from want of proper appliances, through so many of

their friends having died already, had recourse to the most shameless sepul-
chres." Confronted by an incalculable force which defies human reason, men
did what they pleased, *"regarding their lives and riches as alike things of a day."*
(My emphasis.)[49]

Though Pericles is able to rekindle their resolve, the tone of his third speech
is chastened and abstract, the vision less luminous and more foreboding. As if
to confirm this growing distance, Thucydides speaks of Pericles's death and
then of his successors, men whose grasping private ambitions lead the state to
ruin.[50]

Because it was in and by his person that the harmony of thought and action
was sustained in Athens, Pericles's death is the prelude to dissonance and destruction. After his death the harmony of speech and deed, thought and action
ceases. In consequence, action becomes increasingly violent, speech absent or
perverse, and choice diminished. All three can be seen in the Melian Dialogue.

B

In Book V Thucydides tells of the Athenian expedition to Melos, a small insignificant island which had refused, unlike other islanders, to obey Athens.[51]
Though colonists of Sparta, the Melians had remained neutral but could no
longer do so in the face of Athenian plundering of their land. Given the great
disparity of resources and power, the Athenian generals decided to make proposals to the Melians, in the expectation that a realistic assessment will show them
the futility of resisting Athens. But the Athenian expectations are thwarted.
Appearing before the few, the "Athenians" (both they and the Melians remain
anonymous), in keeping with their superior force, set the rules and tone of the
"debate." They insist on talking about the tangible realities of the situation—
"what is present and before your eyes." There are to be no frills to this conversation—no "fair phrases" or recounting of exploits in the Persian Wars, no
bill of particulars of previous injuries or assistance, no solemn incantations of
justice which can be arrived at in human arguments "only when the necessity
on both sides is equal. . . ." Where such equality is absent, "the powerful
exact what they can, while the weak yield what they must." There is no point
in relying on the Spartans; still less on hope of those invisible "prophecies and
oracles, and other such inventions that delude men with hopes to their destruction." Indeed the Athenians claim they may as fairly hope for divine favor as
the Melians. "Our belief about the gods and certain knowledge about men is
that universally, by natural necessity, he who has superior power rules. And it
is not as if we were the first to make this law, or to act upon it when made;

we found it existing before us and shall leave it to exist forever after us; all we do is make use of it, knowing that you and everybody else, having the same power we have, would do the same as we do."[52] Thus the Athenians dismiss all Melians hopes, divine and terrestrial, and remind the Melians that the real choice concerns their very existence.

Lacking other weapons, the Melians must protest in the name of justice, the common good, past unity, and future retribution.[53] But these are mere blades of grass to the knife of Athenian logic and the spears of her soldiers. The Melians choose liberty, honor and independence. Eventually they are defeated, their men slain, and their women and children sold into slavery. A polis with a long, not inglorious history is obliterated. Because her stand against Athens represents a conflict of political ideals, ages (the old and new), and size (smaller and larger agglomerations of power), her demise portends the passing of the polis itself.[54]

Given the consequences, it may well be that the Melians chose wrongly. Her reliance on Sparta does ignore the tangible realities of power and by inference raises questions about her conceptions of the gods. But what about Athens? What is the significance of her arguments and actions at Melos?

Now the choice Melos made to fight Athens, in the name of liberty and independence, is the same choice Athens made when confronting greatly superior Persian forces at the battle of Salamis. Athens too had refused a dishonorable summons, deciding to abandon homes and city to risk all in a single battle against intimidating odds. The physical fact of this victory became the spiritual symbol of not only Greek unity and glory but Athenian greatness and daring.[55] It was Athens who led the Delian League and was proclaimed liberator of Greece. All this is swept away with a weary realism by which the Athenians reject their origins and any interest in justifying their power. In effect they say to the Melians: Do not bore us with talk of justice and honor and we, for our part, will forego the usual ritual about liberating the Greeks, our glorious actions at Salamis, or great achievements afterward. All these are beside the point, mere rationalizations of power and moral fictions believed by our ancestors but known to us to be mere prejudice. Now for the Athenians to say and believe this is to throw doubt not merely on her previous justification of empire, but on her political culture as a whole. In seeing the deeds of their ancestors in purely physical terms, they make the Athenian victory at Salamis, won over greatly superior physical power, literally unintelligible.

Thus the Athenians at Melos repudiate what they asserted in the beginning of the *History*. Now they deny that honor is different from fear and interest.

They seem to have lost "all sense of the difference between honor and success, dishonor and defeat."[56] Their striving for freedom has become its opposite. Neither they nor the Melians have any choice. "As we are compelled and necessity is our master," they seem to say to the Melians, "we shall compel you and be your master." But if both are compelled, then the status of freedom is uncertain. This is made more obvious when the Athenians repudiate moral categories, not on the grounds that their achievement is unique (as Pericles claimed) but on the opposite grounds that they are simply the incidental executors of natural laws of empire, power, and politics, which are impervious to moral considerations and political choice. They are not responsible for what they do, since they do only what others would do in similar circumstances. Hence it no longer makes sense for them to claim that they are unique among men, the educators of Hellas, and a pattern to be imitated by all who love action.

This killing of one's origins and animating vision is paralleled on the concrete level of policy. For in arguing that the logic of empire compels them to make the Melians their subjects since Melos's freedom would be taken as evidence of Melian power, they embark on a suicidal path. As Jacqueline de Romilly has argued, "if the empire really obliges Athens to be constantly showing her strength in order to keep her subjects' obedience, and if this continual show of strength perpetually increases the number of her enemies, then the remedy is simply making the situation worse. . . ."[57] The conqueror is threatened by conquests yet is compelled to go on in spite of herself, increasing her enemies at the same rate as her conquests. Given this "logic" of empire, there is no time for or point to deliberation. At most the political art is a matter of strategy and tactics. Perhaps this accounts for the tone and mood of the Athenians: their attitude of resignation, impatience to get things over and done with, and the crisp, mathematical, even mechanical cadences of their speech. Their physical power is no longer part of an at once limiting and radiant human vision. This is not to deny that this vision also had brutal implications. Nor is it to ignore the cold brilliance of the Athenian arguments or the fact that by making the Athenians justify the rights of the stronger through the law of nature and transform God from the guardian of justice into the pattern of all earthly authority and force, Thucydides gives the realistic policy of Athens depth and power.[58] But it is to suggest that this brilliance is a rationalizing of intellect and a narrowing of the meaning of political wisdom. And insofar as civilization is the successful imposition of Periclean intelligence on the brute manner of the outside world, Melos constitutes a reversal that anticipates the end of civilization. (It remains to be seen how much that intelligence itself contributes to the reversal.)

Furthermore, the policies and arguments expressed at Melos carry forward certain attitudes which, when turned inward, erode that unity of purpose which makes great power possible. At Melos the Athenians justify the right of the stronger through a law of nature. They redefine honor and invest the gods as guardians not of justice but of earthly power. But this realism, though articulated in relation to another polis, does not leave its proponents untouched in their relations to each other within their own polis. In that setting it corrodes feelings of patriotism, loyalty, honesty, and unity which are essential ingredients and prerequisites of power. Lacking this political morality and the moderation it demands, the right of the stronger, enunciated at Melos, becomes an impulse to internal faction and personal aggrandizement, as at Corcyrea or in the "patriotism" of Alcibiades.[59] What Athens does to others she does to herself. In the end, the realism of the Athenians at Melos is unrealistic and cannot simply be redeemed (as hindsight is likely to suggest) by more realism.[60]

In the *History* the reported end of Melos is the beginning of the end for Athens, for it immediately precedes the debate over whether to invade Sicily and the Athenian decision to do so. As Thucydides presents it the unlimited use of violence at Melos is prelude to limitless expansion.[61] Athens has forgotten Pericles's warning that only her own lack of moderation would bring defeat. Now the Athenians fall prey to those passions they warned the Melians against. Hardheaded realists then, they now embark on a virtually utopian venture. Insistent that the Melians be concerned with the tangible realities of the situation, the Athenians are ignorant of the scope of the task they have set for themselves. Again they are convinced by the argument, made here by Alcibiades, that they have no choice.

Is Alcibiades right?[62] This question cannot be disentangled from another: What does it mean for Athens to argue as she did and believe what she does? For the belief in necessity is self-fulfilling. Even if the Athenians are partly right, they have no prospect of not being completely right as long as they believe what they do. Alcibiades is correct in insisting that great power and empire have their own imperatives and vulnerabilities. Pericles, too, appreciated the fact. But he responded by maintaining a defensive position, foregoing precisely the sort of enterprise the Athenians decide on in the Sicilian debate. Only in this way did he think choice could be sustained within the boundaries of necessity. In part political choice depended on human conception and self-conception, even when natural catastrophes like earthquakes, floods, and the Plague were involved. To speak anachronistically, Pericles, and the Athenians under his leadership (as distinct from the Spartans), regarded such chance interventions as both objective and subjective. In their subjective consequences they were not impervious to political intelligence. To regard chance as purely objective leads to political impotence, to regard it as purely subjective leads to a forgetting of the basic fragility of all human achievements.[63] As Melos and Syracuse suggest, the Athenians forget both, ignoring the fragility of their situation in the name of necessity.

Indeed, they seem to regard necessity as a fixed order ruled by some cosmic tyrant.[64] But this is a misunderstanding with crucial implications for the Athenian justification at Melos. For necessity is where no one rules; it is the point where, out of ignorance or arrogance, blindness or obsession, overconfidence or timidity, human intelligence and foresight fail. And this failure is primarily due to the incapacity of human agency.[65] To the degree the Athenians regard themselves as mere executors of natural laws and assimilate their actions to a "natural" causal chain, they deny the possibility of human agency. Preoccupied with the perspective of causal explanation, they begin to lose contact "with the point of view, the conceptual tools, the orientation, that enables man to choose rationally and responsibly, to combine action and thought (speech), to use his mind in the service of his actions."[66]

C

It is clear that Thucydides's and our relation to the speeches are different from that of the speakers themselves and the audiences they address. Whereas the speeches contain the speakers' estimate of the situation, Thucydides's presentation of them indirectly includes his estimate of the estimators. Thus he stands between us and the speakers. From what they say and do not say, in the discrepancies between what they say and do, what they expect to happen and does happen, we learn important things about the limitations of political intelligence, the contingency of political action, and the role of speech in human affairs. For instance, Cleon's speech and the sort of response Diodotus is forced to make under the circumstances display not only how the decision was reached but the grounds for making it and the considerations unnamed, ignored or unimagined in the process.

Of course the speeches are not simply analyses or predictions of events. Since what men think and say is a vital force in politics and war, speech and language are mediums through which men attempt to organize and control their world, convincing their fellow citizens to act on and in the world in certain ways and for certain ends. It is through speech that intelligence becomes the basis for Athenian action and the root of her courage. It is by speaking and talking that mental culture, civic loyalty, and military bravery can be mutually sustaining, that thought and deed can be joined in citizenship. If this is true then the absence of speech and the consequent disruption of the unity of intelligence and action entails the disappearance of the capacity to act. As the discussion of political leadership and Melos have already indicated, this is exactly what occurs as the *History* progresses.

A remark of Herodotus helps make the point. He suggests that the presence of free political speech is identical to the absence of tyranny and goes on to imply that speech itself is a kind of freedom which creates the conditions of life where men are ready to face death and strong enough to overcome forces many times more numerous.[67] Now Herodotus is referring to the tyranny of men, but the discussion of Melos provides another notion of tyranny, the tyranny of events in the face of human resignation.

Ignoring what Jebb calls military harangues, two important things happen to the speeches during the course of the *History*.[68] First of all, there are fewer and fewer of them. Two-thirds appear in the first four books, none at all in three of the last four books. In part this may be due to the unfinished state of the *History*. But this is not the sole reason (nor would it explain the presence and qualities of the Athenian speeches in Book VI). Part of the point is political and can be seen in terms of Herodotus's opposition between freedom and speech on the one hand and tyranny on the other.[69]

An initial reaction to reading the *History* is being overwhelmed by the sheer rush of events (a reaction which cannot wholly be explained by unfamiliarity with names and places). The pace, complexity, and extent of the action make real the frenetic dynamism of Athens and the Athenian historian. The constant movement in the book and Athens gives the reader little rest. What does provide respite from the onrush of events is the interjection of speeches and speech. They give both actor and reader time for reflection and, by relating events to some intelligible purpose, make the world comprehensible in human terms. If true, then the diminishing number of speeches has far-reaching implications. It implies that events have exceeded human comprehension. The world has become a tyranny. In these terms and circumstances it no longer seems inappropriate to talk about a "logic of events," or the rules of necessity and compulsion. Human intelligence appears impotent, capable only of translating the imperatives of necessity into the kind of speech and action we see at Melos.

But in Book V there are no fewer than nine speeches, five by Athenians, including two each by Alcibiades and Nicias.[70] This is the last opportunity for Athens to limit her empire, moderate her daring, and stave off the vise of necessity. In this she fails, as Alcibiades, his patriotism corrupted by vanity, and the impotent Nicias lead the Athenian state to ruin.[71] Here language and speech lose their relation to reality, as words changed "their meaning and to take that which was now given them."

IV

In Part III I indicated some things Thucydides has to teach us about politics, particulary about the political conditions that make for the disunity and disharmony of thought and action, theory and practice. His *History* indicates what kind of theory and what sorts of practices must exist for the unity of theory and practice to be other than a category mistake. It shows how and why the separation of thought and action is a political problem whose resolution is always temporary.

But does Thucydides also have something to teach us about the *study* of politics? What can we learn from his own thought and action about thought and action? If the problem of theory and practice is theoretical as well as political, what might we learn from his way of thinking that could usefully emend the philosophical tradition of political thought initiated by the Platonic Socrates? Can one legitimately make the claim for Thucydides's approach to the study of politics that he makes for the substance of his *History* — that it is useful for the future?

I want to approach these questions indirectly by showing how various theoretical questions emerge from the political issues surveyed in Part III. Each issue points beyond what Thucydides says in the *History* to what he is doing by writing it. Contrasting Pericles with his successors, the Funeral Oration with the Plague, necessity with freedom, and speech with the onrush of events, Thucydides raises questions about thought and action, political intelligence and political education which are also questions about his own thought, intelligence, and status as a political educator. This approach has the advantage of indicating how closely Thucydides's thought is tied to political questions. As such it is a useful beginning for assessing the two dominant interpretations of the *History* — as being practical or contemplative in nature. By trying to determine what is right and what is misleading in each interpretation, I can be more precise (but in the nature of his case not too precise) about what can be learned from the relation of Thucydides's speech to action in a way that supplements the philosophical understanding of theory and practice.

Thucydides shows how Pericles, unable to educate his fellow citizens to carry on his policies after his death, died without a true successor. This fact together with his celebration of Pericles and his blunt criticism of later Athenian political leaders have led commentators to make two related charges: that Thucydides could not or did not want to see that no society could survive by depending on a succession of Periclean personalities; and that he failed to realize that with the corrosion of ethos, no future Pericles could emerge in Athens.[72] In part these criticisms miss the point. The first ignores Thucydides's admiration for heroic politics over a politics of survival. Athens, like Achilles, cannot live on after the supreme climactic contest of its life. It is only in death (and in the Epitaph of the Funeral Oration) that Athens and her soldiers can display the pure ideal of what has passed away. The second criticism tends to be either a tautology (the fact that no new Pericles emerged proved no new one could have emerged) or vague. But the point of the criticisms is really different and deeper. Perhaps Periclean intelligence is limited not only by what it cannot do (for instance, predict the paralogos of the Plague) but by what it does do. John Finley puts the point concisely in his concluding remarks on Euripides's *Hippolytus*: "Intelligence has clarified the world only to find itself powerless before the world's contingencies."[73] Now this suggests that an intellectual attitude, skeptical of myth, religion, tradition, and law and perceiving the world as for human use, creates a situation with which it is unable to deal. If true, then there is a dialectic whereby the process and product of intellectual clarification culminates in power *and* powerlessness. And this raises the entire question of the place and impact of intelligence, including Thucydides's own, in the practice and study of politics.

Similarly, and with a similar result, the problem of necessity, presented in the Melian Dialogue, turns back upon the *History* itself. Here critics argue that Thucydides's book transforms seemingly voluntary actions subject to moral judgement into parts of a long, continuous process conditioned by a higher necessity. Human life, they argue, is thus made to seem subject to laws as inviolable as those of the physical cosmos, and the historian becomes as much a spectator of history as Ionian philosophers were said to be of the cosmos. Finally, the fate of speech in the *History* raises the questions of Thucydides's own speech and its relation to action and of whether the erosion of political limits (from Pericles to Alcibiades, polis to empire) entails a comparable loss of intellectual limits (from speech and thought to theory and philosophy).

Now it is not quite true (as the critics charged) that Pericles had no successors. Alcibiades may not have appreciated the meaning of Athenian greatness and the quality of Periclean wisdom, but Thucydides did. As such he alone can rightly claim to be Pericles's successor. (And Pericles to be his predecessor. For Pericles is a political leader who thinks historically and theoretically. Moreover, both men make comparable claims concerning the future status of their achievements.) But Thucydides, after being exiled, is no longer an actor in the war but a man writing an account of the war. Now this makes uncertain the relation of his intelligence and wisdom to the actors and speakers in the *History* and to speech and action in general. Clearly his deed of speech comprehends and judges the speeches and conceptions, acts and deeds of the actors. Since their speeches were attempts to interpret political reality, Thucydides's speech interprets reality and the possibility of interpreting it.[74] Now, as we saw, the speeches are more than interpretations of the world. They are also attempts to change it. But how is this true of Thucydides's speech? It is not made in the Assembly and therefore its connection with action must be different from those speakers who appear in the *History*. If Thucydides is Pericles's successor, one must account for this distance from space of action.

The first way to do this is to look at what Thucydides says. He offers his *History* not as some momentary display but as a "possession for all time," useful (ophelima) for those "who may desire a clear vision (exact knowledge) of what happened in the past, and what, given the human condition, will at some time, in more or less like manner, happen in the future. . . ."[75] But this leaves unresolved how it will be useful or who will find it so. There are essentially two schools of thought on the subject. Each reads the *History* differently and learns different things from it. One insists that Thucydides conceived his work in the manner of a statesman and rightly understood it as a guide for political actors.[76] Here the emphasis is on the practical and political utility of the *History* (though precisely how, when, and for whom it will be useful is left uncertain). The other regards it as a contemplative, even philosophical work, whose intent is not to effect or motivate action in the future but to present an abiding picture of the past. In this interpretation what Thucydides offers is a clear vision of events, certainly a noble pleasure which may compensate in part for the disappointments of actuality but is far from the realm of praxis.[77] What we can learn from him is how to reflect on the past, not how to act in the present or future.

Certainly it is true that after Amphipolis, Thucydides was an exile writing a book rather than an actor speaking in the Assembly. Not having to confront the question What shall we do?, his speech is indeed distinct from that of the speakers or actors in the *History*. His method in writing the book is not and cannot be a pattern to be copied in action. For he achieves an intellectual coherence denied political actors. Consequently it would confound matters to expect that their failures could be remedied by imitating the intelligence or perspective of the historian.[78]

But it would be wrong to turn the fact of Thucydides's exile into a metaphor for intellectual and political alienation. However much exile lent sharpness to his vision of people and occurrences and thereby enabled him to see actors, cultures, and events as representative; however much his *History* stands outside the contingency, particularity, and partiality of political action; even if, wrenched from what he regarded as the greatest movement in history, the structure of the *History* became his main reality, it is a serious error to conclude that Thucydides was a politically alienated philosopher. He did not choose exile and we have no evidence that he came to like it. He does not seek respite from politics in philosophic life—not only because it is doubtful such a "life" existed but because he is driven to thought by exile and, as I think the *History* shows, by a wish to overcome it. His work is a bridge between thought and action, not a path leading away from the polis to god, nature, or the soul. It is not so much remote from the realm of praxis as different from it. (It remains to be seen in what way this is so.)

It is also misleading to assume that because the canons of Thucydides's historiography are unreproducible in deed, his work is contemplative or philosophical in nature. For Thucydides thinks of his work in political terms. The values, language, and concerns of his thought are primarily those of action and the actor, not those of inquiry or the inquirer.[79] For him theoretical problems arise out of practical ones, and the point of studying the former is to see more clearly the structure in which we are all called upon to act.[80] Hindsight and insight aim at foresight. But they do so without formulating programmatic statements, hypotheses to be tested, or general laws of politics. The *History* is not a handbook, for its wisdom is allusive and unpropositional. Such wisdom involves judging what is significant, discriminating between the essential and superfluous, and sharpening one's understanding of the complex interplay between political experience and thought such that the design of experience becomes intelligible and thought efficacious. This Thucydides displays in his portrait of the precariousness of human speech and action, in his depiction of the efforts of intellect to contain political contingency, in his presentation of political authority and leadership, in his tracing of the corrosive effects of war and imperialism, and in his examination of the relation of speech, violence, and freedom. (He manages all this within the context of a history and story that maintains the beauty of Periclean Athens against the capriciousness of human memory by giving such vivid value and meaning to a moment in his nation's past that his readers, too, feel elation and sadness at the splendor and tragedy of the city that gave him birth.)[81]

Thucydides's relation to praxis, then, is as a political educator. It is true that his thought does not tell us precisely what to do or how to go about changing the world. (That is because he does not regard the political world as an object for technical control and manipulation.[82]) Nor does he offer straightforward authoritative pronouncements on "what is to be done." Only a theory aware of the radical contingency in all political decisions and attainments has, to paraphrase Aristotle, genuine care and respect for its subject matter.

Given that the *History* is not a contemplative glance but a work of political education close to the realm of praxis, is it possible to further specify the nature of proximity? Who are *his* political and theoretical heirs? When will the *History* be "useful"? (being careful not to be too utilitarian in our notion of usefulness). If the achievement of the Athenian Thucydides, like the Athenian achievement, is so rare, what sort of generality can he claim for his work or we for him? What and how can Thucydides teach *us* about politics and political theory, about how to think properly about the problem of speech and action, theory and practice?

In its own terms and for understanding the *History*'s relation to praxis, it is important to see that Thucydides's theoretical heirs, like his political ones, will be those who love action and admire political greatness, even while recognizing the fragility and tragedy inherent in both. Thucydides can teach them to see what is implicit in their theoretical aspirations, just as Pericles in the Funeral Oration revealed to the Athenians what was implicit in their greatness and power. Resisting the temptation to think about politics in technical or ahistorically philosophic terms, they may find in Thucydides an emendation of the way the problem of theory and practice is presently considered. Thucydides is particularly "useful" as a source for emendation given his location in the development of Greek (and Western) thought. He writes at a time when thought has sufficiently emerged so that no thing or idea stands alone but always confronts its opposite. Though these oppositions are general, they are never remote abstractions. They remain individually vivid, unsubmerged by a single dominating idea, balancing intellectual intelligibility and dramatic immediacy. Thus the conflict between political principles and cultures is a war between Sparta and Athens; the impact of violence on politics is exposed in the character of Cleon, the Corcyrean Revolution and the Melian Dialogue;

the relation of speech and deed is explored through the juxtaposition of individual speakers and speaking and action in particular contexts. Ideas and action are never far apart; the former struggle with each other in human fashion and with the vitality of action.[83] Thus Thucydides stands less outside the political forces he studies than most other political theorists. He is less distant and abstracted from the particular desires, claims, interests, and needs of those who are the objects and subjects of his analysis. In large measure (but not completely) Thucydides avoids the temptation to view history as a process realizing itself behind the backs of actors.[84]

It is important to insist on the prephilosophical character of Thucydides's *History*. For seeing him in terms of the later philosophical tradition obscures the political rootedness of his thought and ignores the value of his work for delineating the conditions that gave birth to political philosophy. Appreciating the increasing complexity and pace of polis life, the erosion of political and intellectual restraint under the imperatives of war, the institutional disorder and factionalism of Athens and her fading image of greatness makes the emerging philosophic vocation politically intelligible. Moreover, by providing a political context for the rise of political philosophy, Thucydides enables us to see how the separation of theory and practice is political at inception and presumably political in solution. At the same time, by dramatizing the conflict between words and reality and raising the question of how mind and thought can know and master the whole, his *History* gives us an insight into how the separation of speech and deed, thought and action could become the wider separation of theory and practice. In terms of my earlier image, Thucydides intimates the outer circle of theory and practice, without himself being located on it or writing in its terms. One step removed from the context of action, his critical perspective on the speech and deeds of actors does not diminish his love for politics, action, and his native city. His exile is unchosen. In the end Plato chose the Academy, and Aristotle, from whom we learn so much about Athens and the city-state, is himself a man without a polis.

The unique character and texture of the *History* does not preclude our learning from Thucydides in a way that augments and emends the philosophical study of politics, whether it be Hegelian, Marxist, or Liberal in inspiration. But it does preclude any simple imitation. We must argue for what Thucydides simply did. Contemporary political theorists and philosophers cannot avoid questions of historiography or the philosophy of history that are posed for *us* by the *History*.

V

Thucydides leaves us with some disconcerting notions about whether and when the harmony of thought and action, theory and practice is desirable and possible. Emphasizing a political dimension of the problem largely uncongenial to modern sensibilities, his *History* suggests that any unity or harmony is as rare an achievement as the greatness of Athens or the leadership of a Pericles. (In not one of these cases is the rarity or unpredictability of the achievement sufficient grounds for dismissing its possibility.) There is no historical dialectic that promises permanent resolution. The most we can say is that any unity or harmony of political thought and action, theory and practice requires: first, citizens who share a love of action, and not just some of them but all of them and not just sporadically but incessantly; second, that such love be within a public life that respects human dimensions of space, time, and complexity; third, that thought be firmly attentive to questions of action and that intelligence be integrated into a political tradition recognized as such by one's fellow citizens; and fourth, the presence of a political leader whose political and intellectual gifts enhance the freedom and intelligence of his countrymen so that thought and action are united in citizenship. Where such conditions do not obtain, thought and action must remain separate and opposed. Confronting this argument, one is tempted to dismiss it on the grounds that it is simply irrelevant to our situation. But this is an evasion which fails to explore what is true in Thucydides's argument and lost by any argument that ignores it.

The theoretical perspective of the *History* also leaves us with some notion of what sort of thought could be harmonized or united with praxis and how the vocation of political education might be its vehicle. Or to put it another way, compared to much contemporary political philosophy, Thucydides's thought itself embodies a kind of harmony between speech and deed, thought and action. One can see this in the closeness of his thought to the realm of praxis, in the interplay of his intelligence and patriotism, and in his maintenance of the vitality and uniqueness of human action, events, people, and political cultures against their assimilation by nature, a contemplative glance, or world historical processes. With this sense of theory and politics Thucydides's *History* might usefully emend, or at least give pause, theoretically and politically to, the way the problem of theory and practice is often understood.

III

Plato and Aristotle:
The Unity versus the Autonomy
of Theory and Practice

Terence Ball

The history of philosophy is rewritten in every generation, with the contrast between philosophers drawn and highlighted in different ways. Rewriting that history from the perspective afforded by its own problems and concerns, each generation has its own Plato, its own Aristotle. In the recent past, when it was fashionable to say that political theory had been laid to rest by modern social science, Plato was viewed as the prototype of the "traditional," "speculative," or "normative" theorist and Aristotle as the exemplar of the social-scientific virtues of hardheadedness and empirical-mindedness.[1] This view I believe to be mistaken. My aim in this essay is to show in what ways it is mistaken and to provide a corrective for it. I shall dispute the claim that Plato is the more "theoretical" and Aristotle the more "practical" thinker by showing how their respective conceptions of theoria and praxis differ. My thesis is that Plato's conception of theory entails the unity of theory and practice and Aristotle's, their separation into autonomous spheres of human activity. If my argument holds water, then the claim against which I contend is shown to be not so much false as simply incoherent. That is, it makes no sense to say that, qua theorist, Aristotle is the more practically minded of the two. Instead one might rather say that Plato is the more "practical" and Aristotle the more detached and other-worldly thinker. That too would be an exaggeration but not so entirely wide of the mark.

I

A theorist (theoros) was originally a spectator, an observer of religious rites, theatrical performances, athletic contests, and other public events.[2] And as spectators often traveled considerable distances to see (theorein) such events, the term acquired the connotation of traveler. In later usage the term retained these connotations but assumed a more technical or restricted meaning as well. To distinguish the rude and rowdy spectators from the cultivated, educated, and refined ones, theorist came to mean not only one who "sees" but who has a faculty for seeing farther, for discriminating, judging, comparing, criticizing, and savoring what he sees.[3] A spectator in the latter sense is not one who seeks immediate sensual or perceptual gratification but rather one who seeks understanding and wisdom. Moreover, a theorist in this newer sense will travel farther, will go to greater lengths, to "see." His is the distant vision of a man who has traveled far and seen much not ordinarily seen by most men.

Plato is most emphatic about the kind of seeing done by a philosopher. In the *Republic* Glaucon mentions the resemblance between the sightseers at festivals and the philosopher. Socrates concedes that there is a resemblance but dismisses it as counterfeit.[4] He then goes on to suggest that the task of philosophy is the pursuit and love of knowledge (epistēmē) of what is eternal, immutable, and unchanging. The Forms—the ineffable, noumenal essence of things—constitute the proper object of philosophical contemplation. Such knowledge, moreover, is necessarily incommunicable if not entirely private. Knowledge of the Forms is direct, unmediated by language. In the *Seventh Letter* (if we may grant its authenticity) Plato dwells at some length on the limits of language. What ordinarily passes for knowledge comes, he says, through names, descriptions, and images. That, however, is far from satisfactory for the philosophical mind, which seeks to know a thing not in its mutability but in its eternality:

. . . when the mind is in quest of knowledge not of the particular but of the essential, [names, images, etc.] confront the mind with the unsought particular, whether in verbal or in bodily form. Each of [these] makes the reality that is expressed in words or illustrated in objects liable to easy refutation by the evidence of the senses. The result of this is to make practically every man a prey to complete perplexity and uncertainty.[5]

Every man, that is, except the philosopher. Only he knows the extent of language's inadequacy. Only he knows its limits. And language is, for philosophical purposes, very limited indeed. For all its initial dialectical value, language does not, of itself, reveal or disclose anything of lasting philosophical value;

rather, it forecloses the possibility of gaining true knowledge. And this has profound and far-reaching consequences regarding the very possibility of acquiring and imparting a philosophical knowledge of politics. Plato's conception of philosophy, in other words, not only undermines politics—which is Wolin's argument[6]—but in a sense *rules out the possibility of there ever being anything like political philosophy*. Indeed, I suspect that Plato might have found political philosophy a disagreeable neologism.

If there is to be true knowledge, in Plato's sense, of the political, then there must be an essence of politics. There is perhaps an essence, but it leads us into paradox. The essence of politics is communication: public speech, made possible by a shared language. Without it, there could be no politics but only, as Hannah Arendt has said, "mute violence."[7] If, as de Jouvenel claims, "the elementary political process is the action of mind upon mind through speech,"[8] what are we to do with Plato? Or, to slip into a more comfortable idiom: instead of talking about essences, we might ask, how is political activity *possible* in the first place? If we concede its public character, as surely we must, then language is its conditio sine qua non. That is not to say that a shared language is a sufficient, but only a necessary, condition of political action. Language makes politics possible.

This essential incompatibility between Platonic philosophy and politics-as-speech has some interesting consequences. I shall briefly indicate what these consequences are and suggest that as a result our image of Plato may be in need of some revision.

In the *Republic* we are not so much told what is to count as "political" as we are informed of what is to be excluded. Significantly, participation in any direct or significant sense is excluded, or rather severely circumscribed. The active consent and participation of all citizens is neither required nor requested. Temperance (sōphrosynē) obviates popular participation and consent by rationalizing nonparticipatory silence and acquiescence. Temperance, the particular virtue of most citizens, consists of the multitude's acknowledgement of its individual and collective inferiority, along with a recognition of the rulers' superiority and their fitness to rule. Temperance is a condition of "unanimity or harmonious agreement between the naturally superior and inferior elements on the question which of the two should govern, whether in the state or in the individual."[9] Temperance leads to mute assent, to silent and uncritical acquiescence on the part of the citizenry.

The degree to which Plato's ideal Republic is speechless is quite remarkable. There is no need for *inter*course, that is, speech between and among all the

citizens (as distinguished from the ruling few) about the affairs of the community as a whole. Truly *public* speech and deliberation is superfluous—if not
indeed dangerous—in this ideal Republic. The Philosopher-king speaks in the
imperative voice, instead of the fraternal "tone of expostulation" which Pericles believed to be the proper manner of speech among citizens.[10]

From this a peculiar conception of politics emerges. For politics comes to
exclude public deliberation, speech and debate, participation and argument,
conflict and consent—all carried on, both figuratively and literally, within the
liberating confines of the "public space"—in favor of fear, force, and command. This is surely more a Spartan than an Athenian conception of politics.
Moreover, this conception of politics readily licenses force and compulsion, as
Plato explicitly acknowledges in the *Statesman*. A true Statesman, Plato first
says, can be distinguished from a tyrant by applying a simple rule of thumb,
viz., the Statesman's rule is voluntarily accepted, i.e., the citizens actively consent to his authority.[11] Later, however, Plato not only drops this requirement
but insists that if the Statesman fails to persuade the citizens to comply, he
may "force his better laws upon [them]."[12] It "makes no difference whether
[the] subjects are willing or unwilling . . ."[13]

There is also a rather revealing parallel between Plato's attitude toward law
and his criticism of language. For both language and law "fix" meanings. I have
alluded already to Plato's argument that language stands in the way of true
knowledge (epistēmē), which is the sort of knowledge sought by the philosopher.
In a remarkably similar way Plato contends that a body or system of law, especially one written down and codified, stands as an obstacle to the art of the
Statesman.[14] Law cannot be an expression of true knowledge about governing
because, in its very articulation in *public* form, it repudiates the philosopher's
art, which is the province of very few men.[15] Like language, law cannot make
those fine but crucial discriminations which are so much a part of the philosopher's private communion with the Real. The strictures of language suffocate
the spirit of philosophy; those of law cloud the vision of statesmanship. Both
are in consequence philosophically proscribed.

II

I have suggested that Plato's conception of philosophy raises a perplexing question, namely: How is true knowledge (epistēmē) of the political possible? Or
rather, more precisely, how is political philosophy possible? Plato's answer is
found in the *Republic*. For no true knowledge of the political is possible unless and until the polis itself is restructured to be fit to receive philosophy.[16]

Stated somewhat differently, this means that the possibility of there being such an enterprise as political philosophy presupposes a *philosophical politics*. Only when a philosopher has figuratively and literally remade the polis in his own image, is true knowledge of the political within reach. Just as one cannot have true knowledge of what is chaotic, mutable, and changing, so one cannot attain true knowledge of politics—which is notoriously Protean—unless and until that activity ceases to be a matter of chance and change. If politics is to be a subject worthy of philosophical study and contemplation, it must aspire to emulate and partake of the changeless perfection of the Forms. Only then will political *opinion* (doxa) give way to political *knowledge*. Such knowledge is not open to everyone. It is not only privileged but is indeed essentially private.

Political knowledge is in Plato's view peculiarly self-centered—the self in this case being the philosopher's self or soul (psychē). The Republic, we must remember, is an elaborately structured and richly textured analogy. The whole imposing edifice of Plato's ideal polity begins with an impulse to probe the human soul and to locate justice (dikaiosynē) within it as its ordering and harmonizing principle. This ideal polis is constructed less for the purpose of acquiring political knowledge than for probing the structure of a perfectly harmonized soul, the soul of the philosopher. After the fashion of the Oracle at Delphi, which counseled "know thyself," Plato's overriding aim in the *Republic* is the acquisition of self-knowledge.

It is of course a commonplace and a truism among students of political theory that Plato's ideal Republic corresponds in its structure to the perfectly ordered and harmonious soul of its ruler, the Philosopher-king. Its soul is his soul, writ large. What I am suggesting here is that the analogy between polis and psychē has implications for political knowledge that have been slighted by students of political philosophy. The most important consequence of this analogy is that, on Plato's account, the philosopher's knowledge of the political must, in the end, be a matter of *self*-knowledge.

Other commentators have remarked upon, and roundly criticized, the essentially private character of political knowledge as Plato conceives of it.[17] This criticism, valid as it is, does not go far enough. For it fails to recognize the nature, extent, and implications of Plato's epistemological privatism. If Plato's Philosopher-king were asked, how is political knowledge—that is to say, political philosophy—possible in the first place?, he might well answer: l'état, c'est moi. In a well-ordered and reasonably structured polis like the Republic, only the philosopher can have any genuine knowledge of the political. And that is because the Republic is but a projection of his own philosophical constitution, an enlargement, as it were, of his own reasonable soul. In a fashion that seems almost to anticipate Hobbes and Vico, Plato suggests that one knows best what one has made: and the Philosopher-king has knowledge of the political insofar as his soul is mirrored in its structure. The Republic is reasonable because he has reasoned it into existence. He has made it in his own image. Like God, he sees himself in his creation.

By this act of creation Plato reconciles polis and psychē, political knowledge and self-knowledge. Once the Republic exists as a theoretical construction, political knowledge is no longer secondary to, or derivative from, self-knowledge: the two are then identical and inseparable. By this act of the theoretical imagination Plato joins poleteia and psychē in a timeless bond.

That this imposing achievement existed only "in theory" did not weigh against it. For inasmuch as the theoretical imagination leads one closer to the Forms, theoria is more "real" than concrete praxis in the workaday world of the polis, a world marked by flux and change. "Is our theory any the worse, if we cannot prove it possible that a state so organized should be actually founded?"[18] Plato's implication is that, although his theory is no worse for not being applied in the world, the world is all the poorer for its absence.

<h2 style="text-align:center">III</h2>

What is the place of the philosopher—"one who is so high-minded and whose thought can contemplate all time and all existence"[19]—in a mediocre and mundane world? In what follows I shall consider the concept of praxis and the character of Aristotle's differences with Plato regarding the role of the theorist and the place of theoria on the map of political activity.

Legislators or law givers did not have to be citizens of the polis for which they legislated. Indeed, they were often outsiders, even complete strangers.[20] The philosopher was also an outsider but in a rather special sense. The citizens of his polis regarded philosophy as an alien activity, though for quite different reasons than citizens of present-day America might give. For if being a man was synonymous with being an active participant in the life and affairs of the city, the theorist was only half a man, or, rather, part human and part something else. His activity of contemplation, unlike that of politics, was not wholly of this world; it had an element of divinity about it. On this Plato and Aristotle were agreed.[21]

The "strangeness" of philosophy has been expressed in various ways. Plato made much of Socrates's daemon, with which he communicated while in trance-like states and which advised him to stay out of politics.[22] Plato also emphasizes the sense of loneliness, the isolation bordering on madness, which accompanies the contemplative life.[23] He even suggests that theorizing means taking leave of life, a kind of separation or death.[24] These themes run through Plato's works, especially, as a leitmotif, or better, perhaps, as a defense, the theorist's own apologia pro vita sua. In a poignant and moving passage in the *Republic*, Plato has Socrates justify his abstention from political life. His abstention is not that of a coward or a shirker of his rightful duty; it has a lonely, heroic quality about it. Socrates decries the fallen state of politics, which he has observed largely from the outside. "One who has weighed all this keeps quiet and goes on his way, like the traveller who takes shelter under a wall from a driving storm of dust and hail; and seeing lawlessness spreading on all sides, is content if he can keep his hands clean from iniquity while life lasts. . . ." This outpouring of bitterness, leavened only by an apparent resignation to his fate, seems antipolitical in the extreme. And yet bitterness immediately gives way to a profoundly political lament. For Socrates suggests that serenity, or even divinity, is more suited to a god than to a man, being "far less than he might achieve, if his lot were cast in a society congenial to his nature, where he could grow to his full height and save his country as well as himself."[25] Nevertheless, this reverie is tinged with the harsh light of realism. Plato knows only too well that the fate which awaits the philosopher who returns to the Cave is the fate of Socrates.

Both Plato and Aristotle emphasize the alien or foreign character of theoria, or contemplation. In Plato's later dialogues—particularly the *Statesman*, the *Laws*, and the *Sophist*—the stranger, who has traveled far and seen much, is the central figure. In casting the theorist as a stranger Plato deliberately heightens and dramatizes the foreign character of the theorist, who is given no name, age, or any significant attributes other than his way (aporie). In an almost Jungian fashion, Plato reduces the theorist, as stranger, to an archetypal figure. Similarly, Aristotle remarks upon the alien character of theoria and those whose way it is. He asks, "which way of life is more desirable—to join with other citizens and share in the state's activity, or to live in it like an alien, absolved from the ties of political society?"[26] Yet there is a world of difference between Plato's estranged philosopher and Aristotle's.

For Plato, the philosopher's way is radically incompatible with that of most men. Political society as presently constituted had to be made over, lest it corrupt even the pure spirit of philosophy.[27] Even though the philosopher is the happiest of men, his happiness remains an inward happiness and he is powerless to help others. Instead of allowing the philosopher to grow to his full stature, the city of men would force the philosopher to adopt its licentious ways. Politics and philosophy cannot coexist in harmony, unless and until the political realm is recast in the image of the philosopher. The second-best solutions of the *Statesman* and the *Laws* may be good enough for the run of men, but they are not wholly congenial to the spirit of philosophy.

For Aristotle, however, the theoretical life can more readily exist independently of the political. Politics and philosophy are two ways; it is not necessary, nor would it be desirable, to subordinate the one to the other. The mistake of the Sophists, he suggests, is to make theory dominate practice and to make political choices on the basis of abstract principle rather than past experience.[28] (It sometimes appears that Aristotle regards Plato's *Republic* as a most subtle exercise in sophistry.) A true theorist must have had previous political experience upon which to form the basis of judgment. But it is not necessary, Aristotle argues, to train politicians in philosophy, even if a true theorist must have had previous experience in politics. One's knowledge of the political is practical knowledge; political science is politics done well. The science of politics is the practice of politics. This is not, however, to say that there can be a science of praxis. On the contrary, praxis or action in the political realm is concerned with the application of means to the end of public goodness; the "products" of political activity are laws and other instruments of public virtue.[29] Theoria, on the other hand, is not a means but an end in itself; it "produces" nothing, conduces to no end other than itself. Yet theoria is not the passive vita contemplativa of the Middle Ages; on the contrary, it is highly active – more active, in its own way, than politics itself, or indeed any sort of "production." Theorizing, or contemplative activity, is more continuous than any other form of human action.[30] It is also a higher form of activity than any other because it is not instrumental in character. Theoria is also more independent, more self-sufficient, than political activity; for it does not require the presence of other men in order to be carried on – in marked contrast to politics, which requires the presence of several citizens.[31] Theoria and praxis are thus different in kind; any attempt (like that made by Plato) to subordinate the second to the first would constitute a sophistical perversion of both.

There emerges in Aristotle a kind of functional differentiation between theory and practice. Political activity is concerned with implementing the felicity or happiness (eudaimonia) of the polis. Theory, on the other hand, is primarily concerned with the goodness of the individual, i.e., the theorist himself. More specifically, the happiness of the polis will largely depend upon the degree to which it is self-sufficient (autarkēs). The happiness of the individual will depend upon his having acquired an almost stoical self-sufficiency. The theorist, being self-sufficient, is the happiest of men; unlike the citizen, qua citizen, Aristotle's theorist is, by analogy, the happy or self-sufficient polis. By Aristotle's reckoning, theoria is a more selfish enterprise than it is for Plato. For while on Plato's view the theorist's own ultimate happiness required the enthroning of philosphy in the polis, thereby remaking it and "saving his country as well as himself," for Aristotle the theorist qua theorist does not require a well-ordered polity in which to practice his vocation. So long as Aristotle's theorist is permitted to go his own way, the polis may go its way; for his happiness and its happiness are different in kind.[32] Political activity or praxis is one way, theoria another. Theory is active, but not politically active; the theorist compares, judges, savors, and sometimes even advises, but he does not seek to usurp a function that is not his to perform, viz., the practical activity of politics (or political science).

Given Aristotle's separation of theory and practice, what are the consequences for political knowledge? How, in other words, is political knowledge possible in Aristotle's scheme? It is possible, Aristotle maintains, because there is a distinction to be drawn between different kinds of knowledge, viz., exact or certain knowledge and inexact knowledge. The first kind of knowledge (and for Plato the only true kind) consists of contemplating what is eternal and unchanging, necessary, certain, and precise. But there is in Aristotle's view another kind of knowledge, namely "practical science," which is less precise, subject to revision, and concerned with particular matters "susceptible of change."[33] The latter is concerned with action or praxis. "Political science" is a matter of knowing how to deal with matters concerning the polis. "Political science . . . —politics in fact—is a matter of action and deliberation on policy."[34] Politics, or political science, is aimed at "producing results." And so far as results are concerned, theory is superfluous:

It is in fact experience rather than theory that normally gets results. Practical wisdom being concerned with action, we need . . . the knowledge of particular facts more than general principles.[35]

We acquire knowledge of the political by engaging in political activity. Theorizing, then, does not yield political knowledge. As previously noted, theoria is for Aristotle an activity different *in kind* from praxis. Or rather, political activity is one kind of praxis—that concerned with "production" (poiesis)— and theoria is another—that which is not instrumental or productive of other things but an end in itself. There can be no theoretical knowledge of politics, because political praxis is yielded by deliberation about means,[36] whereas theoria is itself an end.

IV

How, then, is "political theory" possible? From the foregoing it would appear that a theory *of* politics would be out of the question. But there is a way out. For we have been speaking of logical distinctions so far and have failed to consider what might be called the biographical dimension. For although there is no political theory *as such*, there are political theorists. Aristotle suggests that the true political theorist cannot simultaneously be a practicing politician—for the politician's "busyness" is the enemy of contemplation[37]—but that he must previously have been immersed in the immediacy of political activity.[38] The political scientist is the practicing politician; the political theorist is, as it were, the retired political scientist. (This sequence of political immersion and subsequent retirement is a biographical fact for many political theorists, notably Machiavelli, Hobbes, Locke, and even Plato, who never quite became the influential insider he once aspired to be.) The theorist's task is not unlike the music critic's task, whereas the statesman's may be likened to the conductor's and the politician's, to the musician's.[39] The theorist understands the underlying principles of harmony, the causes and varieties of discord and cacophony, etc., whereas the others do not and need not have such knowledge. He may presume to advise the conductor, but he would not become conductor himself. Just so, statesmen and men of affairs "should be willing to hear, and ready to accept, the advice of genuine philosophers."[40] Political philosophy is for Aristotle both a matter of practical know-how as well as "know-why" which comes with reflection, maturity, and systematic inquiry (methodos) into political practice, not only in a single polis at a single time (for the political actor may have to know as much) but in many cities at many times.[41] In the end political theory is neither politics nor theory but a peculiar hybrid for which even Aristotle can find no suitable designation. His taxonomic talent seems almost to fail him, for he can speak only of "proper spirit" and "right habit of mind" as emblematic of the theorist's vocation.

What difference can philosophy be expected to make in the life of a man? Aristotle's answer comes to this: Happiness is the aim of every man and may be pursued in three ways. It may be sought through pleasure; but that is a perverted way, for even the animals do as much. It may be pursued in political activity, which is a noble undertaking and a necessary one; political action yields the shared happiness that comes from living in a self-sufficient or autarkic

polis; but such happiness is precarious and transitory, if history teaches us anything at all. Satisfying as it is, political happiness is of the sort that makes the
individual not wholly self-sufficient but dependent upon others. Therefore the
highest happiness must be one that is intrinsically complete and allows its possessor to be self-sufficient. This is the happiness afforded by contemplation,
by theoria. And even if the theorist is rebuked, and his advice ignored, he can
remain happy; for his happiness does not depend upon the approval of other
men (although such approval would be welcome if it were forthcoming).[42] The
polis need not be made over in the image of the philosopher; it need only leave
him alone, not to intrude upon his contemplation with matters of public concern. Like the "solitary state which is happy in itself and in isolation,"[43] the
theorist is a solitary figure, but one whose solitude is self-imposed and deemed
desirable. For, says Aristotle,

> . . . the life of action is best, alike for every state as a whole and for each in-
> dividual in his own conduct. But the life of action need not be . . . a life
> which involves relations to others. Nor should our thoughts be held to be active
> only when they are directed to objects which have to be achieved by action.
> Thoughts with no object beyond themselves, and speculations and trains of
> reflection followed purely for their own sake, are far more deserving of the
> name of active.[44]

Contemplation is the only self-moved human activity; it requires only to be left
alone and conduces to no further end, public or private. It is not the theorist's
proper task to build ideal cities, much less rule over real ones.

It thus emerges that theoria is for Aristotle in a way more detached than it
is for Plato. Plato's ideal is that of the unity of theory and practice and with
it the end of the philosopher's estrangement. Aristotle's ideal is the real; for
him the real *is* the rational. It is not the business of theory to restructure practice. The theorist's task is not to change the world but to understand it. If he
is to understand the world, the theorist must keep his distance from it.

Plato and Aristotle differ markedly in their respective attitudes toward past
experience, both of a historical and a biographical kind. For Plato the study of
philosophy commences by unlearning what one has learned; if truth is to enter,
error must first be purged. This requires a radical break with the past: "the entire soul must be turned away from this changing world."[45] Of course, later,
the philosopher, armed with a vision of changeless perfection, turns back to
this changing world and attempts to transform it in accordance with his vision.
But where Plato counsels a break with the past Aristotle reaffirms its value.
"The teaching of past experience," Aristotle cautions, "must not be ignored."

"We are bound to pay some regard to the long past and the passage of the years . . ." If a scheme had any real value, it would have been adopted by someone, somewhere, at some time in the past. The task of the theorist is not so much to discover new truths as to sort and coordinate old ones: "Almost everything has been discovered already; though some . . . have not been coordinated."[46]

Thus is Platonic hubris chastened by, and contrasted with, Aristotelian sobriety and "solid good sense."[47] It is this tension between mastery and submission—between changing political reality and "understanding" it—that marks the entire history of Western political thought. The differences between Plato and Aristotle recur, albeit in a different form, in Marx's quarrel with Hegel and, in our own day, in political theory's quarrel with political science. That modern political scientists should look back to Aristotle and regard him as their patron saint comes as no surprise. To praise Aristotle for his sobriety and solid good sense is at the same time to condemn Plato, Marx, and others who would attempt not merely to understand the world but to change it.

V

In this essay I have emphasized several deep and fundamental differences between two great—indeed perhaps paradigmatic—figures in the history of political thought. Yet in emphasizing their differences one must be careful not to exaggerate them. It must be said and underscored that neither Plato nor Aristotle would recognize "theory" in its modern instrumentalist sense, that is, as something provisional, tentative, and forever subject to revision or even outright replacement. Both Plato and Aristotle would agree that a theory is not a means, nor an instrument, but an end in itself. Theory is not a thing to be picked up or put down at will but a way of life requiring total commitment. Theory is to be lived, not used or applied. Theory is to be "practiced" in living one's life properly and well.

Still there is in this ideal an essential, and perhaps inescapable, tension: one's life has to be lived among men, but the bios theoretikos cannot be lived to its fullest in a flawed and imperfect world. If one is to live the bios theoretikos to its fullest extent, one must either leave the world or change it. The former option is implicit in Aristotle and explicit in some later Christian thinkers; the latter is implicit in Plato and explicit in Marx's Eleventh Thesis on Feuerbach.[48] In both Plato and Marx the motive of mastery—of remaking the political world—is paramount. But the similarity extends no further: for Plato, no less than for Aristotle, theoria is an end in itself; for Marx, by contrast, theory is an instrument with which to change the world. And it is in that respect that the classical conception of theoria is at odds with, and light years away from, the modern instrumentalist view of theory and its "relation" to practice.

PART II
Developments

IV

Kant on Theory and Practice

Carl Raschke

I

Kant's moral and political philosophy has incurred its fair share of polemical misinterpretation and abuse within the past two centuries; but perhaps no greater mischief in the chronicle of critical scholarship has been wrought than the Marxian reproach that Kant divorces theory from practice. Indeed, Marxists for generations have touted their philosophical method as bridging finally and incontrovertibly the theory/practice dichotomy; and thus they have tended to malign or caricature earlier schools of thought, which may have arrived at similar, though less refined, insights, as perhaps "bourgeois" or "unscientific" in tenor. The historical defamation of Kant, of course, originates in the profile of the Königsberg philosopher composed by his revisionary heir in the tradition of German idealism and architect of modern dialectical thought—G. W. F. Hegel. In *The Phenomenology of Mind* Hegel meticulously criticizes, without mentioning Kant by name, "the moral view of the world" in which the pure concept of duty is taken "to be the essential reality" and in which "the moral consciousness sees merely an occasion for acting, but does not see itself obtaining through its action the happiness of performance and the enjoyment of achievement."[1] Kant's emphasis on the good will or intention, rather than the utility of the act itself, as the measure of morality was thought by Hegel to involve a denial of the worldly efficacy of one's deeds.[2] The deontological bias of Kant's practical philosophy, Hegel deduced, leads to a sort of ethic of interior virtue, wherein a man can be counted moral without overtly behaving so and without having made some visible impress on the lives of his peers or on society as a whole.

On this same score certain Marxists have seen fit to indict what Kant (perhaps unfortunately) calls his "metaphysics of morals" as passive and privatistic. Kant's presumed "insider's" resolution to the problem of right action, according to the Marxists, tallies nicely with the atomic individualism of bourgeois ideology. The result is that morality became sentimentalized. Yet pari passu the social ethic of humaneness and impartiality, along with personal scruples, is laid aside on entering the busy marketplace.

Second, Marxists swiftly pounce on Kant's ambivalent and seemingly self-contradictory attitude toward political revolution as evidence that his practical philosophy breaks down when confronted with the reality of oppressive social structures. Kant's curious position on this matter, of course, is familiar to many philosophers and intellectual historians. Whereas Kant denounces any resort to armed insurrection as an unacceptable redress for the violation of the rights of a people by their leader (chiefly because, he insists, the people have no more claim to arbitrate constitutional disputes than their appointed rulers),[3] he nevertheless urges that regimes instituted through successful revolts not be resisted as interlopers but fully respected as lawful representatives of the will of the people.[4] In one famous passage Kant lauds the French Revolution and commends the Jacobins not only as deft strategists but as popular heroes who have "fixed their gaze on the *rights* of the people to which they belonged."[5]

Any astute critic might well dismiss such argumentation as slippery enough to escape the Prussian censors or perhaps even as glibly reactionary in its intent. He could point out that although Kant makes it a matter of justice that governing authorities sedulously protect their subjects, he allows the people no effective counteraction (except verbal protest) against malfeasance and misuse of political office. Kant's theory of right, therefore, would seem to apply to real political engagements only under utopian conditions (i.e., those in which the rulers were sincerely and impeccably motivated toward safeguarding the common good) but would have little value in historical practice. Such conclusions can be drawn, however, only if Kant's writings are read with a jaundiced and undiscerning eye. Kant, in fact, was forever defending himself against those who interpreted his ideas selectively without bothering to find out how his thoughts were completely orchestrated. While it would be highly presumptuous to maintain that Kant significantly anticipated the Marxian approach to morals and society, it would be just as unwarranted to demean him as some misty idealist whose philosophy is suitable only for the comfortable scholar's chair and not for transforming the world.

To the contrary, as we shall see, Kant's idealism conceals a model for social and political change that does not stray as far from those of activist philosophies like Marxism as one might suspect. Why such a model is infrequently extracted from the texts by Kant's commentators may be due to Kant's metaphysical diction, convoluted style, and occasional inconsistency. The latter defect is often called against Kant, but we should remember that inconsistencies may not reveal a muddled mind so much as the flexibility of a philosophy in constant evolution. The ontogenetic character of Kant's thought is thus often overlooked by those who assume a unified critical corpus. As Kant himself wryly observed, "consistency is the highest obligation of a philosopher and yet the most rarely found."[6] That certain discrepancies should crop up from point to point in Kant's works (especially in the political writings which are exploratory and topical in nature) should not dull us to the latter's wider impact.

Although one might expect to discover in just about any Marxist history of modern philosophy a rather bad notice for Kant and the "Kantians," most reviews of this kind turn out usually to be ideologically shortsighted or exegetically shallow. There do, however, appear within this tradition (mostly among independent Western Marxists not beholden to party dicta) rather serious and at times sophisticated cases to be made against the general consequences of Kant's thinking. These cases rest on the prima facie import of the language Kant employs—a language which readily suggests a philosophical method that has been disparaged as dualistic or formalistic. The suspicion of such a method breeds the claim that Kant has no workable concept of praxis.[7] Kant's own statements, however, can be cited to spring him from the formalist snare that his critics have laid for him.

II

Now and then Kant himself takes up the gauntlet against those who accuse him of having dichotomized theory and practice. Passages exhibiting the main lines of Kant's defense occur throughout his later works. Kant's most pointed rebuttal appears in an essay composed fairly late in his career (1793) entitled "Über den Gemeinspruch: das mag in der Theorie richtig sein, taucht aber nicht für die Praxis" ("On the Common Saying: This May Be True in Theory, but It

Does not Apply in Practice") and written perhaps in response to insinuations by other authors that his system as a whole demonstrates philosophically the everyday proverb the essay undertakes to disabuse. While not saying so outright, this short tract implies that Kant is seeking to correct a general misunderstanding about the very language he has employed all along in constructing his arguments. In the opening sentence of the essay Kant defines theory as "a collection of rules, *even of practical rules*" which "are envisaged as principles of a fairly general nature, [even] if they are abstracted from numerous conditions which, nonetheless, necessarily influence their practical application."[8] He goes on to state that practice is simply the application of those rules in specific situations. Although this definition may strike the casual reader as plausible and uncontroversial, it nonetheless represents a departure from the use of the term theory in Kant's major treatises. In the *Critique of Pure Reason* and the *Critique of Practical Reason* Kant draws a rigid line between theoretical and practical reason. Theoretical reason is "concerned with objects of the merely cognitive faculty, and a critical examination of it with reference to this use deals really only with the pure cognitive faculty, because the latter raised suspicion . . . that it might easily pass beyond its boundaries . . ."[9] Theoretical reason encompasses the philosophical task, described in the *Critique of Pure Reason*, to descry the limits of scientific cognition by showing the contradictions and inconsistencies into which rationalistic metaphysics must stumble. Such theorizing has a "purely negative character."[10] It does not constitute a world in the same way that the empirical intellect serves to chart through the categories of understanding, a universally valid and objective complex of knowledge. Rather, theory only provides a collection of critical principles according to which the methods of science are prohibited from doing more than merely interpreting sense-data and thereby indulging in speculation, or the practice of making intuitive generalizations without supporting inductive evidence.

Practical reason, on the other hand, does something "quite different."[11] Instead of circumscribing the employment of a priori or metaphysical thinking, as does theoretical reason, by requiring genuine knowledge to be grounded in empirical observation, practical reason permits the exercise of "pure concepts" without the input of sense experience. In the parlance of classical metaphysics theoretical reason affirms the primacy of matter over form (i.e., thought that has been tested by experience rather than developed from mere assumptions), whereas practical reason conversely demands that matter be subordinated to form. In Kant's own terminology theoretical reason denies the knowability of noumena, or objects beyond sense-knowledge; yet at the same time practical reason secures the reality of noumena so far as the term connotes ideal principles of morality. In fine, "pure practical [ethical] reason" succeeds where pure theoretical reason falters.[12] Theory, in the strict sense that Kant allows here with reference to his critique of scientific understanding, can never guide action. Such a disjunction between theory and practice, however, is more a matter of semantics than philosophical substance. In refuting the theoretical claims of traditional metaphysics, Kant is indirectly challenging the ancient Greek notion of theoria as a self-sufficient intellectual activity or passive contemplation. This move is underscored in Kant's celebrated remark from the preface to the second edition of the first *Critique* that his aim is to "abolish [speculative] knowledge to make room for [moral] belief."[13] The trouble with the old metaphysics, Kant says, is that in erecting a monolithic cathedral of a priori conceptions which purport to explain the whole of man and the universe, it left no space for human freedom and moral choice. If all possibilities for man's purposive behavior are foreordained within some "pre-established harmony" (Leibniz) or an eternal system of nature (Spinoza), then the very word praxis, inasmuch as it signifies some kind of autonomous agency, is rendered meaningless. If praxis means (as it would in such a totalistic metaphysics) simply a mechanical repetition of the immutable order of things, then its relation to theory would be trivial. The true theoretician would not be one who sought viable life-policies based on certain rational options but one who merely embraced his cosmic predicament and retreated in a kind of amor fati. His task would not be to discover appropriate courses of action but to justify his own quietism and his acceptance of the world in all its good and evil dimensions within the light of infinity.

In his brief essay "On the Failure of All Theodicies," Kant attacks just this undertaking of speculative reason to "transvalue" moral values by a naturalistic explanation of all types of conduct.[14] The target of Kant's *Critique of Pure Reason*, therefore, is the false theoretical attitude which precludes the exercise of man's rational discrimination between alternatives and the realization of moral purposes. On the other hand, there exists, for Kant, a proper employment of theory translatable into moral practice. This sort of theory consists in the intelligent formulation of universalizable rules of action as well as the necessary *presuppositions* about the context for action that any moral agent must make. In the first instance, Kant is using the word theory, as shown above, to signify the general "collection of rules" that govern all unconditional forms of moral obligation (e.g., the different formulations of the categorical imperative). In the second instance, Kant is talking about such "postulates" as God, freedom, and immortality which enable men to believe that their pursuit of virtue as demanded by reason is not quixotic but accords with the very laws of nature and with the higher telos of the universe.

Theory is not only a system of precepts; it also consists in a set of compelling "moral beliefs" that serve as a rational framework within which those precepts can be obeyed.[15] It is this second meaning of the term that Kant has in mind when in the second *Critique* he comments that the possibility of God's existence and moral freedom cannot be demonstrated by metaphysical speculation and that what "was heretofore [in the first *Critique*] a problem, now becomes an assertion, and the practical use of reason is thus connected with the elements of theoretical reason."[16] Theory is not hampered by a posteriori judgments; indeed, it is vitiated when such judgments are sought. The crucial problem, for Kant, is not how theory can be disengaged from practice but how practice can be regulated by strict theoretical principles that commission universal assent. In short, Kant throughout the critical corpus is really working with three different models of how one should theorize.

(1) theory *for its own sake* or speculative metaphysics;

(2) theory in the sense of logical criticism concerning the limits of scientific cognition (what Kant calls a "metaphysics of nature");

(3) theory as a rational plan for moral activity independent of empirical knowledge and as a scheme of a priori assumptions about what sort of world might be regarded as conducive to such activity (theory taking the form of an enlightened moral conscience sustained by certain "practical beliefs" or what Kant calls "rational faith").

Critics of Kant often confuse Kant's use of the expression theory in the sense of (2) with that of either (1) or (3). As we have seen, though, such confusion can easily be alleviated by carefully inspecting the syntax of Kant's utterances and by recognizing the different problems to which he addressed himself at various stages of his authorship.

III

The reason for the most common misrepresentation of Kant's concept of theory, especially as it involves ethics, lies perhaps in some rather ambiguous manner of speaking through which he describes the foundations of moral freedom in the *Critique of Pure Reason*. The source of all genuinely moral deeds, Kant argues, is a rationally determined and autonomous will conditioned by no sensible or natural incentives, like hunger, thirst, and the desire for sex. On the contrary, the motive for all moral activity must be a pure "idea" of "what ought to be," what Kant calls an "imperative."[17] Whereas nonmoral activity can be generated as a sequence of reflexive responses to the innate biological appetites of the human organisms, or to overt coercion by other persons (and in doing so such activity merely follows the laws of nature), moral deportment breaks with these instinctive or enforced patterns of behavior and creates (according to a paradigm of pure reason) a different series of actions. In his given character, man is a creature inhabiting "two worlds": a world of nature in which he submits to the promptings of physical desire and his general sensory makeup and an intelligible world which he projects and realizes through his definitively human faculty of rationality. On the plane of sensation, man labors in bondage to external forces or empirical circumstances which deny him mastery over his own destiny. Upon cultivating the power of reason, however, he no longer furnishes himself with "those grounds [of action] which are given empirically" and "does not follow the order of things as they appear," but now his rationality "makes for itself with complete spontaneity its own order according to ideas, to which it adjusts empirical conditions"[18] The "ought" prescribed by practical reason demands a change in the natural flow of events (the mere "isness" if things before they are reordered by moral decisions), and through his action the man of virtue imposes on a recalcitrant and amoral universe a new set of laws that were originally determined a priori by the intellect.

The operation of practical reason in transforming the given condition of human life can only be understood, according to Kant, as a special mode of causation. This is the "self-causation" of reason, the activity of the will as causa noumenon. A causa noumenon belongs to a radically different order of explanation than that of nature in which the ordinary rules of causal inference are applicable. By suggesting the possibility of the causa noumenon, Kant is overhauling the common-sense view of causation first enuciated by David Hume. By Hume's dictum, the judgment that one event can be assigned as the cause of another turns on the fulfillment of two fundamental conditions:

(1) the cause must immediately precede the occurence of the effect in time;

(2) the conjunction between the two causally related events must be sufficiently constant (e.g., the regular appearance of lightning flashes together with the peal of thunder) to warrant the expectation that at some future moment the same pattern will repeat itself.[19]

But the causa noumenon, as an expression of rational choice, does not satisfy straightaway these two primary conditions which pertain to that which happens in nature. Instead, the following holds true:

(1) The rational motive of action (i.e., the idea of moral obligation) does not precede its perceptible effect (i.e., the virtuous deed itself), but the two occur simultaneously as complementary aspects of a unitary act. This is only possible, for Kant, because the causa noumenon exists "outside of and above the succession of phenomena" and its "determination of time,"[20] whereas the effect of the rational will (man's phenomenal character) is susceptible to temporal and natural laws of causality. In short, reason, for Kant, "is . . . determining, but not determinable."[21]

(2) Even though every phenomenal effect of the will can be traced ex hypothesi to its noumenal intention by a rule of uniform connection (moral causation being rule-governed in the same manner, according to Kant, as natural causation), the presence of the cause cannot be corroborated by induction from the consequences because all noumena are inaccessible to empirical scrutiny.

In his *Groundwork of the Metaphysic of Morals* Kant states rather unequivocally that "it is absolutely impossible for experience to establish with complete certainty a single case in which the maxim of action in other respects right has rested solely on moral grounds and on the thought of one's duty."[22] Thus inference from cause to effect (which is the object of natural science and is always methodologically possible, since both of the related events occur in nature and can be cognized in the same fashion) is barely feasible for moral action, because only the moral person can know his own motives and the implied cause of every deed is hidden from the external observer. Therefore it cannot be confirmed with any certainty whether an individual's outward actions are consistently and transparently produced by a good will. The freedom to act morally, Kant proposes, cannot be located among experimental facts; since such freedom would then be compromised by the facility of the observer for explaining any given act by some antecedent empirical condition, and hence the act would be "determined" instead of emerging spontaneously. If, on the other hand, man as a rational being exists preeminently in the guise of "homo noumenon," then no further search for the cause of his act becomes possible, save for ferreting out the inner motive. *A* cannot "explain away" the performance of an act of charity by *B*, for example, solely by pointing to such extrinsic factors as *B*'s childhood religious training or the more venal prospect that monetary donations to worthy causes are deductible from one's income tax. Such types of explanation tacitly deny the possibility of genuine morality, because they reduce man to a creature of circumstance as well as discredit his presumed rational discretion for controlling his social and physical environment.

The irreducibility of "ought" to "is" thus is sustained by arguing for the transcendence of moral will over the automatisms of nature.

The emphasis on a transcendent moral will, however, leaves Kant vulnerable to the charge of ontological dualism. If the laws of rational freedom inherently deviate from the laws of nature, how is it plausible that mind can affect its material surroundings? Such was the sort of conundrum raised by Descartes's metaphysics, and the same problem bedevils Kant, so the critics say, in defining the rudiments of ethics. Those leery of Kant's formalism try to interpret the term moral act in Kant's philosophy, as we have seen, as a kind of inward deliberation that does not eventuate in concrete action. But Kant endeavors to link mind and matter, thought and action, through his idea of the will as having both an intelligible and empirical character.[23] The will, as connecting link between the noumenal and phenomenal realms, serves as what E. Ballard has aptly dubbed a "moral pineal gland."[24] The will, for Kant, is both a legislative faculty (which Kant technically terms Wille) that furnishes maxims of conduct and an executive faculty (which Kant calls Willkür) that puts moral ideas into operation. Every act constitutes a complex of deliberation and dispatch which forms a unity of theory and practice.

In consequence, the distinction between noumena and phenomena in Kant can be seen not as an ontological one but as a heuristic principle which inclines the observer to ascribe causal status to moral conceptions of the agent instead of looking for a prior cause among extramental events. Such extramental events, however, may also be regarded without contradiction as secondary influences on the person's act, *once the deed has been committed*. Take, for example, the case of a businessman who decides to renounce his privilege of using his company expense account for his private regalement and who gives as his reason the belief that he is depriving other employees in the corporation of their fair share of available disbursements. From the standpoint of a neutral observer, the man's act of renunciation may be accounted for in two basic ways:

(1) the businessman has given an honest interpretation of why he chose to relinquish his right to company funds: he had a truly unselfish concern for equity.

(2) certain subtle external pressures have come to play on the man's sense of self-interest to abandon his favored position (like the likelihood of ostracism by his colleagues or the threat of an audit by the Internal Revenue Service), and these factors have more weight than any self-professed altruism.

If our neutral observer accepts the second account, he may dismiss the man's rationale for his own action in (1) as either hypocrisy or a rationalization.

The man, he might say, was only behaving out of the "instinct for self-preservation." If, however, he deems the man candid, he may view the existence of external influences or nonmoral facts that *might* have a bearing on the man's decision as merely *circumstantial* to the case. Alternative interpretations of this sort are always available to journalists who find themselves in a quandary about whether to explain a new policy announced by the President either as a conscientious interest in the people's welfare or as a cynical deference to opinion polls. In all events both the "outsider's" explanation of the man's deportment (which appeals to certain empirical criteria as having greater consequence for appraising actions than the subjective "reasons" supplied by the person himself) and the "insider's" account (the self-attribution of virtuous intentions) can be conventionally taken as appropriate causal statements when further kinds of assessments are made.[25] For example, it may be easy to judge if (1) or (2) provides the better report of the businessman's actions if we know something about his proven reputation for integrity.

A similar choice of explanans is authorized by what has been called the "double-language theory of action."[26] According to such a theory, the primary interest of the observer should not have so much to do with the private character of the agent as with what information can be used in appraising his act and what language may be relevant for describing it. Such a theory states that there are really two language-strata that may cover discussions of human agency: those which may be called both mentalistic and behavioristic. Philosophers like Gilbert Ryle who tend to be more comfortable with the latter form deny the meaningfulness of talk about any psychical genesis of behavior, and thus they claim that all mentalistic locutions like motive, intention, plan of action, and thought can be assimilated to overt behavioral processes.[27] But the heart of the conflict between behavioralists and mentalists does not reside mainly in wrongheaded imputations of ghostly mental contents or in some cavalier refusal to admit subjective contributions to conduct; rather, the problem concerns the failure of both disputants to discern *who* is doing the talking about what is happening and *what* his interests are as they affect his behavior. If *A* is discussing his own moral acts, it is perfectly admissable for him to use such phrases as "sense of duty" or "idea of a categorical imperative" to stipulate the *ultimate condition* for his conduct. We might define ultimate condition here as that factor in prompting action *without which* the deed would not have taken the form it did. If *A* was not conscious of his moral obligation, he might readily have acted in an immoral fashion, unless moral action were a habitual reflex of all human beings, something which is excluded by Kant's use of the term morality. On the other hand, if *B* rather than *A* appraises the latter's moral act *M* and *A* does not explain his motive (or if *B* does not believe *A*), then it is reasonable for *B* to look for some other condition with which the proposition *A does M* is consistent. *B* may uncover some general set of circumstances without which *M* would have seemed impossible. For instance, one cannot act charitably unless certain people exist who need charity and who will accept it. These circumstances can be adduced within the grammar of empirical inference as equally necessary as virtuous maxims for *M* to occur. There are two ultimate conditions of the moral act, one internal and the other external, and whether a man cites the former or the latter depends on whether he is more concerned with the occasion for the deed or with its personal motivation. The motive is usually the concern of the agent himself.[28] Our distinction between occasion and motivation may be taken as analogous to Kant's distinction between nature and reason as well as phenomenon and noumenon. Indeed, the double-language theory seems to be adumbrated in what Kant refers to as the "two standpoints" for understanding moral agency.[29] "We can enquire whether we do not take one standpoint when . . . we conceive ourselves as a cause acting a priori, and another standpoint when we contemplate ourselves with reference to our own actions as effects which we see before our eyes."[30] There can be inferred a lawlike connection between the occasion and the moral act just as between the "internal" sense of obligation and the same act.

To return, then, to the larger issue of the relation of theory to practice, it is evident that Kant's division of moral activity into internal and external schemes of causality, not to mention his placing the origin of such activity beyond what is manifest and derivable from sense-knowledge, does not yield any idealization of moral experience; it only leads to a proper recognition of the prerogative of the moral agent to impute to himself rational motives and not to let covering-law types of explanation that exclude free causality suffice as the sole perspective from which his behavior can be evaluated. If this prerogative were not countenanced, Kant seems to be saying, the notion of a moral will that puts the theory of moral obligation into practice would ring hollow; for then it would follow that:

(1) men's actions would be predetermined according to some immutable causal pattern;

(2) any theory would have to consist merely in a *justification* of what individuals invariably do in keeping with their assigned roles under the laws of nature;

(3) the concept of practice as an instrumentation of theory would be tautological and hence immaterial to the concerns of philosophers.

The Marxist objection to the apriority of moral theory in Kant, of course, revolves around the belief that ideas have no practical import unless they can be deduced in some measure from such nonsubjective elements as the dynamics of social development. Theory cannot spring sui generis from the mind, but must reflect the "objective" historical conditions that obtain at the time. But, as we have argued, it is precisely Kant's own contention that, whereas the source of morality must consist in an a priori insight, the necessary occasion(s) for actualizing that insight must be adverted to when formulating a policy of action. As Kant would say, "pure practical reason" must tailor its strategies to what is viable within the order of nature. The necessity of making certain pragmatic considerations when acting is implied in Kant's corollary to the first version of the categorical imperative. Not only is a person obliged to universalize his maxim in conceptu but also "since the universality of the law governing the production of effects constitutes what is properly called *nature* in its most general sense . . . the universal imperative of duty may also run as follows: '*Act as if the maxim of your action were to become through your will a universal law of nature*.'"[31]

The logical implication of such a statement is that the universality of the moral law cannot be formalistically detached from the concrete universality of natural law. On the contrary, nature occasions the possibility for reshaping man's insentient environment to his universal moral purpose. Men do not create a moral world ex nihilo; they are limited in their projects by time and by the resistance of their social and natural environment. Yet they are not limited to such a degree that they cannot consciously innovate at all or by increments of progress gain mastery over their own affairs. In this sense Kant is simply pronouncing Marx's perception of the nature of praxis in a less incisive manner. Marx, in fact, rebuked Hegel for employing philosophical reason only to interpret the world and not to change it. Likewise, the thrust of the critical philosophy is to outfit a systematic critique of existing conditions (to which Kant gives the omnibus designation of nature) by comparing the bare givens of man's moral and social life with inviolable rational standards. Such standards demand a transformation of the status quo to the point where the rational becomes real, yet this transformation cannot come about without the appearance of the proper empirical content to be remolded. Although the nuances of Kant's model of change do not become completely evident in his ethical writings, they take on a sharper focus in the historical and political essays to which we shall now turn.

IV

The bench mark of Kant's moral and political philosophy is his repudiation of utilitarianism. The danger of utilitarianism, in Kant's view, is that it is unable to produce a consistent principle for ensuring equity in the moral and social sense. Utilitarianism claims to sponsor such a principle in the idea of the maximum distribution of happiness. But the principle of happiness, for Kant, is really a kind of shattered glass: from a distance it gives the semblance of unity and clarity yet on closer inspection is revealed to be riddled with tiny cracks and fissures. The illusion of consistency stems from the fact that the demand for happiness can never be converted into a universalizable maxim, as every individual seeks happiness in his own unmatchable way.[32] Consequently, there can be no uniform method for allocating specific satisfactions for individual desires, unless one posits a priori the existence of an "ideal legislator" (as John Rawls terms it) entrusted with efficiently administering the procedures for embellishing every man's felicity.[33] More pointedly, however, utilitarian thinking lacks a coherent theory from which solid practical results might flow. If utilitarian planning is preoccupied with "the natural facts and contingencies of human life" as the yardstick of what should be done,[34] theory must revert to a kind of *technology* of need fulfillment; it must become a grasping for ad hoc solutions to particular challenges as they arise and thus forfeits the status of theory as a broader map of action. No general rules for experimentation are asserted, as in all valid scientific probes, to justify the particular course undertaken. Utilitarianism, with all its professed solicitude for the experience of men, actually fails to give, Kant suggests, order, regularity, and direction to that experience. What order it does furnish consists of a haphazard and possibly skewed allocation of enjoyments and rewards, which may be considered morally good only so far as one acquires a satisfying share of the final apportionment. Since utilitarianism does not try to treat individuals according to the rule of equity so much as it hunts for a provisional balance of wishes and needs, and since one man's happiness may inevitably subtract from the happiness of another, any empirical reckoning of justice in this sense is bound to be a makeshift and highly negotiable solution. Kant's true "man of affairs," however, does not rely on experience to define his social objectives but uses experience "to learn how to apply [theory] in better and more universal ways after . . . [having] assimilated it into our principles"[35] Moral and political theory, for Kant, must be a priori insofar as it does not slide into a mere algebra of self-interest but lays down an absolute charter of certain goods and rights which may or may not clash with particular individual's desires and which the exigencies of pure practice cannot abrogate.

In the sphere of politics, especially, the need for sharply enchased principles of policy becomes paramount in establishing civil rights and duties. The final choice of criteria according to which any given presumption of justice within a society can be measured, Kant insists, must be between (1) legitimation of de facto authority or entrenched power and (2) a theoretically autonomous standard of right derived from self-authenticating rules of reason. Given the first criterion, the very concept of justice becomes too labile for useful definition. Such is essentially the same pitfall, in Kant's eyes, that traps utilitarian ethics. One cannot make the claim, "whatever is, is right," to any consistent end, just as one cannot enshrine the "pursuit of happiness" as a touchstone for general conduct, because the character of existing authority is as corrigible and idiosyncratic as the specificity of each person's notion of his own well-being. The dilemma, again, is the lack of clear and precise theory in utilitarianism, in this instance regarding the boundaries of the term justice. Political theory, therefore, if it is to qualify as theory at all, must first construct certain a priori principles of policy making and then develop the necessary empirical methodology for implementing them. The alleged vacuity of apriorism is only cogent so long as no attempt is made to execute one's fundamental insights; but such a "primitive" apriorism Kant sets little store by. That Kant, therefore, can be said to "leap over the social materiality" (Marcuse) is tenable only insofar as political theorizing becomes an end in itself.

In his essay "Theory and Practice" Kant notes that the problem of choosing criteria for justice rests ultimately on the issue of what should be considered moral. Just as empirical approaches to ethics and politics yield a patchwork of frayed principles, so an even more pernicious consequence of such an attitude is the divorce of political and moral judgments altogether. Kant emphasizes this consequence in his refutation of Hobbes in the second portion of the essay. Hobbes, Kant implies, tries to anchor political right in some "fact" of an original contract between subjects and their sovereign. Whether Hobbes himself, of course, believed the original covenant founding the commonwealth to be an identifiable occurrence is moot among scholars; but Hobbes still saw the underpinnings of firm political order to consist in established *force* rather than any self-validating concept of moral obligation between ruler and ruled. Hobbes argues for the impregnability of the covenant (and hence the absolute discretionary power of the monarch to govern as he sees fit, short of murder) on the grounds that it was sealed by mutually interested parties who surrendered their "natural right" of self-protection to the person of the sovereign, entrusted with preserving them from threats to life and limb with an expertise they cannot attain by themselves. From the *fact* of the original transfer of natural right derives the "DUTY, not to make voyd that volutary act of his own."[36] The creation of the political compact and the concomitant conditions of personal obligation follows directly from what Hobbes calls a "law of nature."[37] Hobbes's own line of reasoning rests on an inversion of Kant's philosophical premises. Every determination of "ought" is contingent on assessing what might be called political precedent; and such precedent tallies with the empirical laws of human behavior. Indeed, Hobbes goes so far as to declare that the "science" of these "natural laws" is "the true and onely moral philosophy."[38] On the other hand, there can be no categorical imperative guiding both moral and political decisions, because the very idea of a moral good is merely a name referring to arbitrary "appetites and aversions" which vary from people to people.[39] Men's calculation concerning what will profit them most in the contest for security becomes the supreme maxim of action.

But the contract binding members of society, Kant holds, can never "actually exist as a *fact*,"[40] for that would mean many tyrannical or oppressive social arrangements might easily be legitimated simply by presupposing that they came into being as a safeguard against strife. The necessity of halting civil disorder is perennially invoked by dictators, and once the iron hand of repression has dropped, the burden of proof that such measures are not peremptory for forestalling future anarchy falls on those who might show that the people were not implicitly willing to surrender their liberties for the sake of peace and order. Anyone who might wish to determine whether the transfer of right to an autocrat was authentic would "first have to prove from history that some nation . . . did in fact perform such an act,"[41] which would prove very difficult under most circumstances. Moreover, lack of historical evidence of an original agreement would not ipso facto discount, on Hobbes's terms, the supposition that the pact had definitely been made. The very existence of civil society and government attests to its making, together with the operation of the inexorable "laws of nature" which necessitate the abdication of liberties in the aim of self-preservation. Hobbes hence is arguing, according to Kant, for the justice of a given commonwealth on the basis that

(x) sovereignty in its empirical form is established by the laws of nature; therefore, the people must consent to it.

But Kant wants to maintain that the contract, the sovereign, and the laws he prescribes must meet standards of justice not reducible to historical or natural precedent. It must not be the case that the people have actually consented to them, but it must nevertheless be logically consistent for them to declare their agreement according to an "idea of reason" alone.[42] Thus, it is Kant's view that

(y) sovereignty in its empirical form must be accepted or rejected on the basis of a transcendental criterion; *only if this criterion is satisfied* must the people concur.

Kant wants a political theory that can support sovereignty without bending to the prevailing customs of civil administration. Hobbes, on the other hand, has devised a theory that logically warrants an existing form of sovereignty but does not allow for criticism of the methods of ruling. All inferences of type (x) proceed from practice backwards to theory (which in historical perspective may perhaps be construed as Hobbes's effort to provide a more stable ideology for the English monarchy), whereas inferences of type (y) go in the opposite direction.

The different connotations that can be attached to the term political theory as it applies to Kant and Hobbes may be brought out more clearly by examining their respective uses of the word right. For Kant, right (Recht) broadly signifies "the sum total of those conditions within which the will of one person can be reconciled with the will of another in accordance with a universal law of freedom."[43] The concept of public right, however, derives immediately from a priori ethical considerations: it is simply the general rule of obligation extended to govern real social circumstances in which practical laws of reason are not obeyed by all persons. The demand that every individual maxim be universalizable as a moral act is enlarged into the supplementary stricture that contrary actions be suppressed. Kant explains that the right of coercion follows according to the "law of contradiction" from the moral imperative that universal law ("right" in the formal sense) be upheld. Thus,

if a certain use to which freedom is put is itself a hindrance to freedom in accordance with universal laws (i.e., if it is contrary to right), any coercion which is used against it will be a *hindrance of freedom* and will thus be consonant with freedom in accordance with universal law — that is, it will be right.[44]

Here right is primarily understood to mean a kind of *positive law* or hindrance, as a check on freedom in the sense of mere liberty to do as one pleases, and it is the principle that can be cited when seeking the means to promote freedom in the sense of rational autonomy within a kingdom of ends. That Kant uses the word freedom in this equivocal sense often leads to misunderstandings of his political thought. For the sake of simplicity, we shall hereafter refer to the former meaning of the term as $freedom_1$ and to the latter as $freedom_2$. In Kant, therefore, political right constitutes the necessary restraint of $freedom_1$ to guarantee freedom$_2$. It becomes the public resort to practical means for realizing on a common level fundamental moral theory, *the theory of autonomy*.[45]

Hobbes, on the other hand, construes right in a different sense, i.e., as "the liberty to do" whatever is seen as fit to preserve oneself.[46] Such a right can be assimilated to freedom$_1$. All rights of this sort, however, are reserved for individuals only in the "state of nature" preceding the formation of the commonwealth, and when civil society has been established, such rights are transferred to the sovereign and can be exercised by the sovereign alone.[47] Right, thus, implies for Hobbes an absolute power of coercion bestowed on the sovereign alone; but it is not the right (in Kant) of guaranteeing reciprocal freedom of action within a moral community. Rather, it is the right of *denying* freedom of action to individuals altogether, since it was the mutual incompatibility of individual rights and freedoms$_1$ (and hence the impossibility of true reciprocity) which led to the creation of public order. The right of the sovereign is to subdue the "natural" rights of the people and does not issue, as for Kant, from a higher principle of *moral right* which entails freedom$_2$ and equality under coercive laws. In Kant's commonwealth, however, everyone "has rights of coercion in relation to all the others"[48] for the purpose of preserving reciprocal interaction between moral agents. While the sovereign has the right of coercion (as in Hobbes) without being coerced,[49] he is authorized only to direct legislation toward fulfilling the higher right of freedom$_2$.

Kant's ideal polis, therefore, is governed by "laws of virtue." The res publica, or civil state, is an executive apparatus formed to restrain those unruly individuals who are likely to disrupt the moral order. In a play upon Hobbes's own lexation, Kant says that for man to leave the physical state of nature and enter into social intercourse is not adequate in itself to elicit justice. A society welded together by force alone, as in Hobbes's commonwealth, turns out to be nothing more than another kind of state of nature in which men still combat each other, albeit by "legal" means. Society becomes a new "ethical state of nature" where "each invididual is his own judge [concerning moral obligation]" and "there is no *public* authority . . . to bring about the universal performance of duty."[50] The sovereign's sword can prevent only chaos, not the erosion of scruples. Instead of battling with clubs and spears, men in society now tend to "mutually . . . corrupt each other's predispositions and make one another evil."[51] The sentiment is similar to that of Rousseau, from whom Kant drew much inspiration in his formative years. Political life tends to make a cunning and selfish beast out of the natural man and to camouflage his perfidy with the pretense of "civilized" government.

Within every "political commonwealth," therefore, it is necessary to work for an "ethical commonwealth" (i.e., a kingdom of ends) that ensures true justice in both the moral and political sense. In a word, Kant is saying that any theory of political justice must be more profound and sweeping than some justification of existing social arrangements, even though such arrangements may satisfy Hobbes's key condition that they preserve domestic tranquility. Justice must comport with the Rawls's requirement of "fairness" which has "the result of leaving aside those aspects of the social world that seem arbitrary from a moral point of view."[52] Once the fairness is stipulated as a principle for social and political relations, no a posteriori defense of absolute power on the pretext that such power is indisposable in quelling conflict can be seen as plausible without first appraising the moral legitimacy of that power. Plain expediency as a rationale for action may lead to reprehensible results.

V

Returning to the Marxist attack on Kant, we can now discern that the charge of empty theorizing in the moral and political writings owes mainly to a misapprehension about the use of the term a priori as it appears in them. Kant seems merely to be proposing that adequate social theory should not underwrite the vested interests of a particular individual, or groups of individuals, in proffering the specious claim that such interests are confirmed by experience. Kant's refusal to separate the right from the good in human conduct appears in this respect as a denial of the moral value of any "objective" satisfactions (like happiness) that might be held out as the goal of men's strivings, were those satisfactions not available to everyone given equal opportunity. Kant, furthermore, clearly sees that equality of satisfactions entails an *equality of means* to attain them; and thus such teleological formulas as "the greatest happiness for the greatest number" means an *inequality* of satisfactions for some (especially for those minorities not counted among the greatest number) to the enrichment of those who might control the channels for accomplishing their private versions of felicity.

A half-century before Marx, Kant pinpoints, without saying so directly, the perils of any program of distributive justice that failed to sublate particular interests (for Marx, class interests) in society. Unable to draw, of course, on the more sophisticated Marxist parlance, Kant nevertheless succeeds in showing how dogmatic empiricism regarding moral and political judgments becomes an ideology. Positing a purely normative world to which all empirical worlds must conform, Kant guards against any defense of the inertia of social institutions.

On the other hand, it has been argued that Kant does not sufficiently grasp the dialectical character of history nor understand how ethics and politics might take into consideration social change and upheaval. Marx's thought would seem superior on this score, because it apprehends all forms of theory as rising out of the configuration of man's material activity, as both an explanation of past processes and an extrapolation toward the future aims of practice. Contrary to Kant, theory, for Marx, "does not explain practice from the idea but explains the formation of ideas from material practice."[53] Thus Kant is engaged, it would seem, in a kind of mystification, since he supposedly does not allow that the ideal of a kingdom of ends or ethical commonwealth may constitute a theoretical response to the fructification of certain historical conditions making such an order of community life possible. Kant seems to pose his a priori ideal of society as an eternally valid construct of reason that requires no temporal realization.

Although Kant's choice of wording may convey such an impression, the converse is true. The sociohistorical sine qua non of such action are spelled out by Kant in a remarkable little essay called "Idea for a Universal History from a Cosmopolitan Point of View" published in 1784, only three years after the *Critique of Pure Reason*. In this essay Kant develops for the first time a naturalistic as well as an evolutionary outlook on man's moral life. Autonomy and rationality are no longer depicted simply as the private and timeless life goals of all men under any given set of circumstances but now are regarded as the products of impersonal historical movements. Moreover, Kant conceives human history in its entirety as the progressive attainment of what from the philosophical vantage point may be interpreted as a purely conjectural moral and political state of affairs but what concretely emerges as a "hidden plan of nature."[54] In other words, Kant is saying that praxis ultimately must be attributed to the inner dynamics of the natural realm, which in his other writings is supposed to encompass the order of moral freedom and decision! On the face of it, such a perspective would seem a volte-face from Kant's celebrated opinion that genuine human activity must proceed according to its own laws and not be guided by some heteronomous principle. But Kant seems only to be saying that any theory of action must descry the concrete shape of the natural environment.

The shape of things, however, is not immutably fixed but is plastic enough for man to leave the impress of his conscious purposes. Thus nature provides man with the wherewithal to bring about a harmony of physical and moral law. Kant makes his case, unfortunately, by employing some rather archaic teleological language. "Nature has willed that man should produce entirely by his own initiative everything which goes beyond the mechanical ordering of natural existence, and that he should not partake of any other happiness or perfection than that which he has procured for himself without instinct and by his own reason."[55] Paradoxically, nature *determines* that man's actions shall be loosed of all determinations. It is nature's purpose that man shall have no other purpose besides the moral purpose he sets before himself.

In a somewhat involuted manner of phrasing, Kant is maintaining that rational autonomy must come to govern man's personal life once, and only once, · the right objective situation has arisen conducive to its growth. Individuals can only act morally when they have adequately matured as a collectivity to perceive the laws of their own generic development and the true agential capacities that nature has destined them to cultivate.[56] In acting in accordance with nature's plan, nonetheless, men are in truth husbanding the natural endowments of reason and conscience. Noumenal freedom, therefore, is not formally estranged from the world of extrahuman objects but stands as a didactic concept for illustrating how the moral character of humanity, emergent from nature, can at the same time transcend and refurbish the very order of nature.

Still, Kant surpasses this basic organismic insight in affirming at a rudimentary level two leading tenets of the Marxist philosophy of history: the eminently *social* context of all human development as well as the *dialectical* structure of progress.

Kant expresses the first tenet as follows: "The greatest problem for the human species, the solution of which nature compels him to seek, is that of attaining a *civil society* which can administer justice universally."[57] For "the highest purpose of nature — i.e., the development of all natural capacities — can be fulfilled for mankind *only in society* . . ."[58] Progress results from the crystallization of a worldwide social order manifesting the conditions for the practice of the moral law, and it is through the realization of this *actually* universal Gesellschaft that the a priori moral universal can be made an operative principle of Gemeinschaft in people's lives. Though Kant fails to anticipate clearly Marx's view that universal justice can only be embodied in a concretely universal class (i.e., the proletariat whose oppression by the bourgeoisie strips them of any privileged rank or pretense that might earn them a special identity over and above the mass of mankind),[59] he at least avoids, again, the formalistic stumbling block of splitting the ethical from the social as well as the amoral stance of Realpolitik which takes the preservation of the ethnic social unit as a strategy to be established at all costs.

Second, Kant avers in its general form the Marxist law of dialectical change: that positive historical movement cannot be carried through without a negation of existing conditions and a fruitful interplay of social contradictions in practice as well as theory. The correlative principle of such a law is that every increment of social progress must ensue from a conflict of parties with mutually hostile interests. Real justice can only issue at the culmination of a struggle between these parties and the elimination of those who perpetuate injustice. Excluding any social tension and the clash of competing wills, the transition from conflict to peace, from the mere form of society to a morally ordered community wherein "a *pathologically* enforced social union is transformed into a moral whole,"[60] becomes impossible. "The means that nature employs to bring about the development of innate capacities is that of antagonism within society, insofar as the antagonism becomes in the long run the cause of a law-governed social order."[61] A global kingdom of ends, ironically, is promoted by those who resist the moral imperative through "enviously competitive vanity, and insatiable desires for possession or even power."[62] Virtue is strengthened when others resist virtue. Man becomes so steeped in the habit of strife that he finally yearns for a cessation of strife.

But the outcome of such warfare must not be a repression of competition, as Hobbes would have it, in the mere political sense. From the caldrons of conflict emerges a new and inwardly regenerated human type—a moral type. Marcuse, for one, objects, however, that Kant's vision of intrasocial struggle (what the latter dubs "the unsocial sociability of man") represents only the historical state of bourgeois internecine fighting while disguising the realities of class antagonism. The question here, of course, is not whether Kant possessed the distinguished insights of later Marxist sociology but whether he fully sketched the conceptual parameters for this kind of analysis. It has been our contention that Kant in a roundabout manner accomplished that end. The construction that Kant puts on the term theory is intrinsically dialectical and historical, as is Marxism, for these reasons:

(1) Kant couples his perspecitve on human progress to a general assessment of certain hidden tendencies or latencies within the *real* contradictions of social life. Such contradictions, however, are inappropriately regarded as everlasting in virtue of their empirical longevity; they can be resolved through detection of the inner meaning and goal of historical conflict. To that purpose Kant distinguishes between an a priori and an empirical philosophy of history. The latter view merely discerns a lot of blood and bluster in the strife of past ages and thereby turns a pessimistic, cynical, or conservative face

toward change.[63] The former, on the other hand, takes a view "from a different angle" and resorts to "prophesying future political changes."[64]

(2) Theory is now placed as an intricate comprehension, not of the timeless makeup of the universe but of concrete material processes. The a priori quality in moral and social theory simply deals with the ability of such theory to penetrate historical appearance to the nascent forms of human intercourse not yet confirmed or institutionalized by trial and tradition. Herbert Marcuse, for example, argues for justification of the "a priori element" in philosophical reasoning alongside the heuristic postulate of a rational essence, because through the concept of essence philosophy now "leads back into history rather than out of it," as would be true with metaphysical idealism.[65] When Kant's ideas of pure reason are construed in this historicist fashion, we can construe them as what Marcuse calls the type of "theory [that] associates itself with the progressive forces of history," and thus "the demonstration and preservation of essence becomes the motive idea of practice aimed at transformation."[66]

VI

In light of the above discussion, it now becomes easier to make sense out of Kant's seemingly self-contradictory utterances about revolution. Kant wants to rule out the worth of any insurrection capriciously instigated for the sake of satisfying some ill-defined general will of the people, once a framework for reciprocal justice has been engrafted within a commonwealth. The yardstick of public right must be insusceptible to a posteriori revisions and cannot be calibrated by mass preference. Otherwise, arbitrary rule may posture as having the collective welfare of the country at heart. On the other hand, revolution undertaken to correct some transient grievances becomes illegitimate when there exists no ethico-legal body of rules that one can name as having been infringed. In neither situation will justice be done, since all forms of the utilitarian quest for justice prescribe no clear social and political duties.[67]

It is obvious from this that the principle of happiness (which is not in fact a definite principle at all) has ill effects in political right just as in morality, however good the intentions of those who teach it. The sovereign wants to make the people happy as he thinks best and thus becomes a despot, while the people are unwilling to give up their universal human desire to seek happiness in their own way, and thus become rebels. If they had first of all asked what is lawful (in terms of a priori certainty, which no empiricist can upset), the idea of a social contract would retain its authority undiminished.[68]

Revolution is not de facto unwarranted, but it is primarily so when it is assumed that a certain fairness doctrine undergirds the web of social agreements and ascriptions. Kant does not offer any genuine rule of thumb for which such a doctrine may be presupposed, and thus he creates the impression that the doctrine is to be postulated for all societies, in which case revolution would always appear impermissible.

On the other hand, we find Kant extolling the French Revolution as a vehicle of moral progress and insisting that "if a revolution has succeeded," the people have "the obligation to accommodate themselves as good citizens to the new order of things," in the sincere belief that the upstart regime is lawfully instituted.[69] These conflicting dispositions toward the practice of revolution, according to one possible interpretation, exhibit a shifting sentiment on Kant's part due to the rush of world events. When Kant wrote "Theory and Practice," the French Revolution was still in its incipient stages, and the leveling of millennium-old traditions seemed an invitation to anarchy and lawlessness. However, several years later, with the publication of Kant's subsequent political writings (and it has been rightly said that German political thinking, including Kant's, was only born with the eruption of 1789),[70] he was able to realize for the first time the salutary effects of this upheaval. Revolutions can be seen in retrospect as teleological "goods."

In his "condemnation" of revolution Kant is only criticizing those enthusiasts who would indulgently and arbitrarily endeavor to upend a rationally sound and legal constitution. A demagogue or a canaille should not be allowed to make impassioned decisions about whether the rights of the commonwealth were trespassed. Many revolutionaries have no perspective on the universal character of justice behind their programs. Revolution that does not bank on a universally valid theory of law and society degenerates into blind practice. On the other hand, to invoke a theory of right without seeking whether a revolution has been adequately prepared by social circumstances ignores Kant's critical requirement that all action follow on its proper occasion. For Kant revolution must be attuned to the dialectic of nature and history. There are, Kant says, "permissive laws of reason, which allow a state of public right to continue, even if it is affected by injustice, until all is ripe for a complete revolution . . ."[71] Revolutions launched willy-nilly lead to the rise of tyranny. There can be no such thing as "perpetual revolution." "But where revolutions are brought about by nature alone, it will not use them as a good excuse for even greater oppression, but will treat them as a call of nature to create a lawful constitution based on the principle of freedom . . ."[72] Revolutions of this kind represent "nature and freedom, combined within mankind in accordance with principles of right . . ."[73]

Kant's concern is that rebellion not be incited simply as a mindless reflex to overt abuses but that is be purposeful and aimed at securing morality and justice. Revolutions in themselves are not an intrinsic good." A revolution may well put an end to autocratic despotism and to rapacious or power-seeking oppression, but it will never produce a true reform in the ways of thinking."[74] Such a true reform, however, can only consist in a revolution of the heart. Kant, nonetheless, recognizes that a violent reorganization of society often sweeps away external obstacles to such an internal reformation of personality. In this sense social revolution is a "natural" precondition of the spread of moral and political right. Yet the enshrinement of such right in the form of a republican constitution makes further revolution a theoretical impossibility, unless that constitution is annulled.[75] Even then, the first recourse of the people must be a campaign of public information and an oratorical assault on illegitimate power rather than the immediate move to arms.[76] "If both benevolence and right speak out in loud tones, human nature will not prove too debased to listen to their voice with respect."[77]

In the main, Kant seems to regard revolution as the practical implementation of the a priori theory of right. The theory must be consistent with both the rule of universalizability and the laws of nature. It is because the satisfaction of these two conditions is not achieved merely in the heat of every battle for the Bastille that Kant casts a wary eye on revolution whose only defense is its emotional catharsis; and hence Kant regrettably has incurred the reputation of being antirevolutionary as well as impractical.

V

Theory and Practice
in Hegel and Marx:
An Unfinished Dialogue

Peter Fuss

Few men have attended to the perplexities of the relationship between theory and practice with as much deliberation and intellectual vigor as did Hegel and Marx. Since the two men were not contemporaries; since there is a widespread belief that, at least so far as the relation between theory and practice is concerned, Marx surely had the last word over his "speculative idealist" predecessor; and since I consider this belief to be quite mistaken, I propose to conduct a thought experiment in which some of the perplexities of theory and practice besetting Hegel and Marx are examined rather more in the form of a dialogue, a dialogue which to this day remains radically unfinished.

I will argue that: (1) the philosophical touchstone of Marx's radical critique of modern society is essentially *Hegel's* concept of human emancipation, (2) Marx's failure to draw the appropriate inferences from this concept—at the very moment he had correctly criticized Hegel for making the same mistake—helped lead him to an incoherent theory of the dispossessed as universal class; (3) Marx thereby not only undermined his own theoretical and practical advance beyond Hegel but remystified the relationship between theory and practice itself; and (4) the ironic consequence of this failure at the theoretical level has been the uncritical practice (by Marxists at least as much as by anybody else) of allowing the burgeoning one-and-only "class" in contemporary society to escape, both in theory and practice, its social responsibilities.

A word of explanation may be helpful regarding the point of view that underlies what follows. On the one hand, I shall presuppose here a general familiarity on the reader's part with what has by now become at least a half-century-old controversy between the so-called scientific and the critical humanist Marxists, a controversy in which the latter may now (and if so then pretty much for the first time) be taking the ascendancy. With this familiarity assumed, I can speak freely of certain philosophical perplexities relating to theory, practice, and their interconnection without having to define and establish as it were from scratch the historical context of this discussion. On the other hand, rather than examine this body of controversial literature directly, I shall instead focus on certain texts in Hegel and Marx themselves. My intention in doing so is not to try to resolve some aspect of the more recent debate; on the contrary, I have become convinced that the very fact that post-Marxian theoretical literature *has* tended to bifurcate into scientific vs. critical humanist (or neo-Hegelian) Marxism indicates a loss of grip on the radically dialectical character of the problematics from which it took its rise: the thought of Hegel and Marx itself.

There is, of course, nothing compelling about the line of inquiry I am proposing here. One may very well become so frustrated (or bored) with this seemingly never-ending squabble that one might be led to seek altogether new paths of social criticism. Or, if one is a philosophical purist, one might reimmerse oneself in Hegelian (or some other) metaphysics, consoling oneself with the notion that if the actual continues to resist becoming rational, perhaps this is because the rational as such is, in the end, the only reality anyway. I can only say that for myself, although I share the frustration, I simply would not know how to develop critical social theory ex nihilo, whereas unbroken confinement within the ivory tower simply is not very appealing to me. At the same time, when it comes to the conceptual foundation of our critical and social thinking, I believe that we have not advanced beyond Hegel and Marx and that the persistence of the neo-Marxist controversy, if nothing else, confirms this belief. Accordingly, my primary aim in this essay will be to tease out those elements of unresolved contradiction and tension in Hegel and Marx themselves that I find rather onesidedly — and therefore even less dialectically, less self-critically — perpetuated in the thought of their epigone.

I. Human Emancipation

The rediscovery of Marx's manuscripts of 1844 almost a century after they were written has become one of the most important events in recent intellectual history. One of the reasons for this, I would urge, is that these early manuscripts reveal a Marx who, devastating critic and revolutionary thinker though he was from the very first, owed the range and depth of his critical perspectives largely to the rich treasury of our classical humanist tradition. Educated in this tradition, Marx understandably had an ambivalent attitude from the very first toward piecemeal reform in neatly compartmentalized spheres like religious worship and political suffrage. To him these are indeed progressive measures but measures which, given the structure of the society enacting them, fall far short of what he repeatedly refers to as "human emancipation."[1] And yet so steeped was Marx in this humanist tradition that he evidently took for granted that his readers already knew what human emancipation was; for he nowhere bothered to explain exactly what he meant by it.

Marx, who was very much under the influence of Hegel at the time, in all likelihood had Hegel to thank for his own understanding of the concept. Hegel had made some effort to explain it, above all in the much anthologized Lord-Bondsman section (Chapter Four, A) of the *Phenomenology*. Familiar as it may be, however, it is presented in Hegel's characteristically difficult prose; and among Marx's several references, laudatory and critical, to the *Phenomenology*, few point clearly to this section, and none illuminate it in detail. How closely Marx attended to this effort by Hegel to clarify the concept of human emancipation must remain largely a matter of conjecture. Yet it is over this particular concept's theoretical implications and practical applications that Hegel and Marx initiated what remains in our own time an unfinished dialogue. We might best begin, then, with an exegesis of the Lord-Bondsman section.[2]

In the Preface to the *Phenomenology* Hegel had defined human experience in general as the self's attempt to escape from the impoverished immediacy of the here-and-now by losing itself in what appears to be other than itself — only to discover in the end that, by having managed to become that other *noetically*, it has for the first time become itself in truth.[3] Now in Chapter Four Hegel's initial and skeletal summary of the achievement of full self-consciousness traces a similar dialectical movement. There are three moments, each having two phases: (1) the moment of self-*loss* — (a) self-estrangement, (b) estrangement from this estranged self; (2) the moment of self-*assertion* — (a) negation of the alien other, (b) negation of the "otherness" of my own self; (3) the moment of self-*recovery* — (a) sublation of my estranged self, (b) restoration of the self-identity of the other. This movement is doubly dialectical because it can occur only if there are at least two self-consciousnesses in mutual confrontation, each of whom does to the other what the other does to it. Each recognizes and confirms its own self only in and through its being recognized and confirmed by the other.[4] After this brief and formal account of the structure of self-consciousness,[5] Hegel proceeds to a more detailed phenomenological description of it. Concretely, the first of these moments[6] takes the form of an unreciprocated polarization. At first, each self is a mere object to the other, and each tries to hold fast to its unmediated self-certainty. But each self must bring its abstract self-assurance to the level of a concrete, demonstrated truth, and this it can do only through a life-and-death struggle with the other. For only by staking my life can I prove that I am free of its determining, enslaving conditions. Yet even while death must be risked, it must also be avoided. The situation is fraught with irony: "ideally" both should die, thus proving their independence of the conditions of life; but if this were to happen they would hardly be in a position to confirm self-consciousness's unbounded powers of transcendence. If only one survives, he will quickly fall back to the position of static self-assurance from which he began. If the two selves *equally* stand the test, nothing happens either; each goes his own way, and they merely "live on" as lifeless, unmediated things. The only progressive resolution is an initial victory of one over the other, congealing into a relationship of dominance and subservience.

Hegel next concretizes the moment of self-*assertion*.[7] It finally dawns on one of the combatants (presumably the more astute of the two) that the privilege of life itself is a necessary condition of selfhood in *any* form. Acutely aware of the need to remain alive, he pays for his insight by his subservience, his loss of immediate self-certainty, to the bolder but less perceptive alien other —the lord. The lordly self is defined by and experiences himself as the negation of what is "outside" himself. But his sense of completeness is hollow and illusory; he *desires* and vainly seeks to satiate his desire in an infantile way—by consuming whatever he encounters. Furthermore, in his lordliness he has his bondsman act as intermediary between himself and things; thus the lord's relationship to things becomes more and more indirect and passive. At the same time, since in his lordliness the lord knows no realities other than consumable things, even his relationship to his bondsman is gradually transformed into one of passivity and dependence, thereby belying the overt, immediate relation of dominance and subservience. Thus the lord-bondsman relationship turns out to be *contradictorily* one-sided: what the lord really desires—and indeed cannot dispense with—is the recognition of an equal. Finally consumption, the lord's essentially passive form of relating to what is other than himself, is inherently sterile, a sterile negation of the other and therefore, dialectically, of himself as well. The lord, who had demonstrated his readiness to die like a man, has shown himself unable to live like one. He has come to a personal and historical impasse. Nonetheless, he is the catalyst of history: *his* truth will emerge in and through the gradual self-emancipation of the bondsman. For Hegel, history as such is the struggle for human emancipation—only in the element of freedom can any man effectuate his concrete truth as a human being. For the lord, freedom seemed actual but was in fact abstract and static; for the bondsman, it was at best potential and latent, but it would prove to be dynamic and, eventually, concrete.

The moment of self-*recovery*[8] is thus the work of the bondsman. Unlike the lord's, the *bondsman's* fear of death penetrated the very core of his being. His was a truly existential dread, because he seems to have been dimly aware that, were he to die, Being as mediated by conscious selfhood, i.e., meaning itself, might be lost. There is much more at stake here than his personal destruction, and, as I understand Hegel's passage, the bondsman (unlike the lord) intuitively senses this. While still at the mercy of the arbitrary will of another he had, without knowing it, already embarked on a course that would take him through many more trials before bringing him to his goal, the concrete realization of the inherent universality of his self-consciousness. In and through his *work* the bondsman achieves something that the lord never actually accomplished: a mastery (albeit limited) of nature made possible by a close familiarity with its materials and processes. Moreover, it is the bondsman who first learns to suspend the immediate gratification of his desires in favor of more significant, long-range satisfactions—unlike the lord, who remains related to things in a *merely* negative, repetitive, and dissolute fashion. The effect of the bondsman's painstaking work is bilateral: his object, the natural world, is rationalized, humanized, and given intelligible form, while his consciousness is objectified in the external world and is thus eventually able to see itself reflected wherever it looks.[9] The two decisive experiences here, existential fear (resulting in servitude) and formative activity, are inseparable from one another. Unless the fear is unconditional, all that is likely to result is dabbling, not genuine form making; Hegel insists that this fear must be absolute if the formative activity is to have the universal resonance which it must have if it is to be definitive of the capacities inherent in being human. Finally, absolute fear is essential for the maturation of a true self-consciousness. Without it, what typically manifests itself is Eigensinn, a self-engrossed stubbornness, instead of der eigne Sinn,[10] a balanced sense of the self's power, limitations, and necessary interrelatedness with what is other than itself—i.e., a full appreciation of its being in a world.

Hegel's theory of human emancipation, then, might be said to have three dimensions: (1) *self-discovery*, an existential achievement effected amidst a community of others who not only precipitate the individual's crisis of identity but, when things go well, empower his self-recovery through confirmatory encounters; (2) *self-alienation* primarily through sublimation, i.e., through the suspension of immediate gratification to achieve long-range and more complex goals; (3) *self-objectification* in and through work (formative activity). The burden of the remainder of the *Phenomenology* is to show that human emancipation, individually and collectively, can be achieved through nothing less than a seemingly endless and enervating series of experiential self-alienations and self-integrations in all three of these dimensions at once. Again and again an immaturely self-conscious individual or community finds what seems at first blush to be the epiphany of its freedom painfully unmasked as ephemeral and illusory — the phantom of a human spirit which in truth is still in bondage.[11]

In its broader outlines, not much of this appears to have been lost on Marx. Hegel deserved the generous compliment that his young critic paid him:

> The greatness of Hegel's *Phenomenology*, then, and of its result — viz. the dialectic of negativity as moving and creating principle — is first of all this, that Hegel grasps the self-creation of man as a process, sees objectification [Vergegenständlichung] as a setting in opposition [Entgegenständlichung] , i.e. as externalization and the overcoming of this externalization; that he therefore grasps the essence of *labor* [*Arbeit*] and comprehends objective man, truly actual man, as the result of his own labor. The actual, active relationship of man to himself as a being who embodies his species [Gattungswesen], i.e. his own manifestation as an actual species-embodying being, as a *human* being is made possible only by the actual bringing forth of all his species-embodying creative powers [Gattungskräfte] — something that is in turn possible only through the cooperative activity of mankind, only as a result of history; — and by relating to these powers as objects — something which again is possible at first only in the form of alienation.[12]

But Hegel equally deserved Marx's criticism of the subsequent development of his mentor's thought:

The appropriation of essential human faculties [Wesenskräfte] that have become objects and indeed alien objects is first and foremost an appropriation that takes place only in consciousness, in pure thought, i.e. in abstraction. It is the appropriation of these objects as thoughts and as *thought-processes*. This is why the *Phenomenology* — in spite of its decidedly negative and critical posture, and in spite of the genuine criticism, much of it far in advance of later developments, which it does indeed contain — already has latent within it, as embryo, as potency, and as secret spring, the uncritical positivism and no less uncritical idealism of Hegel's later works—i.e. a philosophical dissolution and restoration of the empirically existing status quo.[13]

Marx's point, of course, is that making the things of the world (including human capacities and powers themselves) one's own predominantly or even exclusively in thought processes, i.e., at the level and in the form of theory, is not yet to make them one's own in actuality, i.e., in the domain of practice.

But there is considerably more to it than this, and young Marx soon touches the solipsistic nerve in Hegel's "objective idealism":

It is equally clear that a *self-consciousness*, i.e. its externalization, can only posit *"thinghood,"* something that is itself only an abstract thing, the result of abstraction, not an actual thing. But from this it is likewise evident that "thinghood" is by no means something that exists independently in its own right, in opposition to self-consciousness; it is a mere construct posited by self-consciousness; and what is posited here, instead of confirming itself, is merely a confirmation of the act of positing—an act which for a moment, but only for a moment, congeals its energy in the form of a product and seems to bestow upon it the role of an independent and actual being.[14]

To Marx the implications are plain, and so is the dialectical relationship between them. On the one hand, the Hegelian concept of mind is a sophisticated piece of intellectual arrogance: "consciousness (knowing as knowing, thinking as thinking) pretends to be directly its own other, to be the sensual, the actual, indeed life itself—in a word, thought overreaching itself in thought (Feuerbach)."[15] On the other hand, a thought that thus overreaches itself is a thought that in the end uncritically falls back into the status quo: "And so Reason finds itself at home in unreason as such."[16]

Even then, Marx is not quite done with Hegel. He has yet to explain why it was that Hegel, who had sought to overcome man's self-alienation in the religious sphere by pulling the Absolute down from its transcendent pedestal, ended up retheologizing, and thus remystifying, what he had so painstakingly detheologized and demystified.

Hence this movement in its abstract form as dialectic is taken to be authentic human life, and since it is nonetheless an abstraction, an alienation of human life, it comes to be viewed as a *divine process*—but as the divine process of man, a process which man's abstract, pure, absolute being (as distinguished from his actual self) undergoes.

Now this process must have a bearer, a subject; but the subject comes into being only in the form of a result; this result, the subject knowing itself as absolute self-consciousness, is therefore *God*, absolute spirit, the self-knowing and self-manifesting Idea. Real man and real nature become mere predicates, mere symbols of this hidden, unreal man and unreal nature.[17]

This strikes home. Hegel will no doubt continue to have apologists seeking to "contextualize", water down, or somehow explain away his notorious equation of the actual with the rational, of what is with what ought to be—and their efforts will remain unconvincing. For if Marx is right, Hegel's thought cannot escape a dilemma at its very center. His idealization[18] of the concretely actual either dissolves this actuality as actuality—in which case thought has indeed *overextended* itself—or entrenches it as status quo, justifies it in its dreariest positivity by insisting, in the face of any and all evidence to the contrary, that by a higher law of reason what appears for all the world unreasonable must be reasonable after all—in which case thought, by reverting to precisely the kind of conjectural theodicy that Hegel himself had repudiated, has *compromised* itself. Little wonder that Hegel fathered a Left and a Right: their unresolved conflict in historical practice had its roots in a theory that, for all of its dialectical subtlety and comprehensiveness, had never resolved the perplexity from which it had arisen.

Yet even while the young Marx was displaying his undeniable greatness as a philosophical and social critic, he was already becoming entangled in his own nest of perplexities.

II. The Universal Class

Hegel's bondsman is a most intriguing figure but an elusive one, difficult to identify with any familiar individual or class in modern society.[19] He isn't really Marx's absolutely exploited and expropriated proletarian, but then he isn't really the stereotypical rising bourgeois either. For he is more than simply an intelligent, enterprising character, well versed in the ways of sublimation; there are echoes here of the patient instincts of the medieval craftsman and perhaps even foreshadowings of the existential Angst and inner refusal of the contemporary "social dropout". This ideal revolutionary and universally human type, as Hegel presents him, seems to be in the process of activating and actualizing all the capacities required for him to emerge as the harbinger of a Western utopia—at least in theory. But the fact that nothing of the kind had happened by 1850, as Marx rightly insisted (not to mention since) is not enough by itself to invalidate Hegel or vindicate Marx. Despite Marx's frequent objections, there is really nothing wrong with utopian theory provided it remain connected with existing practice by being pointedly critical of it; and the Lord-Bondsman passage certainly is, however much uncritical accommodation there may have been in Hegel's subsequent thought. For if human history is the struggle for human freedom, and if freedom is not only actualized in the formative activity of precisely those who do not rule[20] but consummated in the interpersonal recognition of equals, then any but an ephemeral and retrospective justification for hierarchical stratifications, indeed for institutionalized distinctions of any kind between rulers and ruled, is groundless. It can be said on Hegel's behalf, then, that there was at least one moment in his thinking when *critical theory* and revolutionary practice had—at least in theory—been reconciled.

I am not at all sure that as much can be said for his great critic Marx, in whose allegedly more concrete, down-to-earth thinking the proletariat replaces the bondsman as historical agent of human emancipation. Another early manuscript, "The Critique of Hegel's Philosophy of Right,"[21] provides us with some of Marx's most vigorous statements about why he invested such high hopes in *this* "universal class" and at the same time some of the clearest hints of why these hopes are misplaced.

It is only in the name of general interests that a particular class can claim general supremacy. . . . for one class to represent the whole of society, another class must concentrate in itself all the evils of society. . . . A particular social sphere must be regarded as the *notorious crime* of the whole society, so that emancipation from this sphere appears as a general emancipation. . . .
    Where is there, then, a real possibility of emancipation . . .?
    This is our reply. A class must be formed which has radical chains, a class *in* civil society which is not a class *of* civil society, a class which is the dissolution of all classes, a sphere of society which has a universal character because its sufferings are universal, and which does not claim a *particular redress* because the wrong which is done to it is not a *particular wrong* but *wrong in general*. There must be formed a sphere of society which claims no *traditional* status but only a human status . . . a sphere, finally, which cannot emancipate itself without emancipating itself from all the other spheres of society, without, therefore, emancipating all these other spheres, which is, in short, a *total loss* of humanity and which can only redeem itself by a *total redemption of humanity*. This dissolution of society, as a particular class, is the *proletariat*.

Today no less than in Marx's Europe of 1844 many have good cause to share his yearning for "that genius which pushes material force to political power, that revolutionary daring which throws at its adversary the defiant phrase: *I am nothing and I should be everything*."[22] But as critical theory designed to inform revolutionary practice, Marx's notion of the proletariat as agent of universal human emancipation falls somewhat short of cogency. For if nothing less than a me-and-my-special-devil ideology can rouse the passions of the dispossessed to the needed revolutionary pitch, then Marx's theory of revolution not only comes to an impasse but repeats in its own way the vicious circle that he had already exposed in Hegel. Critical theory—which had just unmasked the self-alienatedness of bourgeois society by seeing through its theological protective cover—would now give way to a revolutionary practice whose indispensable precondition would be a retheologization of concrete social conditions (this time "class warfare") in terms of an abstract and absolute Good vs. Evil. Moreover, one would be naive to suppose that all this is merely a matter of an essentially forward-looking class girding itself for battle by resorting provisionally to a backward-looking ideology which will be shed in due course. Unfortunately, since (as of course Marx himself so powerfully insisted) the proletariat in fact embodies, as victim, the *universal wrong* of modern society, nothing but the most abstract inversion—a piece of pure theory untainted by anything to be found in concrete experience—could render this class the *agent*[23] of what is universally right. Again, since Marx's own concept of human emancipation is a loose amalgam of outstanding moments of theory and practice gleaned from the historical record of the classical humanist tradition, there is something a bit airy, to say the least, about "a sphere of society which claims no *traditional* status but only a human status." It is as though Marx, who had learned so much from and made so many critical contributions to history, were formulating a theory of revolution predicated on the dissolution of history altogether.

In 1844 Marx was still several years away from propping up his myth of the proletariat as universal class with the even more grandiose myth of Historical Inevitability. The manuscript from which we have been quoting ends with a formula for human emancipation whose most noteworthy characteristic is the banality of its Romantic imagery.

Philosophy is the head of this emancipation and the proletariat is its heart. Philosophy can only be realized by the abolition of the proletariat, and the proletariat can only be abolished by the realization of philosophy.[24]

III. The Missing Mediating Term

Although both Hegel and Marx at times claimed otherwise, the essential work of philosophy is not yet accomplished, not even "in principle." The question of the proper relation between theory and practice continues to perplex us— in no small part because of a well-rooted tendency in the modern age to think and act as if they are meant to coalesce.[25] The lesson of experience, however, seems to be that thought that considers its essential function to be its own concretization in action is thought that has already given in to its besetting temptation to overreach itself and put itself in the place of what at first it had simply tried to understand. Conversely, action or practice informed by theory alone is literally boundless and has thus already lost any frame of reference, any context within which its processes and their ramifications could be defined and, when necessary, controlled. What alone can keep thought and action confined within their proper orbits is what awakens them to life in the first place — namely, an object or state of affairs that is decidedly *other* than ourselves as thinkers and actors; that in and through this otherness is capable of engaging and holding our interested concern; and that has within itself the resources to withstand all of our concerted efforts to appropriate it through critical reflection and experimental action upon it. From this perspective — one that I suspect was quite close to Marx's own when he criticized Hegel for eviscerating thinghood[26] — thought, action, and object (thing) form a continuum of three distinct and reciprocally indispensable terms, each of which is able to play its distinctive role only when engaged in a dialectical interplay with the other two. Left to its own devices, any of the three is both destructive to the others and a danger to itself — overbearing precisely because it is so fragile and vulnerable. For the sake of all three of them, one of these terms must alway mediate between the other two.

Historically, there is no fixed structure or sequence to this interplay. Thus it may well be, as Dewey proposed, that *perceived* tensions or contradictions must initially activate the human animal, pressing him to work upon his environment, before his capacity for reflective consciousness can develop to the level of what we call thought. As it happens, this account of thought as a late emergent is not only consistent with the overall structure of Hegel's *Phenomenology* (Consciousness — Self-Consciousness — Reason — Spirit), but reflects the course of things Hegel depicts in his Lord-Bondsman analysis. For the bondsman dimly perceives, then acts (work, formative activity), and only in the end *thinks through* what he has done, realizing fully for the first time who and what he is.

But in a developed, institutionally congealed society, one in which various human capacities have already matured and possibly become overripe, the relationship may well be reversed. Here it may be necessary for thought itself, in the form of critical theory, to illuminate and unmask "objective contradictions" before they can even be *perceived* by the members of such a society. Only when thought has thus reawakened perception will such men *act*, and only then will action in its turn disclose and confront once again an object of shared critical concern: a common cause. In contemporary society it is most often the absence or apparent unreality of just such an inter-personal object that keeps both thought (as distinguished from "group-think") and action (unlike mass behavior) from being anything but rare, exotic, and seemingly aimless, irrational, and arbitrary phenomena. Indeed in a society like ours, the more frequently and widely a cause (nuclear disarmament, social justice, ecological balance) is labeled idealistic or utopian, the greater, in all likelihood, is its capacity to play the indispensable role of alien, unachieved other, of genuine object, of something that can frustrate and thus stem the solipsistic drift of our collective social substance.

The missing mediating term between theory and practice, then, is something other than what we ourselves are and have made, something that is powerful enough to shatter the self-flattering image of a world in which the rational and the actual are put forth as a seamless whole—something, in short, that compels us to think and act.

From a conceptual point of departure like the one I have just sketched, one can understand why the dialogue between Hegel and Marx remains unfinished. Hegel's bondsman passage, utopian though it may be, nevertheless does provide a model of thought, action, and thing in which each of these terms retains its distinctive meaning and relationship within a fluid dialectical process. The bondsman's object, emancipation, is an as yet unfulfilled ideal, prompting his formative activity within a natural world from which he is at first estranged even while he depends on it, in its very difference from him, to reflect back to him the degree to which he is achieving his human essence. It is quite otherwise with Hegel's conception of modern, capitalistic process-society.[27] This society has, by Hegel's own candid admission, an unresolved and seemingly unresolvable problem of poverty—hence an unemancipated and quite conceivably unemancipatable proletariat—at its very core. Unable effectively to criticize this society by providing a plausible agenda for reforming it in practice, Hegel, letting his idealist proclivities get the better of him, tried to *transfigure* it instead. Despairing of a principle of cohesion operative *within* the contradictory phenomenal order, he reposited a Transcendental Subject (the world-historical Absolute) whose "cunning of reason," acting in ways discernible to itself alone (i.e., mysteriously), is here and now, in the face of all experience to the contrary, resolving these contradictions, reconciling all conflicts, healing all wounds. If that is so, what we have here is indeed a theodicy of desperation. Then a highly idealistic[28] body of thought and an actually existing repressive structure of social practice, having been reconciled only "in principle," i.e., on the plane of pure thought itself, are allowed to pretend that they have been reconciled in reality. Marx rightly identified this mode of idealism as a disguised form of positivism. For on such a view unfulfilled revolutionary promises are "kept" in thought alone, which, by rising stoically above the tawdriness of the real and consoling itself with its innate, "spiritual" superiority, ends up sanctioning the appalling lack of critical reflectiveness in this reality.

Marx, then, saw through Hegel's transfiguration of bourgeois society; yet he fell victim to much the same sort of thing—if anything still more uncritically.[29] Convinced that materializing action had to replace idealizing thought—that Hegel must be stood right side up, as the old cliché goes—Marx was driven by the exigencies of revolutionary practice to the fateful myth of Historical Inevitability: a myth whose implications are, if anything, more accommodating than those of Hegel's. For Hegel, after all, had put forth his myth as a *philosophical* (in that sense at least still transcendental) hypothesis, whereas Marx insisted that historical inevitability is *empirically* discernible in the dialectical content of our social institutions themselves. When the social theorists who succeeded Marx found themselves confronting ever more powerful social forces— forces which did indeed seem to move according to laws of their own, quite indifferent to the intentions of those who had set these forces in motion or to the needs of those for whose benefit they had been naively presumed to exist in the first place—their thinking quickly lost its critical thrust. They allowed themselves to arrive at the conclusion that by the law of historical inevitability *all* social institutions and practices are in essence what they ought to be, since what they are and ought to be is always what they must be. In thus sanctifying the status quo as it were from within, they did more than succumb to Hegel's pan-reconciliatory tendencies. They allowed Marx's mythology to overwhelm his critical theory: vindication purchased at the price of betrayal.

The more important lesson to be learned from all this is not so much that the Marxist myth of historical inevitability is insidious (which it undoubtedly is) but rather that it is not so easy as it had once been thought to stand Hegel on his feet. Philosophical idealism is by now not only venerable but very deeply entrenched. Conceptualized by Descartes, its first triumph had come when the testimony of Galileo's telescope at last confirmed what the new astronomy had been trying to teach. Cartesian and post-Cartesian idealism, fostering despair of the unaided senses to advance the cause of unaided reason, played a crucial role in helping to legitimate a science, and eventually a technology, whose spectacular impact on social experience and indeed on nature itself eventually led us to doubt whether it was even possible to distinguish any longer between what is theoretical and what is applied, i.e., between thinking and doing, between theory and practice as such.

The trouble, of course, is that recent "application" has a way of cutting too deep, of altering some long-familiar condition of experience to the point where it becomes very difficult, both experientially and historically, to retrieve such a condition in order to form a critical conception of how much it has been altered, at what cost, and with what long-range implications. The harder this retrieval becomes while social practice remains still pre-Utopian, the more we find ourselves reverting to a sterile oscillation between realism and idealism — now nostalgic for a dependable reality which mere thought and its manipulative outgrowths cannot simply undo, now despairing of such a reality and concluding, not without some of the méchanceté of Dostoevsky's despondent Underground Man, that we, with our hyperself-consciousness, are all that there really is.

Thought's inherent tendency to overreach itself, to appropriate everything it encounters and put itself in the latter's place, seems to meet with little or no resistance in contemporary social practice. This as much as anything else makes idealist theory, in substance if not in name, seem so plausible and so inescapable. But this inescapability is itself the historically conditioned result of too close a fit between theory and practice, with no room left for a "third thing" to limit and in the end frustrate them both. Such a seeming ineluctability is at once cause and consequence of thought's loss of what should be its defining attribute, viz., of being critical. The relapse into positivism that Marx seemed to have correctly diagnosed in Hegel's thought is no mere biographical accident, marking the exhaustion of a great bourgeois intellectual's efforts to free himself from the prejudices of his class and adopt a genuinely "universal" point of view. When theory and practice coalesce to form an unbroken and uninterrupted continuity, thought itself is in danger of becoming so uncritical, so thoughtless, so inert that it does actually begin to reflect, in the sense of purely mirror, mundane conditions. Transmutations of the human image into such grotesque distortions as cold warrior, consumer, and the like, however local or ephemeral these social phenomena may some day turn out to have been, serve only to strengthen the disturbing realization that the dialectical other side of thought's arrogance is its pliability, its all too human proneness to surrender its critical power, its power to *see through*.

But when thought becomes vulnerable to such self-undoing, it can no longer be relied upon to keep action from doing thinghood in. As students of his texts are uncomfortably aware, Marx kept vacillating between (1) the belief that Communist praxis would eventually restore to nature and the domain of the objective (of what is materially *other* than man) its own inherent dignity and meaning; and (2) the view—a thoroughly idealistic, indeed solipsistic one— that there *is* nothing other than man, that *his* thought and action determines and defines all reality. The vacillation is understandable. Once idealistic theory has penetrated, via practice, to the heart of thinghood, it is realism, not idealism, that comes to seem the airier of these two classical philosophical postures. To the unbridled character of thought there then corresponds the utter fragility of thinghood. A revolutionary, yet genuinely self-critical, practice—and one might do well to insist, with Marx, that to be worthy of its name it must be both—can mediate between thought and thinghood only when it itself is already thoughtful enough to be objective, i.e., to give the real its due.

IV. The One and Only Class

In the preceding section I suggested that Hegel, despairing of a concrete rationale for the contradictory forces inherent in bourgeois-capitalist society, was led to transfigure his concept of that society by conjuring up for it a world-historical Absolute and its "cunning of reason." Although I believe that this interpretation, which Marx had already pressed, is in the end correct, Hegel did at least briefly consider a more down-to-earth resolution of modern society's inner conflicts as it were from within. In the *Philosophy of Right* Hegel distinguishes sharply between "civil society" and "the state." Civil society is the domain in which divergent and divisive private and particular interests, predominantly but not exclusively economic, hold sway. The state (at its most advanced stage so far) is a constitutional monarchy whose aim is in part to order and refine these "lower" interests to make them at least compatible with an organic political whole dedicated to the pursuit of "higher" human concerns. This aim is carried out through the agency of a "universal class," a class of enlightened *public servants* (see especially § § 287-297) whose tenure in office is conditional upon satisfactory performance of their public duty and who are rewarded with economic security and public respect as long as they continue to do it.

Now Hegel's universal class, which ideally embodies the "higher" interests of the state, is not at all the "middle class" as we almost universally think of it today—that ever-growing mass of relatively recent winners in the struggle for existence, who collectively reflect a sort of median of private affluence and social prestige between the well-established rich whom they continue to envy and by the poor whom by now they have come to hold in contempt. Rather, it is an *intermediary* class reminiscent of Plato's executive-guardians in the *Republic*. Its role is twofold: on the one hand, to ensure the concrete relevance and the sensitivity of the sovereign's political decisions to the various "corporations" that comprise civil society and, on the other, to encourage the "incorporation" of the lower orders of civil society into politically responsible organizations in whose collective power their otherwise impoverished, isolated, and publicly voiceless members can find their invidivual identities writ large. At the same time, however, this intermediary class requires ongoing pressure from above and below to preserve its integrity.

Civil servants and members of the executive constitute the greater part of the middle class, the class in which the consciousness of right and the developed intelligence of the mass of the people is found. The sovereign working on the middle class at the top, and Corporation-rights working on it at the bottom, are the institutions which effectually prevent it from acquiring the isolated position of an aristocracy and using its education and skill as means to an arbitrary tyranny. (§ 297)[30]

In theory, at least, Hegel's middle class is a class *for* rather than *of* civil society.

For a time, then, Hegel appears to have placed considerable hope in a state, organized around the principle of a social and institutional pluralism, which stimulates as much as profits from the efforts of a class of dependable public servants dedicated to fostering it. I do not know whether Hegel considered his public-spirited intermediary in the *Philosophy of Right* as the descendant of his emancipated bondsman in the *Phenomenology*, although an evolution of this kind strikes me as a plausible one for him to have proposed. What does seem clear, however, is that Hegel did not think enough of his own dialectics of social pluralism and its mediating class in practice to obviate in his own mind the need for those notorious transcendental safeguards which Marx unmasked as elaborate mystifications: the world-historical Absolute and the cunning of reason. In retrospect, this is regrettable, for Hegel's capitulation to "realism" (if that is what it was) in this instance may have contributed something to the impoverished self-conception of the post-Hegelian middle class. Characteristically, the middle class as we have come to know (and be) it acknowledges no public responsibility, plays no mediating role, and feels put upon by even the most modest efforts at social reform when asked to bear some of the cost in the form of tax dollars. So deep-rooted is this attitude that the occasional exception to the rule (a dedicated, underpaid school teacher, a young lawyer taking on poverty cases instead of furthering his career, a Ralph

Nader) is unreflectively regarded as classless, as a somehow admirable but nonetheless quixotic, alien, even suspect phenomenon.

One readily supposes that among Marx and the Marxists, whose social and political consciousness has never wavered from its allegiance to the oppressed, no such capitulation as Hegel's is to be found, either in theory or in practice. But such an assumption, natural as it is, is false. In the remainder of this essay I shall attempt to suggest why this is so.

As always urged on by the need for revolutionary practice, Marx was lured away from his own somewhat hazy but conceptually provocative Feuerbachian concept of "species-being"[31] toward a much more definite, more action-oriented, but at the same time greatly oversimplified notion of class conflict. Marx, the prophet of revolution, has been made to pay dearly for this theoretical shift: there has been no overthrow of the oppressive bourgeoisie by a united and militant proletariat, at least not anywhere in the industrialized nations of the Western world. And it is beginning to look as if there never will be one. For the lesson of the last century seems to be that the capitalistic tendency to widen the gulf between rich and poor is overshadowed by the inexorability with which it turns everything (and everyone) into commodities—a process whose sociocultural, even more than economic, effect is one of leveling and whose eventual outcome would appear to be not the withering away of the *Marxist* state as political instrument of oppression in the hands of a ruling class but rather the degeneration of the *Hegelian* state into the administrative arm of an all-consuming "civil society." With all due allowance for deeply entrenched stratifications which clearly do persist in the highly industrialized West, what we are witnessing is the gradual formation of a one-and-only class, its masters — bureaucrats in one or another guise—drawn not merely from its own ranks but from its own soul. By still another twist of dialectical irony, what can only be described as a theoretical flaw within the context of Marx's own critical analysis, namely the one-sided economic determinism which at times he himself took considerable pains to qualify, has turned out to be impossible to controvert empirically. Bit by bit we have learned to see with what thoroughness man is capable of determining himself in his economic character—how fully he can alienate himself from all his productive capacities when he confuses the fulfillment of his essential needs with what Marx had already called by its right name: the fetishism of commodities.

But there are other lapses in Marxian theory, lapses which continue to mystify human practice because they continue to go undetected. One of these is Marx's failure to distinguish clearly between labor and work,[32] or more decisively still, between labor and what Hegel had called "formative activity." Marx, as is well known, insisted *both* that labor (Arbeit) was human activity in alienated form, the object of man's unending exploitability in capitalist society, and something that would be abolished altogether in the Communist Utopia; *and* that labor (still Arbeit) was man's most distinctive mode of self-expression, the means of his human emancipation, and the concrete manifestation of his universal essence. By stretching the uses of a single concept to such contradictory lengths, Marx once again purchased a kind of descriptive aptness at the price of uncritical theory. For of course the endless resourcefulness of capitalism in exploiting all modes of human activity for profit has itself tended to break down the traditional experiential distinctions among them. One of the conceptual consequences of Marx's conflation of terms is his romance of the revolutionary proletariat as universal class, the drudgery of its labor transformed, as if by magic, into formative activity once it has finally understood how it is being exploited. And precisely this romantic notion has come to present a formidable mental barrier in the path of the only course of revolutionary activity which, so far as I can see, remains open to us at present.

Reconsider for a moment the by now classical dilemma of melioristic vs. radical Marxism: does one, if only because it would be inhumane to do otherwise, welcome and actively cooperate with gradual and piecemeal reform within the established system, or does one ruthlessly oppose and even sabotage such "advances" because, as experience repeatedly shows, they blunt revolutionary consciousness while solidifying, perhaps even perpetuating, the status quo? A perplexity of this sort can be real enough when it is directly confronted by those, namely the radically oppressed, who stand to gain or lose the most whichever way they make their anguished decision.[33] But it is quite another matter when *others*[34] take it upon themselves to resolve such difficulties *for* those who have the most at stake. This is clearly what is going on when self-styled radical Marxists call the proletariat a hard-to-manage "volatile substance": the metaphor itself betrays the manipulative and therefore thoroughly unrevolutionary attitude of these red-shirted masters.[35] And their opponents from within, the softer-headed and kinder-hearted meliorists, are really in the same situation. For by perpetuating the myth of the revolutionary proletariat and the historical inevitability of its uprising, while standing back and waiting for its self-consciousness to achieve critical volatility all by itself (at which point it will presumably show everyone else the way to the promised land), the meliorists are quite simply betraying the cause, replacing their once revolutionary consciousness with one of aloofness and inaction.

But what is most revealing about the radical-meliorist controversy is less its remarkable staying power as a doctrinal perplexity than its sheer presumptuousness. It takes upon itself the right to settle in theory what others will have to achieve, pay for, and live with in practice. As one might expect, social thought of this stripe tends to blind and blunt rather than to inform action; the alleged object of its theoretical conundrums, proletarians in the flesh, have every reason to question the relevance, descriptive or prescriptive, of such thinking to their concrete situation. For it is precisely their concrete situation, the supposed startingpoint of revolutionary practice, which remains unilluminated and un-criticized by such theory when it remains, as it were, once removed.[36] Who can blame a disullusioned proletarian, already the victim of a pervasively thought-less society, for concluding that thoughtlessness is part of the essence of being human and for turning his attention to the problems of sheer survival?

As I have mentioned, Marx's dream of the proletariat as universal revolu-tionary class remains uninterrupted by a single significant instance of its having actually come true anywhere in the industrialized or "postindustrial" West. If even some of the preceding analysis is valid, we can go a little further than the historian's observation that any modern revolution recognized as such has been initiated, masterminded, and led by disaffected bourgeois. True enough; but the *impact* of these revolutions, for better and for worse, has also been con-fined almost exclusively to the condition of the bourgeoisie *as bourgeoisie*. And little wonder. While the socioeconomic middle class has continued to ex-pand and, by every superficial standard, prosper, the extremes on either side of it have shrunk or degenerated (in some instances both at once). From the perspective of social history, we are *redefining* ourselves as the one-and-only "class"—and therefore, as any good dialectician realizes, no class at all. Accord-ingly, either *this* "class" shall somehow have to revolutionize itself, or revolution itself shall presently have become a phenomenon of interest only to historians. From the perspective of this essay, theory and practice will continue alternately to bifurcate and collapse into each other so long as no object of concrete and communal experience can be retrieved to mediate between them. Such an ob-ject, in our world, may well have to be a self-conscious reliving of what had once been the middle class's revolutionary experience.

Unfortunately, this one-and-only class[37] has long since forgotten its original, essentially revolutionary, historical situation, viz., that of putting into social practice the theories of human emancipation expounded during the Enlighten-ment. To this forgetfulness Marxist theoreticians have contributed far more than is generally realized. For by undertaking to program conceptually the revolutionary practice of a class of human beings other than themselves, they have tended to estrange themselves from these others still further and thus indirectly to mystify still more the concrete situation of all concerned. The result is that all the while that we are becoming the only class there is — truly classless if only because the lineaments of "the other" are becoming fainter and fainter — we are still waiting for someone else to do what we all know in our hearts must be done and which we alone are left to do.

Concretely, how *could* an acquiescent, unmediated middle class, given to blunting its critical self-consciousness with the booty of commodities is has spent itself in producing, set forth to retrieve its capacity for revolutionary thought and action? Perhaps (say in the course of an extended "recession") by being forced to internalize, in theory and practice, the experience of the very proletariat whose condition it had once so gratefully eluded and then so callously aggravated and ignored. In that event, by not too great an inversion of his own dialectic, the essence of what Marx predicted might still come true. Or perhaps we shall somehow manage to recover our historical dignity by re-capitulating within ourselves the dialectic of Hegel's lord-bondsman relationship in its more advanced stages. In that event the much more sophisticated but also much more obscure, ambivalent, and doggedly retrodictive Hegelian reconciliation "in principle" would be reflected in revolutionary practice, and then for the first time in history all men would be truly free. But I think that conjectures like these are in the end as unfruitful for us as they are unworthy of the memory of Hegel and Marx. For if I am right that Hegel's idealization of objective reality and Marx's mythification of historical reality disclose a failure to think through a coherent relation between theory and practice in our era; and that this failure is reflected in the domain of action by the tendency of contemporary theory and practice to remain literally up in the air, ungrounded in anything beyond themselves and hence misrelated to one another, then, inspired perhaps by the critical thoughtfulness of which Hegel and Marx were nonetheless capable, it would seem best for us to turn away from the ideological posturings of the neo-Hegelians and the neo-Marxists and begin again.

VI

The Unity of Theory and Practice:
The Science of Marx and Nietzsche

Edward Andrew

The writings of Karl Marx and Friedrich Nietzsche are usually held to be radically dissimilar, both in content and form. Marx was a socialist and Nietzsche an opponent of socialism. Also Marx is thought to be heir to the rationalistic tradition of modern science whereas Nietzsche is considered a critic of scientific methodology and a progenitor of irrationalism or antinomian existentialism. Yet, from Georges Sorel to the New Left, Marx and Nietzsche have been hailed as theorists of action and have jointly been held to be the prime spokesman for the politics of praxis.

The reason for merging the seemingly disparate teachings of Marx and Nietzsche into a theory of praxis will be elucidated by an analysis of the references to the doctrine of the unity of theory and practice found in both men. I do not intend to represent a comprehensive account of the essence or "real meaning" of the two thinkers. Both men have eluded definitive interpretations of their work. For example, a recent book by John Hoffman, entitled *Marxism and the Theory of Praxis*, argues, not without some foundation, that what he calls the "praxical" Marxists, a group which includes every major Marxologist and Marxist of the twentieth century with the exception of Lenin, have distorted the original scienticity of Marxism into an irrationalist voluntarism. Yet Hoffman and other "Engelsian" Marxists have not been able to demonstrate the reasons why Lukács, Korsch, Gramsci, Schmidt, Marcuse, Avineri, Petrovic, and others have rejected the methodology of the natural sciences as the basis of Marxist epistemology. In the absence of such a demonstration, we may assume that there is some basis in Marx's writings for the interpretation that Marxian science springs from the practical transformation of reality rather than from a theoretical reflection upon an existing reality. It is the elements in Marx that warrant such an interpretation with which I am concerned here. In addition, Nietzsche's understanding of science as that which unites theory to practice will be analyzed to clarify some of the implications of Marxist epistemology and politics.[1]

I. Experimentation and Mastery

It has often been deemed expedient to divide Marx's thought into science and ideology or cognitive and prescriptive elements as if there were merely an external or contingent relationship between his scientific analyses of economics and society and his revolutionary political commitment.[2] The thesis advanced here is that Marx's claims to scienticity, like Nietzsche's, were not made in spite of his revolutionary commitment to change the world but precisely because of it.

Science, for Marx and Nietzsche, was not simply an instrument for relieving the state of man but was also a means for ennobling man within that estate. It was not just the means of determining techniques for satisfying existing human desires but was also a method for expanding and transforming human abilities and wants. The central task to be performed by the science of Marx and Nietzsche was the creation of new men, the overcoming of what had hitherto been conceived as human nature. Both Marx and Nietzsche wished to see a science of man replace moral philosophy as the branch of practical reason concerned with the matters of most importance to man.

Marx and Nietzsche saw morals to be that branch of practice which is not amenable to testing, experimentation, verification, or falsification. For example, one may test practical maxims about how to earn money in the stock market, how to achieve victory in guerrilla warfare, how to grow the largest roses, and so on. One tries out the maxim; if it works, one accepts it as practical wisdom; if not, one amends it and tries again. But with moral maxims like one should not lie or steal, there is an injunction against trying them out. If one experiments in moral matters, one is considered immoral.

The difficult and dangerous project of probing and experimenting with morals, laws, and values was an aspect of Marx's and Nietzsche's attempt to create new men. Both men believed that existing moral standards inhibited and retarded human development by undermining man's courage to try out new ways of living, to experiment with new social forms and values, to practice a scientific mode of life. The repudiation of morals, in Marx's and Nietzsche's understanding, would engender a greater determination to test new ideas, to experiment and implement the results of proven hypotheses, to practice one's theories about mankind. Nietzsche prided himself on being the first immoralist; Marx was proud to have supplied a scientific basis for socialism and to have eschewed ethical considerations in distinction to earlier socialists. No longer, according to Marx, is a socialist society to be considered a mere ideal, an "ought", but by means of revolutionary experiments socialist society will become a reality. The determination to probe the structure of society, to test one's hypotheses in practice, to amend one's hypotheses according to one's experiments, in short, to have the courage to apply the methods and practices of the natural sciences to the social sciences, is an essential feature of Marx's transformation of socialism from utopia to science. Nietzsche, who abhorred the thought of the workers winning state power, nevertheless shared Marx's will to experiment, his method of verifying or falsifying socialist theories. Nietzsche writes:

Indeed, I should wish that a few great experiments might prove that in a socialist society life negates itself, cuts off its own roots. The earth is large enough and man still sufficiently unexhausted; hence such a practical instruction and *demonstratio ad absurdum* would not strike me as undesirable, even if it were gained and paid for with a tremendous expenditure of human lives.[3]

Thus the experimental method, which is central to the doctrine of the unity of theory and practice, was espoused by both Marx and Nietzsche. Not only the method but also the spirit animating the research of both men was similar. One might well expect Marx rather than Nietzsche to have quoted the following dictum of Goethe's as an inspiration to research: "I hate everything that merely instructs me without increasing or directly quickening my activity."[4]

Both men scorned "scholastic" "academic," or "impractical" problems. No one could call Marx or Nietzsche disinterested scholars. Both were passionately interested in using their researches for the advancement of mankind. In fact, Nietzsche denounces disinterested scholarship as follows:

I know of nothing that excites such disgust as this kind of "objective" armchair scholar. . . . Such a sight arouses my ire, such "spectators" dispose me against the "spectacle" more than the spectacle itself (the spectacle of history, you understand). . . .[5]

This explosion has a parallel in Marx's fulminations against the young

Hegelian "spectators" of history in *The Holy Family* and *The German Ideology*. Marx's statement that his idea of happiness was to fight and that his favorite occupation was book worming,[6] a combination pertinent to the unity of theory and practice, is similar to Nietzsche's autobiographical statement that he is warlike by nature and that reading is his chief recreation when away from scholarship and writing.[7] "The brave soldiers of knowledge" employ "not a lancet but a weapon." Both Marx and Nietzsche refer to theories as weapons.[8]

One might here wonder how this martial spirit and passionate commitment to a cause are compatible with the scientific claims that Marx and Nietzsche made for their work. If science is considered to be the disinterested observation and cognition of data, the passive or nonvolitional reflection of facts as hypotheses, the testing of the predictions furnished by these hypotheses as a means to eliminate the subjectivity of the observer or theorists, and the elaboration of objective laws to account for the data perceived, then neither Marx nor Nietzsche could accurately be described as scientists. But both men believe the above to be a misunderstanding of the nature of science. As Nietzsche says:

It is only a superstition to say that the picture given . . . man by the object really shows the truth of things. Unless it be that objects are expected in such moments to paint or photograph themselves by their own activity on a purely passive medium![9]

Or as Marx writes:

The chief defect of all hitherto existing materialism . . . is that the thing, reality, sensuousness is conceived only in the form of the *object* or of *contemplation*, but not as *human sensuous activity, practice*, not subjectively.[10]

Scientific knowledge, for Marx and Nietzsche, is the product of active people molding data conceptually for practical purposes, for the mastery of nature and the enhancement of life. Both men adhered to the Baconian dictum that knowledge is power. The function of science is to change the world, not merely to understand or reinterpret it. Or rather a scientific understanding of the world is born of changing it, from experimenting on the world and from the practical application of experimental findings in techniques. Knowledge is mastery; science is simultaneously conquest and understanding. Science is not only a means to obtain theoretical knowledge but also the most effective instrument to obtain practical mastery of the globe. Scientific activity unites theory and practice.[11]

Science is practical, or in the words of Marx, "a productive force." Unlike unproductive modes of thought like philosophy, religion, and other forms of ideology, science does not resign itself to the world as a given but by means of an experimental interaction with it seeks to master and change it. Religion and philosophy are modes of alienation of practical life; they provide a more or less fanciful interpretation of a world they are impotent to change.[12] Science is not passive, receptive, accepting the world as it is. When Marx says that hitherto "philosophers have only interpreted the world in various ways; the point is to change it,"[13] he is demanding that science replace philosophy. Or as Nietzsche says:

The philosophic objective outlook can therefore be a sign that will and strength are small. For strength organizes what is close and closest; "men of knowledge," who desire only to ascertain what is, are those who cannot *fix* anything *as it ought to be.*

Artists, an intermediate species: they at least fix an image of that which ought to be; they are productive, to the extent that they actually alter and transform; unlike men of knowledge, who leave everything as it is.[14]

Nietzsche concludes like Marx that "philosophy, religion and morality are *symptoms of decadence*,"[15] of weakness of will, of impotence.

That science is a practical or productive activity is not, for Marx and Nietzsche, the fortunate and fortuitous by-product of the pure, disinterested pursuit of knowledge. Science not only uses the data provided by the senses but is motivated and given a direction by sensuous needs. Marx asks, "Where would natural science be without industry and commerce? Even this 'pure' natural science is provided with an aim, as with its material, only through trade and industry, through the sensuous activity of men."[16] Science, Marx declares elsewhere, is only true science "when it proceeds from sense-perception in the two-fold form both of *sensuous* consciousness and *sensuous* need . . ."[17] Nietzsche also believes all pursuit of knowledge is directed by physiological impulses.[18] He further asserts that sense perception is conditioned by practical interests or sensuous needs.

Consciousness is present only to the extent that consciousness is useful. It cannot be doubted that *all sense perceptions are permeated with value judgments* (useful and harmful — consequently, pleasant or unpleasant).[19]

Nietzsche, like Marx, rejected the idea of science as the disinterested reflection of objective processes because such an idea presupposes "an eye that is completely unthinkable, an eye turned in no particular direction, in which the active and interpreting forces, through which alone seeing alone becomes seeing *something*, are supposed to be lacking. . . ."[20] Nietzsche wittily pokes fun at "the immaculate perception" of the "pure, will-less, painless, timeless knower."[21]

What Nietzsche articulates more clearly than Marx is that scientific cognition is a mode of volition. If volition or willing is that which prompts praxis, then thinking and acting are alike forms of willing. And it is precisely in the practical nature of science that the unity of theory and practice is revealed; theory and practice, thinking and acting, are both the offspring of willing.

Theory and Practice—Fateful distinction, as if there were an actual drive for knowledge that, without regard to questions of usefulness and harm, went blindly for the truth; and then separate from this, the whole world of practical interests.[22]

Science is born of practical needs and aims at overcoming obstacles to the fulfilling of those needs. It transforms theoretical speculation into practical know-how or technique by means of testing, putting into practice theoretical ideas, amending hypotheses according to practice. Not only is the validity of the theory verified by the testing but also the theorist is elevated by practice, by the experience of repeated experiments—just as the skill of a swimmer or cook is not so much enhanced by reflecting in an armchair or by reading a book as it is by practice. Nietzsche praises the rigor and discipline of scientific activity as a means of ennobling man's character: "it gives an additional energy, decisiveness, and toughness of endurance; it teaches how to attain an *aim suitably*."[23]

Science is a mode of practical and not pure reason. It is not disinterested, will-less reflection but is rather the highest manifestation of the human will. Science is the will to experiment, the will not to accept anything on faith, the will to maintain our convictions as hypotheses to be tested, the will to practice and apply our theories. Social science must be placed on an experimental basis: "it must never again be considered as a disgrace to depart from morality in actions or thought; many new experiments must be made upon life and society. . . ."[24] Since Nietzsche sees natural science as being based on value judgments, one would not expect him to think social science would be value-free. Rather, values, the object of the will and the motive of scientific activity, must be placed on an experimental basis. "Therefore an *experimental morality*: to *give* oneself a goal."[25] The verification of a hypothesis about the best way to live, just like a hypothesis about the operation of submolecular processes, depends on trying it out in practice, on testing.

Political society is an experiment about who can rule and who can obey.[26] That Marx and Nietzsche had different hypotheses on this matter should not obliterate the similarity in their understanding of a science of politics. The question of who is to constitute the ruling class cannot be decided in abstraction from practical experimentation. This fundamental problem of political science is soluble only through political practice. What is required of the man of science is precisely courage. "We are experiments: if we want to be so."[27] Scientists "are men of a daring morality";[28] they must have the courage to experiment, to practice their theories. "To become wise we must *will* to undergo certain experiences, and accordingly leap into their jaws. This, it is true, is very dangerous. Many a 'sage' has been eaten up in the process."[29]

The prerequisite to mastery is the courageous determination, the will to live by experiments.[30] Scientific cognition is a form of volition; it is not the passive reflection of objective phenomena. Theory and practice are united in science since thinking and acting alike arise from willing, from the determination to achieve mastery over one's environment.

II. The Prescriptive Character of Marx's Use of Class

Marx thought that all ideas arise from social practice and are generated by practical needs. Moreover, he provided an interesting account of why thinkers have erroneously conceived their ideas to be disinterested, pure or free of the taint of practice. Insofar as thinkers require leisure, they are members of the ruling rather than the working class — or more precisely, the latter part of a division of ruling class into actual exploiters and ideologists who make their living producing illusions to mask that exploitation. These leisured men, separated from the production of the material requisites of life, see themselves as independent of the production and struggles of practical life. But because they have a practical interest in the preservation of the ruling class of which they are a part, and because their ideas would only be accepted and disseminated by those who control the means of communication, the ideas of leisured men usually express the practical interests of the ruling class, except when there is a strong alternative class competing for hegemony. Thus a major characteristic of ideologists is the illusion that their ideas are disinterested when in reality they express practical class interests. The safegard that a socialist society will provide against ideological illusions is the abolition of the division between mental and manual labor or the union of theoretical and practical activity. All men will be provided with a scientific and cultural education and all men will work in material production.

Science, according to Marx, rather than being disengaged from practical life, requires a comprehension of the practical genesis of theory and an application in practice of one's theories. The Second Thesis on Feuerbach reads:

The question whether objective truth can be attributed to human thinking is not a question of theory but is a *practical* question. Man must prove the truth, i.e. the reality and power, the this-sidedness of his thinking in practice. The dispute over the reality or non-reality of thinking that is isolated from practice is a purely *scholastic* question.[31]

Theoretical problems generally reflect practical problems; they cannot be resolved in a purely intellectual manner but only through practice to remove the source of the theoretical problem. The Eighth Thesis on Feuerbach states:

All social life is essentially *practical*. All mysteries which lead theory to mysticism find their rational solution in human practice and in the comprehension of this practice.[32]

Mankind only sets itself practicable tasks, Marx asserts in his famous preface to *Contribution to the Critique of Political Economy*; the problems that rise from social practice can be resolved in social practice. Marxist theory is then preeminently practical, an instrument or weapon in the service of the proletariat, a guide to action and an expression of the will to act, a prescription for revolutionary praxis.

Yet since Marx frequently presented his prescriptions in the form of predictions, his values in the form of causalities, it has been widely held that Marxian science is not an expression of volition but a pure cognition of objective processes. That this is not the case may be seen in the following example. The first chapter of *The Communist Manifesto* begins with the apparently cognitive statement, "The history of all hitherto existing society is the history of class struggles." This appears to be a purely descriptive statement that struggles between distinct groups of men have marked the pages of all written history. Yet Marx is also asserting that historical development is motivated by the struggle between classes. Shortly before he died, Marx wrote:

For almost forty years we have stressed the class struggle as the immediate driving power of history and in particular the class struggle between bourgeoisie and proletariat as the great lever of modern social revolution. . . .[33]

As yet we cannot clearly perceive an evaluation contained within this purportedly explanatory statement. But if we refer to *The Poverty of Philosophy*, a work written a year before *The Communist Manifesto*, we read: "No antagonism, no progress. That is the law that civilization has followed up to our days."[34] Thus we arrive at the evaluated assertion that struggle is the cause of historical progress. Marx frequently refers to the absense of history as a characteristic of the Orient; despite a high level of technical development and civilization, the East lacks classes and political conflict which characterize and generate the history of the West.

But what precisely is a class struggle? What constitutes a class? Marx never fully answered these questions. His only attempt to define a class is left unfinished.[35] However, we can clearly see from Marx's usage of the term class that it is different from classification according to nationality, race, sex, religion, or creed.

Classes are not based on alleged biological differences, like race or sex, as are castes. Class differences are those which can be overcome. To designate black-white relations, for example, as a problem of class rather than caste is to express optimism about the resolution of racial conflict and to suggest a manner of resolving the problem. To see male-female relations as a class struggle is necessarily to reject the proposition that "biology is destiny." Classes are historical; they can become what they are not.

Similarly, classes are not nationalities, cultural groups, or religious sects. To understand the struggles in Northern Ireland or the Middle East as class struggles is to recommend that the apparent causes of conflict be transcended, that the participants in such struggles have wrongly assessed the meaning and purpose of such struggles. Marx resolved "the Jewish Question" by reducing religious differences to class differences. An unmediated class analysis postulates that no (antagonistic) differences separate humankind except those generated by different functions in a socioeconomic division of labor; it contains the prescription that one should not discriminate on the basis of race, sex, creed, or nationality.

Marx's internationalism is an integral part of his theory of class struggle. A class analysis, far from being a repudiation of an earlier humanism based on a conception of man as "a species-being," is a restatement of it within the framework of his economic interpretation of history. Marx's championship of the proletarian cause is not a partisan interest in conflict with the welfare of the species. For in his introduction to *Contribution to the Critique of Hegel's Philosophy of Right* Marx saw the proletariat as "the universal class," the bearers of the interests of humanity. Subsequently, the materialist interpretation of history located these universal interests concretely, within the economic structure of industrial capitalism.

Classes are economic groupings, but they are quite distinct from income strata. Only "the vulgar mind commutes class differences into 'differences in the size of purses'. . . ."[36] Classes are presented in terms of a relation to the means of production and not to the means of consumption or income. Classes then, for Marx, are groups of men and women with a similar position in a social division of labor, with a common relationship to the means of production.

However, certain groups, like the French peasantry of the nineteenth century, "do not form a class"[37] in spite of a common relationship to the means of production. Peasant interests are merely local; they lack national unity and political organization. The bourgeoisie ceased to be an estate and became a class when it organized itself on a national basis for political purposes.[38] The workers, originally separated by localities and trade demarcations but later brought together by the development of concentrated industrial production and improved means of communication, constitute a class when they organize on a national and then on an international basis. Although competition between workers and between individual capitalists retards class formation,[39] eventually "the collisions between individual workmen and individual bourgeois take more and more the character of collisions between two classes."[40] Before their national organization for political purposes, the workers do not constitute a class.[41] Thus a class is not simply constituted by a common relationship to the means of production but also by political organization and resolution. In short, a class is a potentially ruling group that is united and generalizes its economic interests in a political form.[42]

Now the statement that history is the product of class struggles cannot be taken as an assertion of the ubiquity of class struggles in all stages of human development. For the preceding statements indicate that Marx thought classes come to exist only at particular times in the course of human affairs. These times are the period of class struggle "which carried to its highest expression is a total revolution."[43] Less revolutionary periods are not really "historical," are not times of human development or progress. Without a struggle for power or a determination to engage in revolutionary activity, classes do not exist. "The working class is revolutionary or it is nothing."[44]

Classes, then, are groups struggling for power, but these groups are classified by a relationship to the means of production and the power struggle centers upon control of the means of production. Now why should this be? Marx explains, in laying the foundation for the materialist interpretation of history, as follows:

The mode of production must not be considered simply as being the reproduction of the physical existence of the individuals. Rather it is a definite form of activity of these individuals, a definite *mode of life* on their part. As individuals express their life, so they are. What they are, therefore, coincides with their production, both with *what* they produce and with *how* they produce. The nature of individuals thus depends on the material conditions determining their production.[45]

The character of individuals depends upon the way they express their life, upon their deeds and works rather than their thoughts. Since this depends on individuals' relation to the means of production, class differences are determined by individuals' access to, or separation from, the means of production. The means of production "must not be considered simply as" a means of income but are, above all, the condition for the expression of life, of human abilities and needs. A struggle for mastery over the means of production is a struggle for the conditions of self-expression. Self-determined productive activity is the highest end of mankind.[46] Marx anticipated that, in communist society, "labour has become not only a means of life but life's prime want."[47] Thus class conflict is a struggle between individuals, defined by their preeminently human or productive capacity, for the most worthy objective, self-determined productive activity. The history of class struggles specifically excludes conflict over less worthy objectives.

History as the history of class struggle is then not a purely cognitive description of the course of human events but an evaluation that struggle will engender maximum progress of human development. In fact, if the statement that history is the history of class struggles were purely cognitive, then the exhortation at the end of *The Communist Manifesto* for the workers of the world to unite would be superfluous. And further, if the workers of the world need uniting, then they do not constitute a class. And if the workers do not form a class, then the statement that history is the history of class struggles, if considered a purely cognitive or value-free statement, is patently false. But to understand Marxian science as pure cognition is misleading. The statement that history is the history of class struggles is of the same status as his advocacy of the union of the working class; both express his evaluation that historical progress is best enhanced by the union of men in a struggle for the mastery of the means of production. Both statements are the expression of Marx's will to engage in revolutionary activity, the expression of the worthy objectives he thought would be obtained through class warfare. His descriptions are at the same time prescriptions; his analysis, advocacy.

But if Marx's thinking is indeed a mode of willing, if his analysis is not value-free but is based upon moral prescriptions, how could he claim that his theory is scientific? Precisely by testing these values or prescriptions. In fact, it would not be misleading to assert that Marx devoted his life to the experimentation of his evaluation that human development is enhanced by class conflict. Marx's will to fight is simultaneously his will to test his hypotheses. His science consists in revolutionary practice as the means to verify his theory. The unity of theory and practice is Marx's scientific method. His theories are not derived from passive, disinterested cognition of objective processes; no theories, including those of natural science, are so derived, according to Marx. His theories spring from praxis, from the determination to change the world, from the will to master the obstacles to his ends. Marx, then, like Nietzsche, believed thinking as well as acting derive from willing.

III. Contemplation and Action

To clarify what Marx and Nietzsche meant by the unity of theory and practice, it would be fruitful to explore their objections to the separation of theory and practice. Nietzsche writes, suggesting many of the objections that Marx shared:

Dangerous distinction between "theoretical" and "practical", e.g., in the case of Kant, but also in the case of the ancients:—they act as if pure spirituality presented them with the problems of knowledge and metaphysics;—they act as if practice must be judged by its own measure, whatever the answer of theory may be.

Against the former I direct my *psychology of philosophers*: their most alienated calculations and their "spirituality" are still only the last pallid impression of a physiological fact [or motivation]. . . .

Against the latter I ask whether we know of any other method of acting well than always thinking well; the latter *is* an action, and the former presupposes thought. Have we a different method for judging the value of a way of life from judging the value of a theory: by induction, by comparison?[48]

Nietzsche and Marx are at one in thinking that theoretical problems arise from practical life and that the theorist, no matter how isolated or alienated he is from practical activity, expresses in his ideas and is in fact motivated by practical needs.

The earliest meaning of theorist (theoros) was a spectator, or contemplator of a thea, a sight or spectacle, some public happening, festival, or sporting event as might be witnessed in a theater. The term theoros referred to a man sent to attend the religious festivities of foreigners or to a member of an audience in a theater before the word came to refer to a person who reflects or contemplates on some aspect of human experience. The theoros then was an observer who did not participate in the public happening that he witnessed, a spectator rather than an actor.

Marx and Nietzsche believe that it is a misunderstanding to suppose that a theorist is outside the drama of life, a mere spectator, in the way that a member of the audience is separated from the actors within a theater. Nietzsche refers to the "illusion of the contemplative" as follows:

He calls his nature a *contemplative nature*, and thereby overlooks the fact that he himself is also a real creator, and continuous poet of life,—that he no doubt differs greatly from the *actor* in this drama, the so-called practical man, but differs still more from a mere onlooker or spectator *before* the stage.[49]

Theorists, then, despite their view of themselves, are not outside the practical life about which they reflect; they are a definite part of social life, both as its creature and creator. The experience of the thinker is conditioned by the social circumstances in which he is active. The categories, concepts, and values by which he understands his experience are social products. But thinkers do not passively reflect the social circumstances that condition their thought; they creatively reinterpret the conceptual tools that they inherit in order to master a new historical experience. Thinking is active, creative, but not as the idealists conceive, namely, the activity of rendering something intelligible or comprehensible regardless of practical consequences, the activity of pure reason.[50] The idealist assumption of purely cognitive activity presupposes "an actual drive for knowledge that, without regard to questions of usefulness and harm, went blindly for the truth," a presupposition which Marx and Nietzsche rejected.

The desire for knowledge or understanding as an end in itself rather than for instrumental purposes presupposes the Hegelian or idealist error "that I am a thinking being but not a living one, that I am no 'animal,' but at most a 'cogital'."[51] Marx states the same objection to Hegelian idealism: "For Hegel, *the essence of man—man—*equals *self-consciousness.*" But the thinking self is only an abstraction from man as "a natural, corporeal, sensuous, objective being." As a result of Hegel's idealistic abstraction, the only activity Hegel recognizes is "abstract mental labour."[52] Hegel sees the activity of the theorist as the attempt to render a phenomenon comprehensible; Marx and Nietzsche see the activity of the theorist as the attempt to master the phenomenon. The proponents of the unity of theory and practice maintain that reason is an instrument or a weapon of the living, sensuous man.

Hegel asserts that when the activity of reason is considered to be instrumental rather than an end, "then thinking in general is subordinate to other mental functions. We do not say of our Feelings, Impulses and Interests that they serve us—rather, they are regarded as independent faculties and powers [which comprise our being]."[53] The belief that reason is a servant of the sensuous organism debases what Hegel considers to be the crowning attribute of

men. Theory as a means to practice establishes will as the definitive characteristic of humanity.

Nietzsche remarks that "men use a new lesson or experience later on as a
ploughshare or perhaps also as a weapon, women at once make it into an adorn-
ment."[54] It would appear that men and women never simply wish to understand their experience. The nature of man is a tool maker and a fighter. Man
is practical activity, will; his nature precludes a passive, receptive, "theoretical"
attitude. To be passive, merely reflective is weakness, effeminacy; "for what
is life other than activity?"[55] Passivity is suffering for Marx and Nietzsche.
Marx states:

To be sensuous is to suffer.
Man as an objective, sensuous being is therefore a suffering being—and because he feels what he suffers, a *passionate* being. Passion is the essential force
of man energetically bent on its object.[56]

Thus Marx transforms passivity into activity, suffering into striving or willing.
In a similar manner Nietzsche transforms sensuous experience into willing. "All
feeling suffers in me and is in prison: but my willing always comes to me as
my liberator and bringer of joy."[57]

In neither Marx nor Nietzsche do we read of a noninstrumental reflection
on experience as the function of a theorist. In fact, this constitutes Marx's
criticism of the "mechanistic materialism" of Feuerbach: "Feuerbach's 'conception' of the sensuous world is confined on the one hand to mere contemplation of it, and on the other to mere feeling. . . ."[58] He does not understand,
Marx asserts, materialist practice, the conversion of sense experience to striving
rather than its retention in suffering, yearning, and reflecting.

For Marx and Nietzsche, theory is neither the passive reflection upon experience nor the active attempt to render experience intelligible; the function
of theory is to master experience and change the world. The imperative to
change the world is both ethical—the world is not as it ought to be—and epistemological—"we can comprehend only a world that we ourselves have made."[59]
Thus only by means of human creation, activity which changes the world, can
we understand the world; mastery is knowledge.

The view of the world as "to be changed" rather than "to be understood"
constitutes a different conception of nature and human nature than was held
by Aristotle. Marx and Nietzsche rejected the Aristotelian view that nature
was in the main beneficent, that all parts of the cosmos had a definite role assigned to them by nature, and that man could understand the natural function

of things and men. As a result they rejected the classical conception of theory as the activity of rendering intelligible the natural function of man and his relation to other elements of the world. For Marx and Nietzsche, nature provides no guidance to mankind; nature and human nature are merely the raw material of human practice, something to be overcome by the scientific creation of the world. Nietzsche writes:

Whatever has *value* in the present world, has not it in itself, by its nature, — nature is always worthless: —but a value was once given to it, bestowed upon it and it was *we* who gave and bestowed! We only have created the world *which is of any account to man!*[60]

Man too has no fixed nature; his "nature" is his own creation, the product of his practical activity. For Marx and Nietzsche, man's "nature" is really his history —the continuous transformation of "human nature" by his own practical activity. And history has not come to an end as Hegel's *Philosophy of History* asserts. The core of Nietzsche's teaching is that "man is something that should be overcome."[61] Marx calls for "the alteration of men on a mass scale" in the proletarian revolution, a revolution to be conceived as "the coincidence of changing circumstances and self-changing."[62]

There are no natural objectives of mankind, no inherently choiceworthy goals of human activity, no intrinsic limits to the self-determining man of praxis, of will. The function of the theorist, then, for Marx and Nietzsche, is not to understand human nature but to will a goal for mankind and to ascertain the means to overcome the obstacles toward achieving that goal. Human aspirations must be tested and confirmed in practical activity; values are the product of human creation and experimentation, they do not inhere in human nature. The aspiration to overcome human nature is simultaneously the means to know the extent of human powers and qualities just as the aspiration to master nature was, for Marx and Nietzsche, the source of our understanding of natural forces.

The scientific method requires a transcendence of the separation between theory and practice, of the classical understanding of the theorist as isolated from practice. One cannot know the world from an armchair, even from a chair in the academy. Observation and speculation are insufficient for the establishment of science. Science requires a practical as well as a cognitive interaction with the world; without such working upon the world, trying out hypotheses, testing, application, and so on, the theorist is in danger of concocting myths or illusions which are unverifiable or impracticable.

The overcoming of human nature or the creation of new men was, for Marx and Nietzsche, not only the means to achieve a more livable society but also the means to understand the hitherto unconscious forces in man, to master or control them, and to utilize them consciously for the elevation of the species. Only by the application of science to man himself, by the overcoming of the all-too-human, and by the creation of new men, will mankind obtain knowledge of the worthy ends of human endeavor.

IV. The Mediations between Theory and Practice

The processes that mediate theory and practice are organization and education. That is, the means or tactics to apply theory in practice pertain to organization, and the means to elevate practice to the standards set by theory pertain to education. In this respect, in the means to unite theory with practice, Marx and Nietzsche differed enormously. Marx and Nietzsche had different hypotheses about who would constitute a new ruling class. The means to test these differing hypotheses and the methods to prepare for these experiments varied corresponding to the expected results of the experimentation.

Nietzsche's aim was for a new nobility to rule the world, "to oppose all mob-rule and all despotism and to write anew upon new law-tables the word: 'Noble.' "[63] But Nietzsche did not attempt to organize an aristocratic class in the pursuit of this aim because an aristocratic class, a group of men preeminent in knowledge, grace, and courage, did not exist. "I write for a species of man that does not yet exist: for the 'masters of the earth'. "[64] Lacking a potential ruling class to organize, Nietzsche devoted his time and energy to educating in the hope that some men in future generations would be able to use his writings as a means to master the world.

Nietzsche's teaching is that nothing but the human will, not divine providence or reason in nature or in the historical process, can prevent degeneration or destruction of the species. Progress, including progress in knowledge, depends on courage and strength of will. The future aristocratic class must practice Nietzsche's teaching that courage is needed to break old laws and habits, to experiment in new modes of living, to create new values with the awareness that they are human artifacts, to come to the knowledge that is requisite for ruling well. Nietzsche writes:

The secret of realising the largest productivity and the greatest enjoyment of existence is *to live in danger*! Build your cities on the slope of Vesuvius! Send your ships into unexplored seas! Live in war with your equals and with yourselves! Be robbers and spoilers, ye knowing ones, as long as ye cannot be rulers and possessors! The time will soon pass when you can be satisfied to live like timorous deer concealed in the forests. Knowledge will finally stretch out her hand for that which belongs to her:—she means to *rule* and *possess*, and you with her![65]

Nietzsche demands that thinkers recognize their thoughts as the sublimated expression of the will to power. He advocates that scholars see themselves as creators, scientists as soldiers, philosophers as commanders, men of reason as men of will. "The real philosophers, however, are commanders and lawgivers; they say: 'Thus it shall be!' . . . Their 'knowing' is creating, their creating is a law-giving, their will to truth is —Will to Power."[66]

Nietzsche then believed it was necessary to educate a group of men before they would have the power (the determination, character, and knowledge) to constitute a ruling class. Marx, however, saw in the industrial working class a potential ruling class and thus devoted his energies to organizing them to seize power. Although his organizational activities did not exclude activities, like writing pamphlets and addressing speeches, aimed at educating workers, the most significant aspect of Marx's attempt to wed theory to practice resides in his organization of workers for a revolutionary seizure of power.

Marx perceived in the proletariat a class of men whose conditions of life prompted a determination "to break the old law tables," to make revolutionary experiments on existing society through class warfare. Marx saw in the revolutionary practice of the workers the means to verify his theory by overthrowing the bourgeois state, consolidating a workers' state on a worldwide basis, eliminating class antagonisms, and eventually establishing a noncoercive universal brotherhood of man. The proletariat has the determination to wage class warfare for mastery and, in doing so, will create the new, communist man.

Marx believed that the industrial working class was endowed with what Nietzsche considered a master morality.

The social principles of Christianity preach cowardice, self-contempt, abasement, submission, humility, in a word all the qualities of the *canaille*; and the proletariat, not wishing to be treated as *canaille*, needs its courage, its self-esteem, its pride, and its sense of independence more than its bread.

The social principles of Christianity are cringing, but the proletariat is revolutionary.[67]

Thus Marx believed that the working class rejects "the miserable ease"—the creature comforts, material security, and the consolations of a peaceful hereafter—a desire for which precludes bold new experiments on life and society.

But how are the workers to obtain the knowledge requisite to rule a workers' state or even their own factories once they have seized power? The workers have been denied a satisfactory education in the school system which prepares or "conditions" them for a subordinate role in society. The only school available to the workers, according to Marx, is the school of revolution. In revolutionary activity the workers can test the ideas they have imbibed, accepting and rejecting others when these prove to be appropriate or inappropriate for their purposes; revolutionary practice produces "self-activity," independence from external conditioning. From their own revolutionary experience the workers will become aware of the class character of the state, the dependence of the social structure upon the relations of production, and other aspects of Marxian social science. Moreover, the workers in a revolutionary struggle with the bourgeoisie will develop a sense of solidarity, the communist consciousness essential for constructing a new society. Party and union work will engender in the working class the administrative and organizational know-how required to consolidate their power in a postrevolutionary situation. Marx asserts:

Both for the production on a mass scale of this communist consciousness, and for the success of the cause itself, the alteration of men is necessary, an alteration which can only take place in a practical movement, a *revolution*; this revolution is necessary, therefore, not only because the *ruling* class cannot be overthrown in any other way, but also because the class *overthrowing* it can only in a revolution succeed in ridding itself of all the muck of ages and become fitted to found society anew.[68]

Revolutionary activity is conceived by Marx as a process of self-change, self-development, or self-education.[69] Without the revolutionary practice of "self-changing," the division of society into the educators and the educated will remain.[70] The prerequisite for the necessary alteration of men on a mass scale and for the creation of a classless society is revolutionary self-development and self-education. Marx recognized that the proletariat is not presently equipped to constitute a ruling class, but through sustained revolutionary self-education, they can "become fitted to found society anew." For this reason Marx devoted his energies more to the organization of the workers than to their education. By advocating the union of workers for a revolution and by assisting in its organization, Marx left the education of the workers to their experience in the revolutionary process.

Nietzsche thought the belief in the regenerative effects of a cataclysmic revolution to be a dangerous illusion. "If we wish a change to be as deep and radical as possible, we must apply the remedy in minute doses, but unremittingly for long periods."[71] Marx and Nietzsche then differed in the manner in which they wished to change the world. It must be conceded that the enormous transformation in men that Marx expected is highly unlikely in a sudden, violent seizure of power. But Marx in 1850 envisaged the necessity of perhaps fifty years of civil war "in order to change the circumstances, in order to make yourselves (the workers) fit for power. . . ."[72] Fifty years of sustained determination to fight a civil war might create the alteration of men on a mass scale, the prerequisite of a worker's state, but as yet we have not had the experience to verify Marx's vision.[73]

A further reason why Marx and Nietzsche differed in the means to unite theory and practice is that the latter thought and the former did not think that a reinterpretation of the world was in itself a change in the world. For Nietzsche, the greatest events are great thoughts or fundamental reinterpretations of reality; these generally arise far from the bustle and noise of political parties, public platforms, and the state: "thoughts that come on dove's feet guide the world."[74] But, for Marx, ideas become a practical force only when they have "seized the masses,"[75] an additional reason why Marx thought the organization of men into a fighting force was essential to unite theory and practice.

Theory may be united to practice in various ways. Marx stressed the organization of the workers as a means to implement his theory; he devoted less of his time to their education which, he thought, would be best obtained in the organization and practice of revolution. Nietzsche's teaching is less immediately revolutionary; his writings served to educate those men capable of mastering his thought. Organizing these men into a universal ruling class was left by Nietzsche for future generations.

V. Some Implications of Praxis

Thinking, for Marx and Nietzsche, is a form of action, of praxis. We do not describe an act as true or false but perhaps good or evil. But if we eschew this ethical vocabulary as Marx and Nietzsche did, then we evaluate actions in terms of their results or probable results. Since theory is a form of action, then theory is to be judged not as true or false or right or wrong but as useful or disadvantageous to a particular person or class, as effective or ineffective, as instrumental in bringing about the desired aims or otherwise. The attribution of truth-value to theory, when considered a tool or weapon of practice, is inappropriate; the value of an instrument or weapon pertains to its efficacy or the power it generates.

The doctrine of the unity of theory and practice entails that theory is not a mere opinion to be discussed but is a hypothesis to be tried out, an evaluation to be tested. The greater latitude that many regimes accord to freedom of opinion than to freedom of action is based on the supposition that thought is separate from action, that opinions are not an advocacy to act. However, if the separation between thought and action is a mere subterfuge, if thinking is considered to be a mode of acting, then the realm of free opinion as distinct from the realm of permissible action disappears.

Although Marx and Nietzsche did not consider theories different from their own to be criminal or sinful, they did not consider them to be simply the result of intellectual weakness or error. Since, for Marx and Nietzsche, thinking is an expression of willing, theory pertains more to the character, or the class position which engenders character, than to the reason or intellect. Theory is reactionary or progressive, sick or healthy, cowardly or courageous, ignoble or noble, bourgeois or proletarian, never simply true or false. Opponents' ideas are frequently denounced by Marx or Nietzsche in terms of the poor character of the thinker; they frequently played the man and not the ball, a characteristic of fighters.

The basis of the aggressive character of theory as a mode of praxis may be seen as follows. If thinking is an expression of volition, then theory is an overcoming of the data of the senses and not simply their comprehension. Nietzsche expresses this when stating that

the ascertaining of "truth" and "untruth," the ascertaining of facts in general, is fundamentally different from creative positing, from forming, shaping, overcoming, willing, such as it is of the essence of philosophy . . .

On a yet higher level is to *posit a goal* and mold facts according to it; that is, active interpretation and not merely conceptual translation.[76]

Facts are not just to be ascertained and understood as with a scholar, or to be ignored as with a dreamer, but they are to be chiseled into shape in accordance with the design of the man of action. Sense data are only the raw material for a creative shaping of them by the human will. The shaping of facts bespeaks of lack of trust in the meaning and value of the observable world and a desire to control and command a world one has not created; it is the recreation of an alien and unintelligible world of experience.

The overcoming of facts by the soldiers and sculptors of knowledge entails that conflicting viewpoints cannot be resolved by rational persuasion because there is no objective reference or common basis in fact by which one thinker can appeal to another of a different perspective. Conflicting interpretations of the world can only be resolved through struggle. Thinking as an expression of willing is an overturning of the Aristotelian notion of man as a political and rational animal; it is a reevaluation of the worth of fighting and a denial of the value of pacific conflict resolution, of rational persuasion. It is simultaneously a repudiation of conceptual faculty common to all mankind and hence a repudiation of nomianism and an affirmation of the ennoblement of man through the conflict of opposing perspectives. The theorists of praxis value a good fight. "You say it is the good cause that hallows every war? I tell you: it is the good war that hallows every cause."[77]

Prudence is not a characteristic attribute of the union of theory and practice. The cognizance of obstacles impeding the implementation of theory in practice, and the taking into account of these obstacles when acting, compromises theory. Compromises imply a disunity of theory and practice. A prudent regard for the consequences of action is seen as cowardice, as the unwillingness to experiment, to try out one's theories. The unity of theory and practice possesses what Nietzsche calls "the magic of the extreme."

The confirmation of Marx's and Nietzsche's theories consists in the testing and application of their hypotheses about the new men to be created through praxis. However, if theory is an expression of willing, it is more difficult to conceive how a theory can be falsified. Failure to implement a theory may be seen to result from a deficiency of will rather than from an inadequacy of theory. Thus practice may be the means to verify theory but may not be the means to falisfy it. Lacking the usual verification principle of the sciences, Marx and Nietzsche may be inviting us to unite theory and practice in a permanent revolution.

PART III
Dilemmas and New Directions

VII

Hannah Arendt: The Ambiguities
of Theory and Practice

Richard J. Bernstein

I

The nature and the role of political theory has been and continues to be one
of the deepest and most troubling intellectual perplexities of our time. We
can almost date this perplexity from the time of Marx's ambiguous and controversial thesis, "The philosophers have interpreted the world only, the point
is to change it." We know that Marx was not a mindless activist, nor was this
a call for uninformed action. He was—to the end of his life—ruthless in his
criticism of those who were ready to man the barricades without a proper comprehension or theoretical understanding of the dynamics of what was taking
place and what its historical roots were. However difficult it may be to articulate what Marx meant by the unity of theory and practice, the synthesis he
proposed has proved to be extremely attractive and dangerous. Its attractive-
ness is evidenced by its appeal to intellectuals since Marx's time and by the
way in which the best thinkers in the Marxist tradition have returned again
and again to explain and defend the unity of theory and practice. And its
danger is manifested in the way in which some versions of Marxism have degenerated into dogmatic creeds which supposedly provide infallible guides to

Note. This paper is based on a lecture given at York University on 24 November 1972. The
conference, "The Work of Hannah Arendt," was sponsored by the Toronto Society for
the Study of Social and Political Thought.

action. Whatever stand we take concerning the viability of the unity of theory and practice—and what precisely this means—we must admit that the unstable synthesis that Marx sought to achieve has broken down for us. The fragmentation and confusion that remain have shaped our own immediate intellectual heritage.

There are those who have claimed that political theory is dead or that it is nothing but the study of the past and outdated political theories which have now been replaced by a more modest, empirical, tough-minded political and social science. One of the dogmas of mainstream political science is that we must carefully distinguish empirical theory from normative theory. Although there is widespread skepticism about the legitimacy and rationality of normative theory, there is a confidence that empirical theory has full epistemological validity. The task of political science, like other social or natural sciences, is to uncover and discover significant regularities, and the role of theory is to formulate those hypotheses, models, and systematic interconnections that can increase our explanation of these regularities. Ideally such a theory will increase our ability to make empirical predictions based on our understanding of these regularities. According to the position that I am characterizing there is a basic acceptance of the positivist conception of the symmetry of explanation and prediction. Any concept of explanation or understanding, like verstehen, that is not tied directly to prediction is rejected as "unscientific." It is the direct connection between explanation and prediction that provides the basis for the possible control and manipulation of events. Most defenders of mainstream political science will readily acknowledge the modesty of what has been achieved to date, but they are staunch defenders of the claim that in principle there are no a priori limits to what can be eventually achieved by the development of empirical political theory. Whatever practical difficulties may confront us, there are no good reasons why we might not expect the progress, cumulative growth and development, and increased quantitative sophistication that are characteristic of other more mature sciences. According to this essentially positivist conception of political science, the true inheritor of the great tradition of political theory is empirical theory. For supposedly we can now do in a careful, empirical manner what has heretofore been done in a rather confused, vague, and speculative fashion.

From the perspective of this mainstream bias, we must also make a sharp distinction between theory and practice, thought and action. The function of the empirical political scientist is to describe and understand significant regularities and to test his hypotheses and models which formulate the ways in which these regularities are interconnected. Qua scientist, the political scientist is not (and ought not be) an activitist. If he allows his own political interests substantially to influence his research, he is violating the canons of objective research. Or, as a policy scientist, he can—on the basis of his empirical understanding of regularities of behavior—formulate hypothetical imperatives about what is likely to occur if certain courses of action are initiated, but he cannot qua political scientist issue categorical imperatives concerning what ought to be done. There is no intrinsic logical connection between the facts that he describes and the "oughts" proposed for what should be done, although he is firmly convinced that practical decisions concerning what ought to be done should be informed by an empirical understanding of what is likely to occur.

In theory—or in principle—when such a defense of the nature and role of empirical theory is put forward, it appears eminently reasonable and convincing. We cannot underestimate the extent to which it is implicitly or explicitly acknowledged by many professional political scientists. Yet in practice many problems and perplexities arise, and it is all too rare to find political science as it is actually practiced conforming to its self-understanding of what it ought to be.

One of the persistent themes in Hannah Arendt's work is a critique of the conception of political theory sketched above. Unlike some others who have attacked this conception of the nature and role of political theory, her criticisms are diverse and subtle. She does not engage in a philosophical sleight of hand that tries to argue that in principle such an understanding of empirical political theory is epistemologically faulty and impossible. On the contrary, she sees clearly that this is what political theory is in the process of becoming. But she shrewdly notes that such a development of empirical political theory presupposes and encourages the development of a world in which repetitive regularities come to dominate behavior. Ironically and tragically, this would be a world in which political action—in a sense soon to be characterized—comes to play an increasingly insignificant role.

Speaking of behaviorism in social science, she puts the issue forcefully in *The Human Condition*:

The unfortunate truth about behaviorism and the validity of its "laws" is that the more people there are, the more likely they are to behave and the less likely to tolerate nonbehavior. Statistically, this will be shown in the leveling out of fluctuation. In reality, deeds will have less and less chance to stem the tide of behavior, and events will more and more lose their significance, that is, their capacity to illuminate historical time. Statistical uniformity is by no means a harmless scientific ideal; it is the no longer secret political ideal of a society which, entirely submerged in the routine of everyday living, is at peace with the scientific outlook inherent in its very existence.[1]

She also shows in graphic detail how the mental set of the social scientist who is convinced of his ability to understand and lay out the hypothetical courses of action that confront policy makers can lead and has led to distorted and tragic results. This is clearly one of the main points of her analysis of the Pentagon papers.[2]

But the deepest and the most interesting line of criticism is that insofar as political science and political theory develop in the manner sketched above — to the extent that political science becomes a "behavioral" science — it fails to study and comprehend the distinctive subject matter of political theory: political action. For political action, properly understood, is of such a character that it does not lend itself to the techniques and methods of the behavioral sciences.

If the mainstream view of empirical political theory is rejected as well as *its* conception of what constitutes normative theory, what is the alternative? It is already clear that if we are to make progress in answering this question, we must explore what Hannah Arendt takes to be distinctive about action as it pertains to politics.

But first, two preliminary points must be emphasized. In clarifying and adumbrating the meaning of action, and what we can and cannot comprehend or know about action, we are dealing with basic metaphysical and epistemological issues. Metaphysics and epistemology are not terms that frequently occur in Arendt's writings, but I am using them here in a perfectly straightforward sense. If metaphysics is taken as the study of what there is and epistemology as the study of what we can and cannot know, it is essential to realize that at the heart of Hannah Arendt's thought is a metaphysics and epistemology of action. In describing and characterizing what action is, she is not simply stipulating or proposing a new definition. Her intention is to lay bare the essential features of action. What she has to say about action has important consequences for almost every aspect of her thought, including her conception of the nature and limitations of political theory. I stress this aspect of her work, because we shall see how many issues lead us back to what I am calling Hannah Arendt's metaphysics of action.

The second point that I want to emphasize is already implicit in what I've said: it is to note the systematic quality of Hannah Arendt's thought. The term "system" is one which has been much abused in our time and tends to evoke an image of a closed deductive scheme. But this is clearly a caricature. If we think of systematic philosophy in the sense in which what a thinker has to say concerning any one central theme or issue has direct and indirect logical and theoretical implications for other themes and issues, a sense in which we can speak of Aristotle as a systematic thinker, Arendt's work is clearly in this tradition. This is an aspect of her work that has not been frequently noted or understood: indeed she has been criticized for not being systematic. Yet I would argue that not only in her more theoretical works like *The Human Condition* but also in those works where she has attempted to come to grips with the most pressing and baffling events of our time, there is a systematic web of concepts which is constantly being elaborated, refined, and put to the test. I stress this aspect of her work because unless one grasps the main threads of her systematic explorations, one can gain only a superficial understanding of her work.

In attempting to clarify the outlines of her theory of action, one should start at the beginning, and with her notion of a "beginning." Although I do not intend to follow the career of Hannah Arendt's intellectual development, one should remember that her first major work was a study of St. Augustine. Her study was concerned with an examination of the concept of love in St. Augustine, but it is clear that Augustine had a permanent influence on her thought. One theme that pervades her work is that of beginning. Its importance is emphatically stated in *The Human Condition.*

To act, in its most general sense, means to take initiative, to begin (as the Greek word *archein*, "to begin," "to lead," and eventually "to rule," indicates), to set something into motion (which is the original meaning of the Latin *agere*). Because they are *initium*, newcomers and beginners by virtue of birth, men take initiative, are prompted into action. *[Initium] ergo ut esset, creatus est homo, ante quem nullus fuit* ("that there be a beginning, man was created before whom there was nobody"), said Augustine in his political philosophy.[3]

She goes on to affirm that "with the creation of man, the principle of beginning came into the world itself, which of course, is only another way of saying that the principle of freedom was created when man was created but not before."[4] This linkage of action with the principle of beginning and freedom already indicates why the concept of action is so central to her thought. "Men," we are told "*are* free—as distinguished from their possessing the gift of freedom—as long as they act, neither before nor after; for to *be* free and to act are the same."[5] In speaking of a beginning, Arendt does not mean a *mere* beginning, a moment which is singled out in a continuous series of events, because "it is in the nature of beginning that something new is started which cannot be expected from whatever happened before."[6] Not only then is action essentially linked with beginning and freedom, but the systematic web of concepts reaches out to include genuine novelty, the unexpectedness inherent in all beginning. "The new always happens against the overwhelming odds of statistical laws and their probability, which for all practical, everyday purposes amounts to certainty; the new therefore always appears in the guise of a miracle."[7] Here, too, a theme is introduced that has played a major role in Arendt's outlook. For if "to be free and to act are the same" and all action involves genuine novelty or unexpectedness, then there is a radical opposition between the realm of freedom and that of necessity. Action in this distinctive sense is outside of or beyond the realm of necessity. From Arendt's perspective the confusion of the realm of necessity with that of freedom, or the belief that somehow freedom emerges out of—or merges with—necessity has been one of the most serious and disastrous confusions in modern history—especially since the French Revolution. We have here the basis of her quarrel with Hegel and Marx, for it is her claim that both have been guilty of just this confusion. But the issue is by no means solely a theoretical one, it is precisely this confusion—the false belief that necessity is operating in history and out of necessity freedom will emerge—that is central to her interpretation of the failure of both the French and the Russian revolutions.[8] For when revolutionary leaders come to believe that they are being guided by necessity operating in history, they have betrayed the revolutionary spirit.

The consequences of Arendt's metaphysics of action for an understanding of the role and nature of theory also begin to appear. If we accept her characterization of action; any theory that claims to discover or has recourse to the concept of necessity in accounting for action is mistaken. This is just as true for theories, like Hegel's, that claim to exhibit necessity after the fact, as for theories that claim there is a necessary link between the past and the future—a view Arendt ascribes to Marx. But it is not only the Hegelian and Marxist traditions that she criticizes; this is a cardinal point in her criticism of political science or social science conceived as the study, explanation, and prediction of regularities. If action "always happens against the overwhelming odds of statistical laws and their probability," it is a mistake to think that one can perfect a science that has as its aim the prediction of *actions*.

This claim may appear to be paradoxical, especially since we can and do make predictions about what people will do, predictions that can be confirmed by what happens. But this is not what Arendt is denying, and it helps to bring into focus what she considers to be distinctive about action. For it would be silly to deny that we can and do make predictions about human behavior; it is hard to imagine human interactions without this capacity. But the key term here is behavior, which is not to be confused or fused with action—the two concepts are antithetical, for behavior involves a "leveling out of fluctuation," a world in which action has less and less of a chance of stemming the tide toward conformism, behaviorism, and automatism. This is why the triumph of behaviorism in political science — which is a real possibility — would have the threatening consequence of eliminating what is most fragile and vital about politics, viz., action.

II

Several years ago Hannah Arendt, speaking of her own intellectual origins, wrote, "If I can be said to have 'come from' anywhere, it is from the tradition of German philosophy."[9] In what we have said so far about her metaphysics of action we can see the truth of this claim. For the identification of action with freedom, involving genuine novelty which is not determined by the past and which excludes the realm of necessity is a theme that has been central to the existentialist tradition and finds its echo in two of Arendt's teachers, Jaspers and Heidegger. Little we have said thus far cannot be found in the Augustinian themes that are at the core of Kierkegaard's thought. Kierkegaard — or rather his pseudonymous creations — makes almost the same points in *The Philosophical Fragments* and *The Concluding Unscientific Postscript*. Quite independently, we can also find their origins in Nietzsche. But there is one absolutely crucial difference between the way in which Kierkegaard and others affected by the existentialist tradition develop these insights and Arendt's thought, a difference which can further clarify her metaphysics of action. Kierkegaard's dialectic, which is also anti-Hegelian, opposing freedom and becoming with necessity and being, carries him to a point where action becomes identical with inwardness.[10] There is a radical subjective turn in his thought, one which has become the obsession of many existentialist thinkers. It is not only existential themes in German philosophy that influenced Arendt but also the inheritance that classical Greek philosophy bequeathed to nineteenth-century German philosophy. In opposition to the subjective turn which is not only characteristic of Kierkegaard and Nietzsche but has pervaded so much of modern thought since Descartes, action for Hannah Arendt turns out to be essentially a public and *political* category. Action both presupposes and can be actualized only in a human polity. This becomes clear in the close linkage between action and speech. Although action is not identical with speech, "no other human performance requires speech to the same extent as action."[11]

Without the accompaniment of speech, at any rate, action would not only lose its revelatory character, but, and by the same token, it would lose its subject, as it were; not acting men but performing robots would achieve what, humanly speaking, would remain incomprehensible. Speechless action would no longer be action because there would no longer be an actor, and the actor, the doer of deeds, is possible only if he is at the same time the speaker of words.[12]

Strictly speaking, acting in this distinctive sense is not properly predicated of isolated individuals. This is clear from the introduction of the concept of action in *The Human Condition.*

Action, the only activity that goes on directly between men without the intermediary of things or matter, corresponds to the human condition of plurality, to the fact that men, not Man, live on the earth and inhabit the world. While all aspects of the human condition are somehow related to politics, this plurality is specifically *the* condition—not only the *conditio sine qua non*, but the *conditio per quam*—of all political life.[13]

In this respect it is difficult to imagine a more radical divergence with the existentialist tradition, especially the subjectivist bias characteristic of so much work in this tradition. Individuals may initiate action, but action "goes on directly *between* men." Without the "human condition of plurality," there would be other forms of activity including labor and work but not action. It is part of the very ontology of action that it is essentially political.

Given this distinctively political turn in Arendt's analysis of action and speech, other central concepts emerge. For action and speech require a genuine *plurality* of men and not just an aggregate of individuals; and they require a *public space* in which they can be realized, a public space in which men are both *equal* and *distinct*. The essential political nature of *history* is indicated by its being the story of actions, deeds, and speech.

Further, what many political theorists have taken to be the most central political category—power—is illuminated from the perspective of Arendt's metaphysics of action.

Power is actualized only where word and deed have not parted company, where words are not empty and deeds not brutal, where words are not used to veil intentions but to disclose realities, and deeds are not used to violate and destroy but establish relations and create new realities.

Power is what keeps the public realm, the potential space of appearance between acting and speaking men, in existence.[14]

Power exists or is actualized only as long as men act together. And power must be carefully distinguished from force, strength, and violence.[15] Violence can destroy power, but it can never be a substitute for power. Once again, it is Aristotle whom Arendt credits with the theoretical insight into the nature of political power.

It is this insistence on the living deed and the spoken word as the greatest achievements of which human beings are capable that was conceptualized in Aristotle's notion of *energeia* ("actuality"), with which he designated all activities that do not pursue an end (are *ateleis*) and leave no work behind (no *par' auta erga*), but exhaust their full meaning in the performance itself.[16]

If the characteristics we have listed are those that single out action, we can see how frail and ephemeral it is and how all sorts of forces and trends threaten its existence. We can see too why the evocation of the Greek polis plays such an important role in Arendt's thought. Although fully aware of the comparative smallness of the Greek polis, the brief period of its flourishing, and the fact that except for those who were citizens of the polis, its principles did not apply, Arendt believes the polis still stands as one of the most remarkable historical moments in which deeds and speech flourished. "The *polis*," she tells us, "properly speaking, is not the city-state in its physical location; it is the organization of the people as it arises out of acting and speaking together for this purpose, no matter where they happen to be." It is the public space in which a genuine plurality of men as equal and distinct personalities appear to each other. It is a public realm in which the function of speech is not to manipulate or to dominate but to persuade. No man can live in this public space all the time and a great deal of human life falls outside the polis. It includes neither the private affairs of men nor the concerns of pure thought or theoria. One of the major factors involved in Arendt's diagnosis of the ills and crises of our times has been the failure to appreciate—for all its possible glory—how fragile and limited the realm of politics really is and the dangers that result when this realm of freedom and political action is confused with the pressing needs and demands of social life.

We have seen enough to justify the claim I made about the systematic character of Arendt's thought: how a core of interrelated concepts provides the basis for a fully articulated metaphysics of action. Further, I can also indicate what I meant when I said that this systematic core is developed, refined, and put to the test throughout her work. For example, we already have the key for understanding her approach to the study of revolution. The basis of her praise for the founders of the American Revolution is the awareness they displayed of the conditions necessary for the flourishing of political action. And the same criteria are operative in her severe judgment of the fate of both the French and Russian revolutions, because they systematically crushed and undermined the public space required for political action and freedom. Even her attitudes toward recent protest movements are shaped by these underlying themes. She has a high opinion of the early civil rights movement precisely because it exhibited the virtues of genuine political action, but she tends to despair about recent radical movements because despite their talk of liberation and freedom they undermine the public space of political freedom. But I want to return more explicitly to the primary concern of the paper, Arendt's understanding of theory and practice and their interrelationship.

I have already mentioned Arendt's opposition to Hegel concerning the nature and role of necessity in history and her attack on the notion that the aim of theory is to reveal the necessity operating in history. But her relation to Hegel is more subtle than this opposition indicates. For in other respects she is much closer to Hegel, especially in the way in which Hegel can be taken to represent the culmination of the classical tradition of theoria where the highest aim of thought or theory is to interpret, to understand, to comprehend what is. Further, she shares with Hegel the conviction that the realm of becoming, process, change, and history is not a realm which eludes the categories of comprehension but is rather the ultimate concern of political theory, for without a comprehension of what is and what has been, thought is in danger of becoming abstract and consequently false. But even these similarities with Hegel's self-understanding of the nature and role of theoria help bring out the sharp differences between Arendt and Hegel. For if it really is true that action introduces genuine novelty into the world and is not simply a vehicle for actualizing what already is implicit or an sich, the theorist has the obligation of attempting to forge and explicate new categories that are adequate for this understanding. To perform this task intelligently requires, of course, an understanding and appreciation of what is past, of what has been, for otherwise it is not possible to locate, conceptualize, and understand what is new and distinct. This is an extremely difficult task that requires the virtues of imagination, courage, and a willingness to engage in independent thinking. For there is something deep in all of us that constantly attempts to categorize and understand the unfamiliar and the unexpected in terms of what is psychologically and conceptually familiar. We can see how consistent Arendt's major concerns are with this self-understanding of the role of theory and the theorist. Consider two phenomena that are the subject of major studies — revolution and the origins of totalitarianism. In both instances she is concerned with showing how these phenomena have been genuinely novel and cannot be appreciated or comprehended by using categories evolved before their appearance in history. And the burden of her argument is to single out just those distinctive characteristics which reveal the uniqueness of these phenomena. I think too that much of the furor stirred up over her Eichman book can be accounted for by this characteristic of her role as theorist. In her graphic report of the trial she shows us the inadequacy of traditional and conventional categories for adequately describing, comprehending, and judging Eichman's crime. She was by no means exonerating Eichman or his crime but challenging the conventional framework for judging him, and in the process she revealed a basis for judgment which was far more severe than the conventional "monster" theory.[17]

The mention of Arendt's study of totalitarianism and her report on the Eichman trial can help correct what is likely to be a misinterpretation of her metaphysics of action. For the emphasis on the novelty, freedom, and lack of necessity involved in action may be misread as an essentially optimistic doctrine. And it *is* optimistic—or better, realistic—in contrast to doctrines that claim nothing new happens under the sun or the future is so related to the past and the present that everything that will occur is determined by or is implicit in what has already occurred. But as Augustine appreciated and emphasized so long ago, the capacity and actualization of the principle of beginning, freedom, novelty, is the source of both human glory and evil. It is the same capacity in man, the capacity to act and initiate, that gave rise to not only the Greek polis but also the nightmare of twentieth-century totalitarianism. We are never in a position—before the fact—to know whether the virtues of political action or its terrible vices will be manifested. This systematic ambiguity lies at the very core of Hannah Arendt's metaphysics of action; it is rooted, so to speak, in the ontology of action, and it signifies the essential epistemological limits of political theory. Let me be perfectly clear here. In speaking of the systematic ambiguity of action, I am singling out what is an attribute—one is inclined to say, the most essential attribute—of action itself. There is no way of eradicating or diminishing the ambiguity of action without eliminating action itself. This ambiguity is not due to some espitemological deficiency on our part which could somehow be overcome if our knowledge were perfected. On the contrary, it is the systematic ambiguity of action itself which sets the limits on what we can legitimately claim to know. This systematic ambiguity is dramatically illustrated in the concluding paragraphs of Arendt's massive study of totalitarianism.

There remains the fact that the crisis of our time and its central experience have brought forth an entirely new form of government which as a potentiality and ever-present danger is only to likely to stay with us from now on, just as other forms of government which came about at different historical moments and rested on different fundamental experiences have stayed with mankind regardless of temporary defeats—monarchies, and republics, tyrannies, dictatorships and despotism.

But there remains also the truth that every end in history necessarily contains a new beginning; this beginning is the promise, the only "message" which the end can ever produce. Beginning, before it becomes a historical event, is the supreme capacity of man; politically, it is identical with man's freedom. *Initium ut esset homo creatus est* — "that a beginning be made man was created" said Augustine. This beginning is guaranteed by each new birth; it is indeed every man.[18]

III

If I am correct in what I have said thus far about both the practice of political theory and the self-understanding of the nature and limits of theory in Hannah Arendt's work, other pressing questions arise. What role, if any, can theory play in illuminating, guiding, or directing future action? What is the relation of theory to the past? It might appear that we have already answered the first question. For if we expect or hope to have from theory some basis for predicting the future, our hope is a false one because it is of the very nature of political action to exclude this possibility. Nor can we hope to discover those patterns, laws, or necessary forces operating in history that will provide a guide for future action; because they do not exist. But it would be rash to conclude that political theory has no relevance for future action. If we accept Arendt's metaphysics of action, we can see how her theoretical explorations exhibit the oldest and most classic virtue of theoria — the conviction that with genuine comprehension men can achieve the freedom and self-determination that comes with wisdom, with the knowledge of their own ignorance. For with this knowledge we can escape superstition, false beliefs, and false expectations. I do not think this is solely the solace of the philosopher or theorist, for it has enormous practical consequences. Our times are characterized by the many who have claimed that there are inexorable laws of history, that the future is already implicit in what has occurred, that necessity is operating in history, and that it is within our power to predict the course of political action. But whenever she detects these "false idols," Arendt sets out to smash them, and the "message" that emerges from her work is that every end in history is also a beginning and with a beginning there is also a promise and a hope. There is nothing in the past, present, or what we can know of the future that can exclude or preclude the possibility of concretely realizing those virtues of political action which have illuminated brief moments in history. It is for this reason that, despite the systematic ambiguity at the core of Arendt's metaphysics of action and her own major preoccupation with the darkness of our times, her work has provided so much inspiration for those who have have hoped and worked for the creation of a new public space in which speech and deeds are realized. By her own account, all that the theorist can do for those who are concerned with the future is to clarify what is *possible*. If one does this honestly, the theorist has the obligation to clarify and describe the dark possibilities as well as the ones that promise light and hope. But to know what is possible and to guard oneself against all those who pronounce necessities or impossibilities is to be prepared to face future action in a more intelligent and informed manner.

Implicit in what I have said about the relation of theory to the future is the answer to the query about the relation of theory to the past. But it is important to spell this out. Arendt tells us, "If it is true that all thought begins with re-membrance, it is also true that no remembrance remains secure unless it is con-densed and distilled into a framework of conceptual notions within which it can further exercise itself."[19] We have seen already that one essential task of the theorist cannot be performed without an act of remembrance and an under-standing of the past. For unless we understand what has been, there is no stan-dard or measure for grasping what is new and different in history. A knowledge of the past and of previous political theory is not an idle curiosity or a nostalgia for what has been and is long gone but the only basis for coming to grips with what is present. But remembrance plays a more profound role, and here we can detect a certain Heideggerian strain in Arendt's work. We are always threatened with the danger of forgetfulness. The past does not stand as an open book to be read by any who would read it. History as the story of men's actions is only available to us as long as men talk about them, try to understand them, re-cover them. "Experiences and even the stories which grow out of what men do and endure, of happenings and events, sink back into the futility inherent in the living word and the living deed unless they are talked about over and over again. What saves the affairs of mortal men from their inherent futility is nothing but this incessant talk about them, which in its turn remains futile unless certain concepts, certain guideposts for future remembrance, and even for sheer reference, arise out of it."[20] But why should it be so important to recover and talk about the past? The interest here is more than a purely theo-retical concern with what is over and done with. On the contrary, it is for the present and the future that it is so important to understand what has been. For in this understanding, whether it be of the Greek polis or the American Revolution, we gain a clarity about what can be, not because history will re-peat itself in any automatic or predetermined fashion, but because of the real possibility of creating in new and different ways those permanent possibilities achieved by human initiative. And here we have still another perspective not only for comprehending Arendt's self-understanding of the role that the theorist can play but for understanding much of her own work. For we can conceive of it as an act of recovery, an attempt to clear away the dross and obscurity that overlay our understanding of political action. Her endeavor is a descriptive one—although not in the emasculated sense of description so fashionable with mainstream political scientists—for she is attempting to describe and uncover for us what can and has been achieved through political action. But it is a description which has powerful normative consequences. For in the act of recovery which describes for us the human freedom, dignity, friendship, joy, and immortality that can be realized through political action, as well as its limits and frailty, we are not simply describing what is past. We are describing and remembering a human possibility which is as relevant to our lives as it was to those who actualized these virtues. I mentioned Heidegger before in noting the sense in which so much of Hannah Arendt's work can be conceived of as an act of recovery and a battle to overcome human forgetfulness, but one might also mention in this context Aristotle, whom Arendt so admires. For Aristotle profoundly understood the lure and power that a description of what a truly and fully human life can exert in shaping men's character and actions. This act of recovery, this reminder of what politics can be, this battle against all those subtle forces conspiring to forgetfulness and thereby resulting in a loss of our own humanity is Hannah Arendt's most enduring contribution to political theory.

IV

Thus far I have attempted to articulate—as sympathetically as I can—the self-understanding of political theory that emerges from Hannah Arendt's work and how it is related to her metaphysics of action and to her actual practice as a theorist. I have contrasted her view both with her understanding of the Hegelian-Marxist tradition, in which the central emphasis is on necessity and the supposed emergence of a realm of freedom from this necessity, and with the conception of empirical theory characteristic of mainstream political science. Like Hegel—and indeed the classic conception of the telos of theoria— her essential aim was one of comprehension and Begreifen of what is, but because of what we learn from her metaphysics of action, this requires the attempt to develop categories and concepts that can illuminate what is genuinely new. I have indicated how some of her major concerns, like the study of totalitarianism and revolution, exhibit this dimension of theory. I have suggested that whereas theory can never hope to predict the future course of *action*

—and that we become fools of history when we attempt to do so — nevertheless theory is not irrelevant for future action. For it serves the vital function of destroying myths about what is deemed necessary or impossible and illuminates for us what are real possibilities for action. And I have tried to indicate the sense in which this conception of political theory can be understood as being both descriptive and prescriptive or normative (although not in the sense in which these terms are frequently taken by mainstream political science). For in clarifying the web of concepts involved in understanding what action is, how it is essentially a political category involving freedom, novelty, initiative, and a public space in which men as equal and distinct can reveal themselves in speech and deed, she helps us overcome the forgetfulness so characteristic of the crisis of our times and performs an act of recovery which serves as a reminder of what men together have achieved and may *still* achieve. In all this Arendt herself displays imagination, courage, and independent thinking, Selbstdenken, which has brought light to these dark times.

But I would like to conclude with a brief indication of what I take to be some important weaknesses in this self-understanding of the role of political theory — or rather lacunae which I find require a further systematic development of her own central categories. The issue here is one of emphasis, but I think that in political theory a matter of emphasis can make for fundamental differences. In brief, I am more concerned here with what Arendt does not say and treat rather than with what she does say, for I find myself in agreement with many of her claims. The major point I want to make can be expressed in several different ways. I sometimes think Arendt's skepticism about the role that the theorist can play in guiding future actions leads her to an extreme and mistaken position, that concerning the issue of what is to be done, the theorist must always be silent. We can understand the dialectical reasons for taking this position, for we have witnessed in the twentieth century the terrible consequences of those who explicitly or implicitly believed that they had some infallible guide to direct action. But suppose we take the position of the actors in human history who are convinced of the various forces and trends that are dehumanizing man, that are undermining human action and freedom, that are transforming man into a creature of political behavior rather than action. However much one wants to emphasize the spontaneity, unexpectedness, and "miraculous" quality of action, Arendt herself knows all too well that the participants, the actors, require an understanding of the world in which they live — what are the evils that threaten the realm of freedom, what concrete steps are likely to create here and now a public space in which deeds and speech can flourish? This does not mean that one is looking for a theoretical understanding that can provide an infallible guide for action but rather for a concrete theoretical understanding of our immediate historical circumstances that can inform our actions. For without this, action can become dumb. In one sense, it strikes me that Arendt knows all this and there is a way of reading her work that further substantiates the importance of informed beliefs for political actors. But I do not find in her work an adequate attempt to confront the issues of the demands this can place upon political theory. For theory, critical theory, or critique can set itself the task of describing, comprehending, and criticizing existing social and political reality with the explicit aim of encouraging and informing those extant tendencies for concretely realizing freedom and action. The "either/or" that seems to hover in the background of so much of Arendt's thought concerning theory and practice—*either* silence *or* fallacious prediction and dogmatic blueprints for the future—is oversimplified and ultimately spurious.

I can make my point by noting a possibility that Arendt has failed to take seriously, one which I believe emerges from the work of Hegel and Marx. I am not interested here in entering the tedious scholastic game of debating whether Arendt has interpreted Hegel and Marx correctly (although I do believe she has distorted their views).[21] I mention Hegel and Marx as a point of reference, and whether views sketched here are considered authentic or a form of revisionism is irrelevant for my purposes. But I do think that one can find in Marx, especially in his dialectical criticism of Hegel, an alternative—or more accurately a supplement—to what we learn from Arendt. When Marx declares "that we do not anticipate the world dogmatically, but rather wish to find the new world through criticism of the old"; that "even though the construction of the future and its completion for all times is not our task, what we have to accomplish at this time is all the more clear: *relentless criticism of all existing conditions*, relentless in the sense that the criticism is not afraid of its findings and just as little afraid of the conflict with the powers that be"; and that "the reform of consciousness exists *merely* in the fact that one makes the world aware of its consciousness, that one awakens the world out of its dream, that one *explains* to the world its own acts,"[22] we can see the emergence of a conception of theory as critique that has a very different emphasis than we find in Arendt. Such a critique is not directed to anticipate the world dogmatically or to construct a blueprint for future action, but rather to provide for that self-understanding of our present historical situation which is a necessary condition for achieving the political freedom Arendt herself has so subtly illuminated for us.

And as Marx so acutely emphasized in his criticism of Hegel and the Left Hegelians, self-understanding itself can be impotent and false if it is not directly linked to concrete action—to praxis. I do not believe this is ever a task that can be finally completed, nor do I think the unity of theory and practice is finally achieved; rather, it serves as a regulative ideal where one strives for a self-understanding or true consciousness which can speak to men's deepest needs and desires and thereby inform their actions.[23]

I can phrase my quarrel with Arendt in a slightly different manner. Much of her theoretical work is concerned with delineating and explaining the differences between the social and the political, the private and the public, the contrast between those forms of the vita activa that are manifested in labor and work, and action proper. And here, too, Arendt's concern with careful conceptual distinctions has significant practical consequences. Her interpretation of modern history is concerned with the terrible consequences that have resulted from the fusing of these different realms and from the false expectations and hopes that arise when it is believed that satisfaction of men's private needs and social necessities is sufficient to achieve freedom. Even when we take Arendt's warnings with full seriousness, the fact remains that our problematic is one in which the social and the political are inextricably connected. And whatever fault she finds with Marx, I think she would have admitted that no one has demonstrated more brilliantly than Marx that any attempt to solve the "political" question, any attempt to achieve genuine political freedom that ignores the social question or turns its face away from the question of social poverty and misery, is doomed to failure. We can agree with Arendt that social liberation does not automatically lead to political freedom and that the belief that it does can be disastrous in both theory and practice. But we cannot avoid the consequence that political freedom—which is not to be delusory or infected with hypocrisy—can no longer be achieved for us without an attempt to solve the serious social issues that confront us, or, to use the Marxist turn of phrase, to create those material conditions which although *not* the sufficient condition are at least the *necessary* condition for real political freedom. But if this is so—if it is true that for us living now, there cannot be genuine political freedom without a commitment to social liberation—the theorist who still cherishes the ideal of political freedom and is concerned with its realization is under the obligation to understand and to foster those social conditions that must be realized if freedom is to flourish.

I realize that in these concluding remarks I have provided only hints and suggestions for a critique of Arendt's understanding of theory and practice.

They are offered in the spirit not of pitting one view against another, but rather of suggesting how following out the dialectic of her own thought can carry us beyond what she has already accomplished. If I understand Hannah Arendt correctly, it is only by "incessant talk" about such possibilities and alternatives that we will keep the great tradition of political theory alive, a tradition intimately tied up with our own humanity and already more vital and secure because of Hannah Arendt's own contributions.

VIII

Rebels, Beginners, and Buffoons: Politics as Action

Raymond L. Nichols

> Our purpose is to find out whether innocence, the moment it becomes involved in action, can avoid committing murder.
>
> —Camus, *The Rebel*[1]

In his effort to grapple with the continuing slaughter of our century, Camus is archetypal. His superb reflections on rebellion are essential to our topic— and to our times. For both theory and practice, we must see where we are in order to see what it means to go elsewhere. And in the midst of an activistic era, the investigation of revolt assumes paramount importance. Many men, protesting outraged innocence, feel driven to say "no"; many agonize over the possible outcomes of acting.

But innocence and action both have many faces; and murder is not the only question their conjunctions pose. Innocence can range from inoffensiveness to naiveté—in the academy as well as in the streets. And action spans an even greater range. Its cognates (act, active, agitate, actuate, actualize, actual: see the *O.E.D.*) give some indication. Action has some close affinities with creation— innovating, originating, producing, initiating and commencing, beginning and starting; it involves doings of a certain kind, bringing things into being, bringing them forth, setting them in motion. But it is not solely concerned with things; it also can deal with meanings, symbols, relationships. And not all motion is action in a creative sense. (The action of a rifle bolt is simply its operation, its mode of movment.) Nor is all "human action." It may simply connote risky movement (in gambling, a piece of the action; in military parlance, action stations, being in action). It may be sheer agitation. Or it may be *mere* performance (an act—mere entertainment; mere dissimulation; or mere enactment of something already set forth, carrying out without initiative or innovation). Activity has diverse forms, both negative and positive; and if there are modes of creation, there are modes of destruction as well. So with political activism. Concentration on the question of murder actually tends to obscure the nature of rebellion— and of action. Ironically, Camus's very moralism, his opposition to the slaughter which too often passes for politics in our day, shows that we have largely lost a sense of what politics *can* be—of what it means to go somewhere politically and of what activities can take us there. And if this is true even of Camus, it is far more true of the recent outpouring of studies (especially in America) on the problem of violence, and the still-growing literature on revolution.

I do not mean that violence is not an agonizing issue—but it is not the only one—and even it is not best seen in isolated prominence. And by contrasting moralism and politics, I intend neither to use the term moralism pejoratively nor to draw a crude fact/value dichotomy. I mean that it is high time for us to focus on *politics*. What that involves is no simple thing: the whole of this essay is involved with it. For I propose to investigate *varieties* of activism. Our task is literally that of finding "where the action (really) is"—the nature of the modes through which political worlds are made. And rebellion points the way; for even revolution (surely a term to conjure with) produces more excitement than clarity, more sheer frenzy and more motion than it does action. Briefly, my thesis is that rebellion presents the apparently paradoxical picture of a tradition; that the tradition of rebellion has been undermined by an extreme form of innocence, a modern notion of new beginnings; and that this modern notion springs from the degeneration of the terms action and revolution in both activistic and academic discourse. Analysis of this tortuous collapse, through such diverse figures as Camus and Marx, Hannah Arendt, yippies and situationists, and contemporary social scientists, is necessary for us to recover a full sense of politics—and of its contemporary sources. For, paradoxically, there well may be germs of renewal in present-day excursion and alarums, which neither activists nor their critics can easily detect, precisely because of those linguistic filters I have just named. Terms are significant in what they signify—in what they symbolize, thus order and bring together or apart. The decay of politics as action is far more than purely semantic. To lose a political language is to impoverish one's concrete practices as well as one's theories.[2]

I. Opposition: Revulsion and Rebellion

I have suggested that Camus is an essential starting point for our inquiries. He provides us with the first clues both to the contemporary problem of political action and to its solution. The original title of Camus's key work, *L'Homme révolté*, points more directly to his central theme than does the English title, *The Rebel*. For le révolté, says Camus, "in the etymological sense, does a complete turnabout." Le révolté experiences a form of existential disgust. He feels revulsion, is revolted, acts in opposition to, turns against: in Camus's phrase, he says "no." The point is both apt and fundamental. Yet Camus makes it in order to transcend it. Something else, more subtle, is also involved. For Camus, rebellion must not be purely negative. "What is a rebel? A man who says 'no', but whose refusal does not imply renunciation. He is also a man who says 'yes', from the moment he makes his first gesture of rebellion."[3] The rebel also says "yes." The revolted man must not be moved simply by Sartrean "nausea." It is this positive aspect of Camus's conception of l'homme révolté that is most significant, for it generates some distinctions of fundamental importance for our subject.

The origins of Camus's "positive" notion of rebellion are crucial for both understanding and assessing it. Camus, as many moderns, thinks the modern world is profoundly disenchanted. Old gods are dead and new faiths problematical: personal despair and social terror threaten to dominate an existence from which sense has fled. Thus Camus begins his analysis of rebellion, not with his primordial figure, the "servile rebel" (slave), but with "the absurd"—the notion of man in a universe devoid of human meaning, where both life and death seem pointless. "The absurd": here was Camus's central motif, inextricably linked with him. (*Le Monde* even headlined its report of Camus's own death, in an auto crash on 14 January 1960, with the word "Absurde!") It was a long preoccupation, only gradually worked out, into politics, in the pages of *The Rebel*.

From the outset, absurdism for Camus was something to be confronted rather than surrendered to. In his review of Sartre's *La Nausée* (in the *Algier républicain* during 1938), he had written: "The realization that life is absurd cannot be an end in itself but only a beginning. . . . It is not this discovery which is interesting, but the consequences and rules of action which can be derived from it." In *Combat* during 1945, he had proclaimed: "No, everything is not summed up in negation and absurdity. We know this. But we must first posit negation and absurdity, because they are what our generation has encountered and what we must take into account."[4] In a series of works throughout this period, Camus presented concrete instances of men's responses to absurdism: the bloody and demeaning tyranny of *Caligula* (first written in 1935); the indifference and ultimate defiance of Mersault, *L'Etranger* (1939); the suicide of Marie and the primitive "rebellion" of Martha—"Mary and Martha"—in *Le Malentendu* (1944). Successively, *increasingly* in these works, Camus groped for some "positive" beyond the "negative." And in *The Myth of Sisyphus* (1940) he undertook an explicit analysis of the absurd. He enumerated concrete situations wherein intimations of absurdism arose. He specified three possible responses to it: suicide, which was mere escape and defeat; philosophical faith, which was mere intellectual suicide; and "living with it"—Sisyphus, making his fate his own by internalizing it, becoming conscious of it, and thus "happy."[5]

Here, indeed, there was not simply a progression but a major reversal, itself a "turnabout"—from Camus's early belief that there was no life without despair of life, to the suggestion that there was no despair of life without life. Indeed, Camus added: "I said that the world is absurd but I was too hasty. The world itself is not reasonable, that is all that can be said. But what is absurd is the confrontation of the irrational and the wild longing for clarity whose call echoes in the human heart. The absurd depends as much on man as on the world. . . . The absurd is essentially a divorce. It lies in neither of the elements compared; it is born of their confrontation. . . . the Absurd is not in man . . . nor in the world, but in their presence together."[6]

This was a crucial movement, the ultimate basis of Camus's developed notion of rebellion. But only ultimately. Thus far it was incomplete, its implications not yet fully developed theoretically or practically. In his preface to the new edition of *Sisyphus* (1955), Camus himself would note that this work was only a beginning for *The Rebel*. This was very true: for Sisyphus possessed only consciousness, only awareness. Camus as yet had drawn only the conclusion that absurdism must be preserved as a first truth; and he noted, "The preceding only defines a way of thinking. But the point is to live."[7] The active import of the dual bases of absurdism, in man and the world, remained to be grasped.

That grasp, the full confrontation with absurdism, emerges only in *The Rebel*; and only in rebellion. Here, beginning with the absurd, Camus swiftly moves beyond it. Absurdism, he tells us, is the existential equivalent of Cartesian doubt: it is "an experience to be lived *through* [my italics] ." It begins by wiping the slate clean. Initially, as a rule of life, it permits all things, by reducing virtue (and vice) to mere caprice. But this is true only initially, for, *as* a rule of life, absurdism is contradictory. Logically, the denial of all meaning, of all belief, must ultimately turn on and transcend itself. To cry "Absurd!" is just that — to cry out, to protest. Only utter silence would be consistent with absurdism. And thus revulsion against meaninglessness creates a "minimum of coherence" and has consequences. Absurdism itself generates a turnabout. Here, rebellion is evidence for the limits of absurdism. The claim that one believes in nothing must itself be believed — and lived. To live is already, implicitly, to judge. Human life emerges as a necessary good, simply for there to be a continuation of what Camus calls "the desperate encounter between human inquiry and the silence of the universe." And if life is good, it must be so for all men: the protest against the absurd, articulating life, is categorical. Hence, both suicide and murder must be repudiated. Thus rebellion itself, rather than the "absolutes" of religious or secular doctrine, already begins to indicate a sort of *limit*, a "rule of action."[8]

Derived from an encounter with the absurd, rebellion is a matter of saying "no" and "yes" simultaneously, of affirming in denying, of negating mere negation. Camus's analysis provides a double, reverse twist, to both credo quia absurdum est and the Hegelian dialectic of man and nature. And in the same way Camus reexplores the relation of man and man, of master and slave. He indicates his "debt" clearly enough: "Only a god, or a principle above the master and slave, could intervene and make men's history something more than a mere chronicle of their victories and defeats. . . . There was infinitely more in Hegel than in the left wing Hegelians who triumphed over him."[9]

The wanted principle is the same as that found in encountering absurdism. The rebellious slave's (unphilosophical) "no," Camus argues, is also an affirmation of a border line, of limits which must be respected by the master. The slave discovers something in himself which he wishes to have respected, which he sees as "preferable to everthing, even to [his own] life itself." And just as with absurdism, Camus says, this analysis of servile rebellion suggests that orthodox existentialism is wrong, that there is some sort of common human nature. (But only some sort: fearful of the way abstract formulation may lead to categorical murder and not wishing to depart from his immediate, concrete "evidence," Camus refuses to spell it out.) To be sure, Camus notes, social rebellion can remain motivated by merely negative resentment or egoism; and he seems to imply that this is often true of the slave. He singles out Spartacus as prototype

of the servile rebel: demanding equality, then translating that into a demand
to become master and make the master his slave, Spartacus enunciates only a
reversal, no positive transcendence. But even here, Camus contends, there is a
potential in rebellion which is not essentially individualistic nor a merely negative turnabout. Insofar as the rebel accepts his death, he is drawn out of his
egocentric solitude: he demonstrates "that he is willing to sacrifice himself for
the sake of a common good which he considers more important than his own
destiny." In social terms, the spectacle of oppression, not only the experience
of it, can be an occasion for rebellion. A sense of identification with other men
is involved, not psychological nor in terms of interests but in terms of common
human destiny. Men are together in confronting the universe. What the rebel
seeks to defend belongs not to him alone but to man's "natural community";
and the rebel demands respect for himself only insofar as he identifies himself
with that community. Again, the principle involved is quasi-Cartesian; and the
solidarity is (as Camus himself describes it) ultimately metaphysical.

In our daily lives rebellion plays the same role as does the "*cogito*" in the realm
of thought: it is the first piece of evidence. But this evidence lures the individual
from his solitude. It founds its first value on the whole human race. I rebel—
therefore we exist.[10]

   "I rebel—therefore we exist." This is a vast move from Camus' early recognition (in his review of Sartre's *La Nausée*, mentioned earlier) that "I write,
therefore I am" is not enough. Yet, as we shall see, this conception of rebellion has profoundly ambivalent political consequences, and its origins mirror
Camus's stark vision of the politics of our century. At the same time, Camus's
argument is productive. In the first place, the notion of absurdism allows us
to draw a distinction between le révolté and (to use one of Camus's famous
earlier titles) l'étranger. Le révolté does not commit "gratuitous acts." For him
it is not true that "everything is permitted." It is rather l'étranger (the stranger,
the outsider, the alien) who remains a prisoner of absurdism without transcending it. As a result, he is truly isolated, alien not only to the universe but to all
other men. His outbreaks are random, spasmodic, and nihilistic—even at best,
they know no bounds and themselves create nothing.

   We shall consider the implications of this distinction and its divergence from
Camus's politics, later in this discussion. But before that, it is essential to note
that Camus is all too aware that his conception of rebellion (involving both
rejection of homicide and affirmation of human community) is not universal
either in the present or in the past. Men in opposition may remain tied to egoism
or resentment; as the record of modern history especially shows, they also may

become mired in the "absolute negation" of nihilism or in the equally deadly "absolute affirmation" of fanaticism. It is precisely for these reasons that Camus proceeds to draw a distinction himself between rebellion and revolution. Forcefully, he denies that rebellion is merely a primitive form of revolution. The two are essentially different. Revolution, Camus argues, is the denial and destruction of rebellion. Nevertheless, he sees a certain vicious connection between them: a move from social to metaphysical rebellion, from metaphysical rebellion to metaphysical *revolution* — and thence to *political* revolution. The social rebel (e.g., the slave) protests against his immediate condition in society; the metaphysical rebel protests against his condition as a man in an inhuman universe. The true form of the slave's rebellion offers a positive (ultimately metaphysical) aspect, affirmation of human community or unity; so too, in its initial stages, does metaphysical rebellion. But metaphysical rebellion need not stop there. For rebellion *leads into* the realm of ideas (awareness); but revolution only *begins* in that realm. Metaphysical rebellion moves from defiance, to blasphemy, to denial; and then on to secular theism and the deification of man. The metaphysical rebel, e.g., Prometheus, begins by defying an unjust god; ultimately, the metaphysical revolutionary proposes totality, the reshaping of the entire cosmos in accordance with his theory. And finally, revolution moves from pure metaphysics, through "appearances" (exotic life-styles), to politics. Here, Camus notes, the term revolution retains its astronomical meaning: it is a *circular movement*, leading from one government to another. Be it bourgeois, Stalinist, or Fascist, the revolutionary government attempts to stabilize society on its model by realizing, through force, its new doctrine (formal equality, rationalist history, or sheer irrationalist dynamism). In its political form, supported by its totalistic "ideology," revolution undertakes "logical crime." Breaking with its rebel origins, revolution abandons limits and both commits and sanctions murder—"crime dons the apparel of innocence."[11]

Here, Camus has returned to the question posed in the introductory quotation. Human life is a necessary good; the rebel is identified with men's natural community.

Man's solidarity is founded upon rebellion and rebellion, in its turn, can only find its justification in this solidarity. We have, then, the right to say that any rebellion which claims the right to deny or destroy this solidarity loses simultaneously its right to be called rebellion and becomes in reality an acquiescence in murder.[12]

But if rebellion rules out murder, how effective can it be? Camus's answer is that "there are two sorts of efficacy: that of typhoons and that of sap." A risk *must* be taken—rebellion, existentially concerned with life, remains concerned with concrete realities and relative values, not with abstract absolutes. Specifically, for the rebel murder must be truly exceptional, a limit which can be reached by any man only once. The rebel-murderer is no longer entitled to refer to that natural community which justifies rebellion. Only if both his victim *and the murderer himself* disappear can the natural community (without them) provide its own justification. "The rebel has only one way of reconciling himself with his act of murder . . .: to accept his own death and sacrifice. He kills and dies so that it shall be clear that murder is impossible." The same reasoning, Camus contends, applies to violence generally. Systematic violence destroys man's natural community. But absolute nonviolence only serves as the negative foundation for the violence of slavery. Hence, violence cannot be rejected absolutely. But if the rebel resorts to it, it too must be accompanied by "personal responsibility" and "immediate risk." And it too, unlike revolutionary violence, must be provisional and exceptional, being used only momentarily and only to combat another's (the master's) violence. "Authentic arts of rebellion will only consent to take up arms for institutions that limit violence, not for those which codify it. A revolution is not worth dying for unless it assures the immediate suppression of the death penalty. . . ." Like unrequited murder, revolutionary terrorism (whether of incumbents or of newly established insurgents) must be rejected. In both cases rebellion must be self-consistent. Indeed, for Camus, rebellion must apply the limits which it initially reveals, in all its spheres of action. Liberty and justice, virtue and cynicism, rationalism and irrationalism, idealism and realism—rebellion cannot lapse wholly into either alternative but demands the constant tension between opposites which is the substance of life. And the same is true of art, which can be a pure form of rebellion: neither sheer formalism nor mere realism, neither total escapism nor total acceptance, art must be a process of reconstruction, of the rectification of the world. The path of rebellion is the path of true moderation, the avoidance of hubris. Rejecting both excessive self-righteousness and excessive fastidiousness, rejecting both absolute affirmation and absolute negation, rebellion must continue to say "yes" and "no" simultaneously.

Does the end justify the means? That is possible. But what will justify the end? To that question . . . rebellion replies: the means.[13]

Brutus must turn his knife upon himself; violence must be used only as an exceptional and ultimate (self-terminating) countermeasure. These conclusions are based on a chilly but compelling logic. Whether it is a sufficiently *political* logic, however, is another matter. To be sure, Camus's distinction between rebellion and revolution prompts us to an invaluable skepticism about the adequacy or finality of any political solution. There is eternal tension, there are contradictions but no final sublation; and hence the need for activity as a *constant* and *continuing* one. Rebellion, says Camus, is one of the "essential dimensions" of human existence; "rebellion will die only with the last man . . . it is the very movement of life and . . . cannot be denied without renouncing life."[14] And Camus's insistence that rebellion must be positive provides a reply of sorts to the notion (heralded by such moderns as Sorel, Sartre, and Fanon) that violence is a creative force which welds men together. But the reply is incomplete. Camus's own notion of rebellion presents problems of its own.

Camus has indeed *dissolved* the paradox of rebellious violence (the only way a paradox can be dispatched) in terms of his own argument. In these terms, only an apparent paradox remains concerning the murderer's own fate. If both murder and suicide are excluded, the murderer-rebel surely cannot be murdered (executed) himself—that way lies an infinitely bloody progression. It would seem, then, that he must commit suicide: such an act, at such a point, is only the compounding of his own sin (and martyrdom)—rebellion continues without him. But how fortunate if this difficulty can be avoided by the murderer dying in the course of his original act of homicide! And how fortunate if men willing to accept the murderer-rebel's fate can always be found when needed. By Camus's own logic others cannot simply call for them ("charge!" is not the rebel's idiom; only "follow me!"). And by his prime example, the Russian terrorists, murderer-rebels compose only a tragic and transitory "community."[15]

In fact, community is the central problem. The most elementary type of servile rebel does indeed undertake a turnabout—but he only attempts to reverse the existing order, not to create a genuinely new community; he is servile even in rebellion, to that which he attacks. But is Camus's positive notion of natural human community (the metaphysical link) sufficient to transcend this? It would be inaccurate to treat it as purely visionary—it has its roots deep in classical Western tradition—and as Camus employs it, it is not simply a pure ideal. Nonetheless, even if men are together in this sense, they are only abstractly so: they share no substantive ties. The anarchic streak in Camus is deeper than he may have realized. By itself, the notion of natural community is *politically ethereal*. It is the notion of an Augustinian community of saints, not to be confused with the earthly city of man. As in Augustine's heavenly city, one cannot imagine what the term citizenship would mean in it, in the absence of any conventional and institutional bonds. And as in Augustine's temporal body of the Church, there is no certainty that members of this natural community know of or act in terms of their common membership. (Camus himself vaguely sees this, without seeing its implications: "The community of victims is the same as that which unites victim and executioner. But the executioner does not know this.")[16]

Similarly with Camus's concept of limits. Gore Vidal says somewhere that there are no ends—only means. Camus removes the cynicism from this notion and shows a classic sense in it, brilliantly. But his argument is based solely on the supposed logical consistency of rebellious action with its origins (the discovery of natural solidarity)—it makes no reference to the fragility and unexpectedness of action. Is natural solidarity either necessary or sufficient to show where talk of means and ends breaks down? Is it only through Camusian rebellion that hubris can be seen to be a political sin and only in such rebellion that true moderation can be practiced? And do art, justice and liberty, etc. fit neatly on the single base of natural solidarity in life? Limits would seem to need somewhat different foundations from those which Camus provides.

Similarly, again, with ideology. Camus uses this term pejoratively throughout—he certainly wishes for the end of the ideological age. Thus he takes his place in the notorious modern debate over the "end of ideology." This is not the place to summarize or explore that tortuous controversy. Granted that totalistic secular theology is dangerous, does Camus's response suffice? Is the notion of human unity, and opposition to slavery and injustice on that ground, enough? Some more richly detailed or textured *political* conception surely is needed (whether one calls it ideology or not). Even a sense of *in*justice, if it is effectively to transcend existing patterns and prejudices, must be founded on some vision of justice—and this is true even if one is not so naive (or criminal) as to believe that one can make that vision fully concrete, eternal, and forever adequate, forcibly or overnight.

In brief, what Camus offers us politically is a *mode of coping* rather than a mode of creating, a way of making out rather than one of making up (and one which, regarding concrete acts and relationships, is individualistic in the extreme). Certainly this is better than nothing. And Camus's mode is superb in avoiding cynicism, timidity, and complacency. He persistently reminds us (we should not need to be reminded) that rebellion is a desperately demanding as well as an urgent undertaking. Associated with life itself and denying final solutions, rebellion is not primitive, stagnant, or parasitical upon its enemies— here is no mauvais foi. However, to settle for a mode of coping (even for one like Camus's) does indicate a certain *lack* of faith. And for Camus that lack of faith arises from his view of the politics of our era. "We can act," he tells us,

only in terms of our own time, among the people who surround us. . . . The important thing, therefore, is not, as yet, to go to the root of things, but, the world being what it is, to know how to live in it. . . . In the age of ideologies, we must examine our position in relation to murder.[17]

We must cope, *because* the political world is what is has become. "Politics is not religion, or if it is, then it is nothing but the Inquisition."[18] Secular religion ("ideology") and "politics"—Camus's jaundiced conjuction of the two is sadly appropriate for many of the paramount events of our time: Buchenwald and Hiroshima, slave labor and terrorism, nihilism and fanaticism. . . . But to assume that this negative conjunction is essential, to take pathological examples as definitive, is far less appropriate. Of course politics is not everything—but is it nothing, or purely negative? Camus's preoccupation with violence (murder, terrorism, capital punishment, the universal death sentence which all men live qua men) is too disenchanting—and too restrictive. He has largely turned his back on politics and sought refuge beyond (or before) it, in the absurd, the human condition, and human nature. Even if, as Camus says, rebellion is one of the essential dimension of human life, it is not sufficient on his model. Even its positive aspect—the notion of limits, the affirmation of community—remains too abstract. Here, Camus's revulsion is ultimately antipolitical. Disillusioned but struggling to wrest at least some moral guidelines from the chaos, Camus himself remains l'étranger to the possibilities of politics.

Camus is a modern archetype precisely because of his profound ambivalence. Many others have shown a fear of ideology and politics, but their understanding has been far more restricted, and less tortured, than Camus's. That so resolute and thorough an enemy of complacency or timidity manifests revulsion against politics is a poignant comment on men's reactions to the historical events of our time.[19] The question is whether we, in turn, can go beyond this—whether we can at least indicate an affirmative conception of politics which offers concrete possibilities. And here too, Camus's very ambivalence suggests the lines for our further explorations. His continual reminders about rebellion and his view of revolution indicate the ultimate basis of the problem. But to see how, we must look beyond Camus. Here, we can compare his analysis with another classic treatment of modern activism.

Consider André Malraux's revolutionary parable, *Man's Fate*. The novel begins with Ch'en, gripping his knife before his victim's bed. In the background, the night city already sounds distant and unreal; the consummation of Ch'en's act plunges him completely into another microcosm. Striking, the ravisher is ravished. He is wedded to death and becomes an isolate from normal human life. Ch'en becomes as imprisoned in his new world as is any man in the normal cosmos he has left behind — perhaps even more so. He is caught up in the nature of his deed. With Hegelian logic, Ch'en becomes what he does. His "fate" is of his own making — even to his eventual annihilation.[20]

Ch'en is not simply The Terrorist, a stereotype to rival those of empiricist social analysis. And if his violence produces a Camusian sundering of community, it is not merely a metaphysical breach. We learn of Ch'en's beginnings only fragmentarily and later in the story. His opening scene is a rite of passage, a new beginning which buries the old. (When he goes to see his old teacher and mentor, Gisors, they are no longer capable of speaking to one another. Here two traditions, that of the Chinese teacher-disciple relationship and that of Gisors' western revolutionary doctrine, have been eclipsed.) Ch'en loses his innocence but also gains it anew: his opening act is at once baptism and rebirth into another world. The initiator initiates himself. He creates a new world and simultaneously re-creates himself. Fearsome innocence, inhuman birth, starkly isolated new world — but Ch'en's figure, though extreme (and negative), is exemplary. Not simply novelty, but the *notion* of new beginnings has assumed paramount importance. Not the phenomenon of violence, but its conceptual surround has altered radically. Even for Ch'en, violence is ancillary. It is an initiating mode of a certain kind.

Ch'en, the new man in his own new world, is the extreme étranger — in a *concrete* sense. To extend the distinction between le révolté and l'étranger, in nonmetaphysical terms, we can say that l'étranger is isolated from every concrete community (of idiom, continuing contact, belief), including that within which he finds himself living. Treating that community, not simply the universe, as meaningless, he can find no resources for his action there. Le révolté, however, needs and uses a concrete communal heritage, both (in its immediate manifestations) as a point of clearly focused opposition and (as a cultural tradition) as a source of armaments. Not only must he really *know* that against which he rebels in order to be sure that he really opposes it both now and in the future (that much is, or should be, obvious); he also must find resources (moral, symbolic, analytic) for his action within it. An individual can hardly find resources for rebellion by himself, de novo — too much time and effort is needed to master external sources and then to explicate them to his fellows. (A *series* of such entrepreneurial efforts obviously can arise through scholarship or direct experiences. As elements of one culture or subculture become readily accessible to another, they become part of its own traditions.) Events and terms, the idiom of example, explicit comparison, and symbolic reference — these form the armory of the rebel. They provide resources for direction, attack, persuasion, and redefinition of the situation. In this crucial sense, as a cultural tradition of resource, rebellion indeed does have a positive aspect.

"Cultural traditions." When they hear these words, our self-conscious moderns reach for their bulldozers. The vehement reaction indicates a modern confusion and a political peril. A tradition is neither static or monolithic. Rather, it has continuity and variety. A society aware of traditions need not be traditionalistic, view all things as authorized repetitions of timeless precedent. As I have suggested, tradition is a basis both for what exists and for visions of alternative acts. And *ignorance* of a cultural tradition of rebellion may approximate the absurdism of l'étranger in both its attitudes and its actions. Today we can witness a veritable cult of the outsider, not confined to characters of fiction. Jean Genet is the prime example; a more recent (although embroidered) one is Henri Charrière, "Papillon."[21] Obviously, men may be ignorant because their particular society has made them so: they may be outsiders as members of a victimized minority. And for this very reason their society may become a target for rebels who act on their behalf. But on the part of these rebels (if they are to deserve the name), ignorance is not only in no sense excusable — it is disastrous. Neither with widespread ignorance nor with ignorance as the forced possession of a minority is the issue one of *conflicting* cultures: it is one of *culture*, of a knowledge of the situation and resources of a tradition. Of course, men (including minorities) may have good reason to reject the immediately prevalent or dominant meanings of their society. Much rebellion involves precisely this sort of rejection. But rejection is not enough. And a cult is not a culture. The loss of a sense of rebellion as tradition leaves little room for truly positive resistance.

These observations allow us to bring together the strands of our analysis thus far. Camus becomes doubly revealing. On the one hand, his essay can be read as the recounting and marshaling of a particular heritage, the western tradition of rebellion. It serves as a concrete example of my notion of tradition and the potentials which knowledge of its resources can bring. Camus presents exemplars, episodes, the mutual effects and blendings of subcultures. Prometheus (Hellenic and Romantic), Sade, the Dandies, Dostoievsky, Nietzsche; Spartacus, Saint-Just, the Decembrists, Bakunin, Marx — we need neither complet the list nor add a detailed commentary on it. Camus frankly admits that both his selections and his interpretations are partial, neither the only ones possible nor all-explaining.[22] But this in itself should suggest the varied nature and uses of a tradition.

Yet, on the other hand, these suggestions are clearly developments *from* Camus. While there is continuity and variety in the balance of his analysis of western rebellion, Camus refers only to the past—for him, as for so many moderns, tradition is a pejorative term. In fact, for him it means only what I have characterized as traditionalistic: it is "the sacred" rule by "myth" which eliminates all problems by a set of "eternal answers."[23] This points to a fatal flaw in Camus's analysis. His lack of an adequate notion of tradition is both source and symptom of his difficulties with rebellion. It is this lack which makes the turnabout of Camus's rebel too complete, his acts too abstracted and still too negative.

How does this fatal flaw arise? And how can our notion of rebellion as tradition be developed in more explicit terms? The answers to both questions concern Camus's other central term, revolution. To be sure, in speaking of revolution Camus is not so much concerned with general historical description as with constructing a polar opposite to his notion of rebellion. (Other acts could violate this notion without being fully revolutionary in his sense.) But the fact that Camus can use "revolution" negatively suggests the ambiguous degeneracy of that term, a degeneracy which affects his own "rebellion." With both terms Camus's return to etymology (révolte as turnabout, revolution as Thermidorean circular motion) is actually misleading. Indeed, Camus's treatment of Spartacus shows this: Spartacus's desire to replace masters with slaves indicates that circular motion per se does not depend on metaphysical vision. Camus's view of revolution as founded on a proposal of a total new creation is far more to the point. And it does contrast strikingly with our notion of rebellion as tradition. Only in a sense can we speak of a tradition of revolution — one which rather destroys than is nourished by its ancestors. The revolution devours its fathers. It is this which makes the notion of rebellion as tradition so difficult to recapture and develop. But although a modern notion of new beginnings is indeed the culprit, revolution is not its sole source; and it is not simply or even primarily a matter of explicit doctrine, of full-blown ideology. Indeed, Camus's stress on doctrine, especially his emphasis on Rousseau as a prime figure, is almost identical with that in one of the earliest modern theoretical grapplings with revolution, of classic date and provenance: Insard's *Observations sur le principe qui a produit, les révolutions de France, de Genève, et d'Amerique dans le dix-huitième siècle (1789).*[24] The problem is deeper than Camus, or Insard, saw.

Reflect on Camus's overall thesis. We can restate it thus: only *between* primitive (servile) revolt and full revolution—in "true" rebellion—can there be any escaping from the circles. But given circles, *how* (and where) is a "between" to be located? Camus's terms indicate a certain collapse, incipient in his own analysis. *Even his own thesis*—the move from social rebellion, to metaphysical rebellion, to metaphysical revolution, to political revolution: from social to metaphysical to social—enunciates circular motion. Even Camus's analysis revolves: circling, the terms come home to roost. Failing to see this, Camus perpetuates a modern set of false alternatives. By *reducing* "action" to his brand of "rebellion," Camus actually contributes to the destruction of both as positive, political terms. He thus takes his place in a strange lineage which includes some of those he criticizes—the lineage, ultimately, of Ch'en. To comprehend and reckon with this, to see how the creation of political worlds need be neither ethereal nor totalistic, to see how concretely affirmative rebellion depends on the *breaking* of the circles—to do all this, we must venture into a yet more tangled jungle, where revolution and action are curiously intertwined.

II. Motion: Revolving and Beginning

> Being, as to our bodies, composed of Changeable Elements, we, with the World, are made up of and subsist by Revolution.
>
> —Penn, *Maxims* (*Works*, 1726, I.841)

> The French Revolution is but the precursor of another revolution, far greater, far more solemn, which will be the last.
>
> —"Manifeste des Egaux" (Paris, 1796)

Between them, these two quotations mark the tangled field of revolution—they are rather curiously linked than diametrically opposed. The history of theories (and histories) of revolution remains to be written. But for our purposes we can best start with the present and work backwards. For modern efforts to construct a theory of revolution (whatever the validity of such efforts per se) are especially revealing of the complexities that underlie the notion and of their tortuous implications for political activity.

If few modern theorists have been overly troubled by the deeper roots of their central term, they have been bothered by its slippery magic. Does all revolution involve violence, or terrorism? Totalistic, secular religion? Thermidorean reaction? At best, such questions are ways of asking about the different types of phenomena we tend to lump under a single name. And surely some distinctions would seem necessary. What is striking, however, is the enormous variety of lines on which they have been drawn.

American, French (1789), English (Puritan), Russian—these have been the preferred, the classic examples. But the dominance of these examples (especially that of France) well may seem restrictive. What of other events, in Europe in the nineteenth century, or in Spain, Italy, Germany, Yugoslavia, China, Cuba in our own? Or, more antique, the English Great Rising of 1381, or Thucydides's description of the events of Corcyrea, Athens, and Samos—or the struggles of the Gracchi? Crane Brinton, for his limited range of (classic) cases, relied on the model of fever (marked by five stages: prodromal signs, full symptoms, crisis, uneven convalescence, recovery), which he noted had unfortunate "pathological" connotations. In some ways his model is remarkably similar to Thucydides's analogies among plague, war, and internal upheaval. On much grander scale, ranging from Rome and the Crusades to the nineteenth century, Jacob Burckhardt treated "the theory of crises and revolutions" as a whole—"the theory of storms."[25] Fever, plague, storm—the similarities of conception indicate a deep-seated urge to make analogical sense of great events. But at first glance, at least, they are hardly persuasive. The notion of process involved seems to beg some crucial questions. Pre-revolutionary situation seems teleological, whereas postrevolutionary reaction (or exhaustion) seems tautological. And the homogeneity of the process or stages (The Terror; the "end" of revolution) even of the classic cases seems highly problematical. Generally, modern English-speaking theorists have vaguely thought the Russian and French cases to be more truly revolutionary—more violent and issuing in greater change. But Hannah Arendt has given first place to the American case, on diametrically opposed grounds. It was *less* violent, she argues, precisely because it undertook no great change in the distribution of wealth ("every attempt to solve the social question by political means leads into terror"). And it was *more* truly revolutionary, because it issued in the establishment of a new constitution for the body politic. For Arendt, this is a sign, not of Thermidor, but of a true "new beginning."[26]

Arendt reminds us that the establishment of a new polity can be a creative act of a kind, rather than a mere reaction. But there is more to new beginnings and to the intersection of politics and society than meets her eye. For there is an obvious problem of *scope*, in both conception and example. How *long* and *large* can a revolution be? Revolution or evolution? Political or social? Industrial, technological, moral, philosophical, fashionable, managerial, consumerist—the usages seem to expand indefinitely. And to overlap: Thomas Kuhn's "Scientific

Revolution" explicitly plays on an analogue with political revolution; Tom Hayden's "Triple Revolution" reverses the analogue.[27] As a consequence of these complexities, some theorists have desired to delimit a distinct subject matter. Some, picking up the familiar notion of terror, have insisted that "creative violence" is the key and that such phenomena as "industrial revolution" are not parallel. Others have taken a similar line, more systemic if less ecstatic, seeing a focus on violence as allowing them to delimit coups, palace revolts, guerrilla struggles, civil wars, and great social revolutions as species of the same genus—internal war. And one set of authors has taken it further, to modern urban violence: "the hypotheses contained in a very long intellectual tradition—the study of revolution—are equally applicable to riots."[28]

Still other theorists have argued that this sort of delimitation is misconceived —that the focus on violence directs attention toward efforts to monopolize power, ignoring the more dynamic element of beliefs and expectations which is indicated by the various social revolutions covered by the broad, modern usage of the term. On this view, what matters is *fundamental* change. But here too there are problems: political revolution is seen as coming to the non-Western world with Westernization and bound to be replaced everywhere, West and non-West, when men accept social revolutions (modernization) as regular parts of their lives.[29] And from this, in turn, it seems no great move to the view that a great social revolution is a change in the "systems" of a society. Here revolution is seen as an upset in the "equilibrium" among systems (but equilibrium, though apparently held to be something other than a theoretical norm, is never specified concretely); violence is reduced to "violation of expectations" (so that beating native workers, one supposes, may be nonviolent, but native workers' peaceful demonstrations may be violent); and the reference is solely to the social, never the political, system.[30]

Given these tangles, another extreme proposal begins to seem hardly surprising: all is really flux, revolutionary and evolutionary change are matters of perspective; fundamental change in *any* realm (scientific, philosophical, political) is a matter of theoretical interest, of the analyst's decision to make an arbitrary stopping point on the basis of the sector of norms carved out for analysis.[31]

Having spoken so often and so broadly of an "age of revolution," social scientists ofen seem compelled to find themselves a part of it—if only in methodology. For ultimately, by these devices political revolution (indeed, revolution in any meaningful sense) seems to be eliminated, not illuminated. Generally, with the stress on systems and society, politics appears epiphenomenal; rebellion becomes a term designating minor or primitive upheavals; and tradition becomes a pejorative, especially in contrast with the great (methodological) "revolution of modernization."[32] The analyst and the participant too often part company; and the scope of the company makes a difference. It matters considerably whether a system, a stopping point, or fundamental change is perceived as such — and how — *by those involved* in the events. Violence and belief; political and social — the social as analogue for the political, the political as analogue for the social. The reversals seem interminable. Though lacking the drama of illness or storm, these usages too hark back to Penn, with his talk of the world and men's bodies subsisting by revolution. And *they* are what prove illuminating.

It is precisely "those involved" through whom revolution reveals an immediately relevant range of meanings. The famous modern European dates suggest a progression quite in keeping with the Manifesto of Equals: 1789, 1830, 1848, 1871. . . . "Come the revolution!" *The* revolution came to be regarded as just that — a single, continuing process, unfinished and due to break out once more. Even a massive failure like 1848 was regarded as a turning point where history only momentarily failed to turn. It was simply somewhat premature, only a temporary stoppage in an ongoing process. Edmund Wilson has brilliantly protrayed the impact of this vision on the great historian of the revolution, Michelet, who coupled it with Vico's theory of curso and recurso. Michelet replaced the notion of mere repetition with that of progress — "the reawakening idealism of the tradition of the great revolution gave purpose to Vico's cycles." But with unintended irony, Wilson adds:

It is strange and stirring to find in the *Scienza Nuova* the modern sociological and anthropological mind awakening. . . . Here, before the steady rays of Vico's insight . . . we see the fogs that obscure the horizon of the remote reaches of time recede, the cloud-shapes of legend lift. In the shadows there are fewer monsters; the heroes and the gods float away.[33]

Ironic — for *have* the mists and myths dissipated? And *can* they really do so? There is much more than a trace here (in Vico, in Michelet, and in Wilson) of the model of bodily motion or natural cataclysm — the language, a conception, has an impact on the analysts themselves. And the impact is a continuing one. On recent American events: "The present generation is learning anew a lesson which many generations have learned in the past, sometimes too late: there are in human affairs great natural forces, comparable in their power to destroy to hurricanes or earthquakes. . . . [But] the wrong attitude can generate a self-fulfilling prophecy. The disorders that threaten us are far from apocalyptic." The added disclaimer seems oddly forced; the notion of natural forces is a persistent one. On Paris in 1968: "Then came the days of wrath. Nanterre was aflame. . . . The State seemed to dissolve. Society was cracking up. . . . The old order has grown old . . . the Latin Quarter, swept as it is by a tonic gale. . . .'' On 1848: "There was an intense consciousness of revolutionary tension, and no one seems to have had the strength, or even the will, to stand up to the storm when it broke." And, to a contemporary observer, the young Walter Bagehot, writing from France shortly after Louis Napoleon had finally "finished" the events of 1848:

Five weeks ago, the tradespeople talked of May, '52, as if it were the end of the world. . . . I was present when a huge *Flamande*, in appearance so intrepid that I respectfully pitied her husband, came to ask the character of a *bonne*. I was amazed to hear her say, "I hope the girl is strong, for when the revolution comes next May, and I have to turn off my helper, she will have enough to do." It seemed to me that a political apprehension must be pretty general, when it affected that most non-speculative of speculations, the *reckoning* of a housewife.[34]

Nonspeculative—in an important sense, revolution is indeed just such a notion. Besides the varying contexts and contingencies, the bewildering multiplicity of issues and events, of course there is human imitation and self-fulfillment. But beneath even that, there is a notion with ancient roots, which both precedes and subtly influences both theoretical efforts and activistic forays. The implicit but candid teleology of the famous European dates, the "amazement" of a Bagehot—these elements are not mere surface dressing; they are of central importance. For they point back to a truly mythic complex of associations and assumptions, to a specter which continues to haunt—process, beginnings, resurrection, and new creation. The new birth and new innocence of Ch'en is only an extreme and recent manifestation; revolution can hardly be grasped without seeing this.

To be sure, the notion of rebirth and recreation is an extremely ancient (even primordial) one. But its very antiquity is revealing. For once upon a time it was inextricably linked with another notion, that of eternal return—the recurrence of the seasons and the cycles of the ages, the harmony of earthly patterns and celestial reigns. "As is the generation of leaves," says the *Iliad*, "so is that of humanity. The wind scatters the leaves on the ground, but the live timber burgeons with leaves again in the season of spring returning. So one generation of men will grow while another dies." In timeless symbolism, life follows death, creation follows decay—the initiate's old life is given up for a new one; the year's end is a time for its regeneration, by ritual reenactment of the world's beginnings. But with the erosion of the notion of returning, both natality and cosmogeny subtly alter. Heavenly portents begin to suggest a radical notion of novelty; history appears differently. Greater cosmic cycles, extensions of the year, suggest total transformation rather than regeneration — cataclysms symbolize the return to primordial chaos; the purity and potency of origins (Eden, the Golden Age) is transferred to the new cosmos of the future.[35] Finally, the cycles broken, time begins to flow in linear fashion — the final battle, the Last Days, the New Jerusalem are awaited. In Augustine's classic formulation, history becomes ultimately providential: time is the product of eternity, forming a series of *points* with a definite beginning (Genesis) and end (Judgment Day), with the deus-homo as the great, calendrical pivot. Temporal progression, along the points, is in one direction only. The day of judgment is literally the *last* day of (profane) history; the final returning of all to divine unity is also a new beginning, the ultimate transcendence of the temporal realm. And the revolt of the angels, paralleled by Adam's, establishes the two cities whose struggle is the tale of history — revolt serves to wrest apart the sacred and the profane.[36] By a strange transformation, returning (as a last, or ultimate stage) itself begins to take on the connotations of beginning: there is only a faint echo of the original complex, a deadened emphasis, in *re*birth and *re*creation. Here, innocence becomes absolute.

And Milton's Lucifer and Shelley's Prometheus already await in the wings, along with Hegel: politics recapitulates cosmology. For before there was a revolution, there was a *Re*naissance and a *Re*formation: the terms come trailing antique clouds. The ancient Greek theorists generally used stasis (Thucydides) or metabole (Plato, Aristotle) for political upheaval — and they did so in explicitly cyclical contexts.[37] And the Latin revoltus/revolvere and revolutare simply meant revolve, roll again; for political events, the Romans used such terms as rebellis and res novae (new things). In Renaissance English, revolt took on the connotations of falling *away*, going over (to the other side); revolution longer retained its connotation of returning motion — a time period, a recurrence, a turn or twist, a bend or winding. Here the new physics and astronomy entered in. And as Hannah Arendt has reminded us, the English events of 1660 (candidly called "The *Restoration*") and 1689 (more subtly, "The *Glorious Revolution*") were indeed viewed — at least by the victors — as circular motion back to preordained or preestablished orders; Machiavelli spoke only of renovazioni ("return to the first principles of the constitution"); and Tom Paine could reply to Burke by praising the French and American events as "counterrevolutions." But this is not the whole story — and it alone gives a distorted picture. Other connotations — and visions — already were being absorbed and had been present in the Cromwellian struggles. Indeed, the slow and uneven process of intermingling had begun perhaps as early as the fourteenth century.[38] Biblical eschatology obviously offered much ampler scope for res novae than did Roman (or Greek) thought: there could be a new *world*, not simply novel objects or incidents. And even the motion of the new science could be politicized by a Hobbes, in strikingly noncyclical and radical ways—despite Hobbes's claim to total novelty—ways of subtle fusion in which old cosmology lingered amidst new science. For all that Hobbes's Leviathan was an artificial man, it was still a man. The image of the body politic continued its suasive impact; and Hobbes still presented macrocosm, microcosm, and body politic, not as "vain tropes" but as *literally* ("substantially") identical.[39]

The "Manifeste des Egaux" itself clearly shows the composite. As well as proclaiming the doctrine of revolutionary progress and the triumph of the future, it contains much older notions: "The evil is at its height, it covers the fate of the earth. Chaos has reigned there under the name of politics too many centuries. Everything must be in order and resume its place. . . . The days of restitution have arrived." Within another ninety years, another Frenchman, provoked by yet another upheaval, could stringently and explicitly deny that the etymological roots of revolution were revealing: rather than periodic movement, the term denoted "bouleversement," "déracinements . . . sur les éléments constitufs et organiques de toute société."[40]

Here, to be sure, the social question does enter in—but not for the first time and not in merely one way. The reference to politics in the 1796 Manifesto, like so much else, is prophetic. And here, Marx (whom I have carefully skirted until now) shows himself truly to be the central figure in modern revolutionary theory. His theory is indeed a synthesis of revolution: in a way strangely in keeping with his own professions, Marx sums up the relevant conceptions of the modern era. In his theory socialism and sociology, those two great modern neologisms, come together with explosive force. Civil society, not the state, is the true source and theater of history; history is no metaphysical entity, it is made by men—but not just as they please; consciousness does not produce life, rather life *produces* consciousness; objectification is a *progressive* process, ultimately liberating—the realization of philosophy and the humanization of nature, the unification of theory and practice, the end of ideology, of alienation, of class society, of division of labor. . . . Production and generation, beginning and ending, birth and death, the womb of the old and the seeds of the new. Revolution is *social*, the very stuff of history, a fundamental sea change rather than a sudden event. The fatal contradictions in society grow apart over years; their eventual synthesis marks the end of one stage of history and the beginning of another. Social life is essentially a matter of praxis — materially productive (and humanly transforming) activity. And praxis is inherently revolutionary in its development: the historical process brings the production of revolutionary consciousness. Indeed, only such action is truly revolutionary. Politics, in all senses, becomes epiphenomenal. Even violence is merely the midwife of revolution, not its source. The seizure of the state comes only as an epilogue to the basic, social-revolutionary process; and the last revolution of all ultimately brings the end of politics itself. Marx refrains from giving any blueprint, any specific doctrinal model for the ultimate postrevolutionary society; he chooses the historical "is" (dynamic process) rather than any idealistic "ought." The Owl of Minerva only spreads its wings at the fall of dusk — Marx's final (proletarian) revolution is literally and figuratively a *last act*. It is a return (to an advanced form of communism, the product of capitalism) which is also an ultimate beginning. It is no accident that Marx alternatively describes the proletarian revolution as the end of history and as the end of prehistory (the beginning of truly "human" history). Action, released from productive imperatives, is projected vaguely into the final postrevolutionary future. Revolution, as spiral rather than circular motion, leads to last things which are simultaneously the first of a radically new beginning.

With Marx the revolutionary metaphor takes on the flesh of contemporary apocalypse: the word revolution retains its primacy and its slippery magic. *Hence*: far from being one of the oldest terms in our political lexicon, revolution is a phoenix — it rises from the smoldering embers of earlier manifestations. Temporal cycles, astronomical motion, astrological correspondence, millenarian vision, physical upheaval (tempest, storm, deluge, earthquake, eruption, conflagration) — revolution absorbs all these and leads to a radical notion of "new beginnings," spawning strangly unpolitical breeds of action.

Commentators, including Camus,[41] have discussed the apocalyptic element often enough. But what is crucial is the *fusion* of this element with its companions, their really *pre*theoretical nature, and their joint link with action. However faded or submerged, these elements remain to be used by (in a sense, to *use*) different men and theories. The theories, the doctrines, the full-blown ideologies are none of them primary; the available *language* acts as a filter (not a mirror) for experience and as a mode and mold for thought. In this case, the word revolution, with its complex connotations, is crucial. Revolution is an especially striking example of the general phenomenon of the literalization of figure and of the birth and death of cultural idioms.[42] For what is at stake is men's vision and speech: the (political) language they use as an instrument to wrest order from their experience and to present it, in a compelling fashion, to their fellows. To speak thus of language is to suggest that it has consequences for action—and this is correct. The modern efforts to recombine Marxism with other doctrines (positivism, existentialism, structuralism) seem to indicate a continuing, truly mythic appeal in the underlying notions of beginning, returning, and social moving. Indeed, the tangled roots and connotations of the word revolution come together in Marx's synthesis with mordant impact. Even for those who are not in any sense Marxists, Marx's theory seems to state the *terms* of ensuing arguments and efforts. For the notorious failure of the proletariat to revolt as forecast proved both theoretically and practically compelling. Different parts of Marx's vision can be seen as models of alternative efforts to grapple with revolution and politics—efforts of quite varied logics. There is an echo of Marx's notion of the last revolution even in Camus's comment that there as yet has been no "real" revolution, for there could be only one such— "definitive," "stabilizing" everything in heaven and earth.[43] We are already well on the track of Camus's poignant antipolitics and the decay of action.

And not just in Camus. Conceptually and analytically, if not intentionally, contemporary academic theorists have taken over Marx's praxis. For coupled with the eclipse of politics before society is the embarrassment that action has become a technical term of Parsonian sociology. Here action is reduced to patterned, systemic activity (albeit no longer materially productive, and no longer liberating). Analytic theory, despite its nonmechanist claims, returns to an almost Hobbesian position—activity appears as nothing but "civic motion," and "motion produceth nothing but motion."[44]

But it is the activistic side which deserves primary attention here. It can be seen as a complex alternative to the academic treatment of action—and as a parallel degeneration. Sorel already suggests the pecularities of Marx's legacy. By proclaiming Marx's final proletarian revolution an invaluable example of "social myth," Sorel in some ways penetrated more deeply than he knew. However, his notion of myth (an emotionally charged picture of final battle, literally untrue but crucial for mobilizing men) was none too profound. And his proposal of the general strike as a substitute myth for Marx's revolution signaled a decay of Marx's theory. The general strike, for Sorel, was more appropriate for conditions where violence must be used to *force* the classes apart. Here the historical production of consciousness was replaced by the intentional *production* of consciousness, and praxis became the action of the proletarian warrior-hero. With the emphasis on such action, Marx's sense of the profound importance of concrete historical analysis was submerged. Sorel never explained how men could move from the fighting ethos of his warriors to the new "ethics of the producers" which he envisaged as the basis of a new society. The notion of historical synthesis (spiral motion) to which Marx's new beginning had been tied vanished here; pure novelty remained. And the avoidance of blueprints became a blind faith in the efficacy of heroism. If Sorel's contempt for the parliamentary "palship" of Third Republic France was justified, his identification of that with politics per se and his vague substitution of warfare were far from satisfactory. The case of Sorel's greater contemporary, Lenin, is more subtle. Lenin's use of the term economist as a condemnation, his emphasis on political education and agitation still had roots in a vivid sense of concrete conditions. And Lenin, of course, claimed to be Marx's faithful descendant: here, at least, revolution was not treated as a mobilizing myth. But unlike Sorel, who still claimed that the myth of the general strike was not his own "intellectual" creation but the spontaneous product of the syndicalists themselves, Lenin's own famous call was for a professional vanguard to override mere trade-union consciousness by raising embryonic flashes of understanding to a true revolutionary consciousness. ("There is spontaneity and spontaneity.") And if Lenin did not exalt violence, neither did he deny its efficacy when carefully and selectively used. He ended his call to arms with the demand that the existing, erroneous period of revolutionary activity be "liquidated" so that a new one might be begun. Once more, praxis had become directly activistic, "tactics as a plan" in opposition to (historical) development. With Lenin, too, the guiding image was not of inherently revolutionary praxis (and not just of politics) but of the embattled band, marching down a narrow path, threatened on every side, with every member of the unconverted to be seen as a reactionary enemy. The vanguard; l'avant garde. . . . More recently, with Régis Debray, the military imagery becomes completely literal: the embattled band take to the hills. The rejection of economism and spontaneity, the Manichaean vision of a world with only two alternative forces—Debray uses these elements in such a way that they only sound Leninesque. His war cry goes beyond Lenin's. Failures, not theory, teach how to make a revolution. The stress is on pure tactics, not tactics as a plan (not "strategy"—Debray's rejection of such "intellectual" constructs is almost Sorellian). Praxis becomes military action, which must control every form of the political; the word proletariat comes to designate members of the rural guerrilla, bourgeoisie includes urban workers. To *make* revolution —the phrase is telling. The invocation is at once a distorted echo of Marx's emphasis on material fabrication and a departure into the realm of pure, immediate social creation. Violence as destroyer, purifier, creator—the symbolism is ancient. Violence replaces material productivity and becomes the key to politics, the means for initiation and for new beginnings.[45]

The classic tale of activistic revisionism need not be elaborated further. What is important even in these examples (which are familiar enough in other contexts) is the way they show the curious transformation of both revolution and action and the extraction of a notion of *absolute* beginnings. And the transformation does not end there. The very titles of our previous examples are indicative; so are contemporary ones. Revolution is now forthehellofit. Action becomes a matter of *doing it*. Here, the works speak best for themselves.

Revolution for the hell of it? Why not? It's all a bunch of phony words anyway. Once one has experienced LSD, existential revolution, . . . one realizes that action is the only reality; not only reality but morality as well. One learns that reality is a subjective experience. It exists in my head. I am the Revolution. The other day I took some LSD. . . . There is no way to run a revolution. Revolution is in your head. You are the Revolution. Do your thing. . . . Be your thing. Practice. Rehearsals come after the act. Act. Act. One practices by acting. . . . Only a system has boundaries. . . . A true revolutionist carves the revolution out of Granite Rock. . . . Environment is in your head. Your head is a granite rock of neural impulses, get some dynamite if you need it. . . . The problem is not what to do in the revolution but what to do in between the revolution. . . . The only way to support a revolution is to make your own.[46]

The Revolution is rock and roll; the Revolution is Telegraph Avenue, Berkeley; it is a social and "head" revolution:

Experience taught us to believe in the *Apocalyptic Action*. History could be changed in a day. An hour. A second. . . . Revolution meant the creation of new men and women. Revolution meant a new life. On earth. Today. Life is the act of living. Revolution is the act of revolution. . . .

Amerika says: History is over. Fit in. . . . But for the masses of people throughout the world, history is just beginning. We kids want to start again too, rebuilding from scratch. . . . Act first. Analyze later. Impulse—not theory—makes the great leaps forward. . . . What the yippies learn from Karl Marx . . . is that we must create a spectacular myth of revolution. Goals are irrelevant. The tactics, the actions are crucial. . . . Do. Do. . DO. . . . We are interested in creating a new world. . . . I support everything which puts people in motion, which creates a disruption and controversy, which creates chaos and rebirth. . . . The only exciting and meaningful thing to do in Amerika today is to disrupt her institutions and build new ones.[47]

The Revolution is in your head:

Le rêve est réalité. . . . Mes désirs sont la réalité. . . . Soyez réalistes, dé-
mandez l'impossible. . . . L'imagination prend le pouvoir. . . . Blow up
your mind [sic]. . . . La révolution est incroyable parce que vraie. . . . La
révolution, c'est une initiative. . . . Le nouveauté est révolutionnaire. . . .
Révolution, je t'aime.

Act, do it—

L'ennemi du mouvement c'est le scepticisme. Tout ce qui a été réalisé vient
du dynamisme qui découle de la spontanéité. . . . Il n'est pas de penser Révolutionnaire. Il n'est que des actes Révolutionnaires. . . . L'acte est spontané.
. . . L'action ne doit pas être une réaction mais une création. . . . Créativité,
Spontanéité, Vie. . . . Vibration permanente et culturelle. . . . Ici, on spon-
tane. . . . Frontières = répression. . . . Ne vous calorifiez de vos actes!!!. . . .
Héraclite revient. A bas de Parménide.[48]

Birth, creation, apocalypse, spontaneity, novelty, beginning; doing and Dada,
ideal and surreal, medium, message, myth—a seething stew of witty paraphrase,
half-remembered phrases, ancient allusions. Heraclitus returns—all is beginning.
The resurrection is a perfect symbol. Swirl is king; "The Movement" is all.
Movement *makes* the revolution. Mental dynamite, creative action—there is
only one kind of spontaneity. One no longer even need ask, what is to be done?
You don't need to ask the weatherman which way the wind is blowing.

But what does this mean for politics? "We have learned that Revolution can
be fun, and such wonderful fun that we can use it for our cause. When the
people see how much *spass* it is to throw eggs at America-House, then they'll
be joining us." "Do it all fast. Like slapstick movies. Make sure everyone has
a good time. People love to laugh—it's a riot. Riot—that's an interesting word-
game if you want to play it. . . . I think fun and leisure are great." "The
yippie's idea of fun is over-throwing the government."[49] Epater le bourgeois.
But there are no boundaries, no frontières—and this applies to words too: they
are literally seen as *terms*, things that set limits. Hence words are phony, de-
luding "word-games," la répression grammaticale. And, by the same token,
detailed social doctrine, "ideology," is emphatically rejected. There is only
practice, not theory. Play's the thing. With this license politics is fun, is art, is
life. "The revolution is *now*. We create the revolution by *living* it. . . . We
gotta reduce politics to the simplicity of a rock'n'roll lyric. . . . Our politics
is our music, our smell, our skin, our hair, our warm bodies, our drugs, our
energy, our underground papers, our vision. . . . Politics is how you live
your life, not whom you vote for."

What the fuck does political mean? PO-LI-TI-CAL . . . what if you consider doing your thing as your definition of politics? And what if your thing is what you call politics? We meditated at the Pentagon. How can you define joy — Festival of Joy? . . . Joy is doing what you want to do. Joy is living in history — change that, Joy is *doing* in history. . . .

Politics to me is the way somebody lives his life. . . . I'm more interested in art than politics but, well, see, we are all caught up in the word box. I find it difficult to make these kinds of distinctions.

"L'Etat est chacun de nous. . . . L'action est dans la rue. . . . La politique se passe dans la rue. . . . La poésie est dans la rue. . . . L'art est mort, libérons notre vie quotidienne."[50]

There is more than simple heroism (Fidel, Che, Mao, Ho) here and as much of Groucho as of Karl Marx. But it is an extreme reaction against the reduction of action to materially productive praxis and of revolution to long-run social (productive) process. At the same time, teleological history, dimly absorbed, becomes transmuted into the notion of instantaneous new beginnings; objectification and self-realization becomes dehistoricized and individualized; and in the opposition to ideology, there is a tattered remnant of Marx's opposition to idealist futuristic blueprints. If politics is no longer epiphenomenal, it has become more ambiguous than even in the military imagery of a Lenin, let alone of a Sorel or a Debray. As life, now imitating art, it is both chronology and the absolute birth of "doing." "The Movement is both social process and instant creation — revolution, extended to the last degree, retains a protean compulsion. Praxis becomes the pure creativity of Marx's ultimate postrevolutionary society — but is no more political. *Motion* is omnipotent, sometimes as constant flux, sometimes as apocalyptic frenzy — but is either of these *action*? Paradoxically, motion reigns supreme in activistic as well as academic discourse. A metaphor can decay long before it dies.

It is easy to condemn such manifestations out of hand; and the condemnations have come from many places. For example, from André Malraux, whose words are especially pointed:

You quoted the slogan, *l'imagination au pouvoir*. But that is a joke. Are we, who know the meaning of political reality, to forget the lesson of the whole of our lives? Political power is gained, not by imagination, but by organized political forces . . . we all know, after all, that building a barricade is pure theatre. What are barricades, what are they for? . . . barricades might be called a symbol, but a nineteenth century symbol. A real revolution always develops its own symbols.[51]

But this is all *too* easy. Here one portion of the revolutionary metaphor is opposed to the other; the invocation of "political reality," of "organized political forces" merely begs the crucial questions of vision and rejection of purely patterned activity. And there are potentials, even in the "pure theatre" of recent, massive manifestations of the cult of l'étranger, for recovering a positive sense of politics—as action and as rebellion. More than one metaphor is involved. In Paris, in 1968:

Les barricades . . . délimitent un champ clos, à l'intérieure duquel se creé une conscience des groupes et d'action commune. . . . Le mouvement qui se constitue n'est pas un mouvement politique, attaquant les institutions, mais il est plus qu'une révolte. . . . Il y eut beaucoup de théâtre en mai, à l'Odéon qui ne voulait plus en être un après son occupation . . ., à la Sorbonne, dans la rue. . . . Tout ce théâtre voulut détruire spectaculairement la séparation de l'acteur et du publique. . . .

And in America, in 1967:

Social work theatre is out; play for your own kind—you understand them, and they identify with you. . . . The public is made up of all those who think they see you in them and all those whom you know. . . .

And in Germany, Karl Marx in 1843:

The comedy of despotism being performed with us is just as dangerous for him [the king] as the tragedy once was for the Stuarts and the Bourbons. And even if for a long time we would not see this comedy for what it is, it would still be a revolution. The state is too serious a thing to be made into a harlequinade.[52]

Theater as politics—politics as theater. The dramatic metaphor reverses readily. But the reversal becomes too familiar: degenerating into cliché, it loses both point and impact. Role, performance, action—all remain bothersome. Can an actor really be other than apart from his public? What is an actor's "own kind" —simply the audience of those who already agree with him and merely watch him? A space for the creation of thought and action but not yet political—how political can it be, if confined to the closed, interior, transitory community of the happening? And yet, if comedy can be dangerous, is it not a serious thing indeed? Theater/politics—the *reversal* is crucial: it requires serious scrutiny. Which term is primary and which is analogue? Theories and practices: each term plays off the other, and they generate an infinite series of reflecting mirrors. To see how this is so, how it can be made political, and how it can illuminate action, we must turn from the detailed turmoil to theory of a different kind.

III. Public Action: Buffoonery and Harlequinade

Opposing and moving, revolving and beginning, living and making—these form the background against which we must try to locate action. Here, Hannah Arendt's *The Human Condition* speaks directly to our purpose. While scarcely activistic in conventional terms, it is by no means purely academic—it cuts across that division in provocative ways. For Arendt's aim here is to revive a sense of action and to do so by distinguishing it from other modes of activity. And, in an irony of a sort which by now should be familiar, her own analysis illustrates just how profound the decay of politics and action has become.

For Arendt the human world is indeed a human creation, but its modes of constitution are multiple. She contrasts action, labor, and work as three phenomenologically distinct activities, corresponding to different conditions of human existence. The way of the actor is not only distinct from (and superior to) that of animal laborans and homo faber; the latter two figures have virtually obscured the former in modern times.

Labor corresponds to mere (animallike) life, the cyclical, repetitive biological processes of the body. It is prompted by *necessity*. It assures survival and is thus a constant activity with neither a definite beginning nor a definite end; its products are consumed as a means for continued living, and the process itself ends with the exhaustion of labor-power (with death). And work corresponds to the unnaturalness of human existence, to man's existence in an artificial world of fabricated and enduring things, which provides him with a home. Work is prompted by *utility*. It is a process with both a beginning and an end—a product (a *use*—rather than a consumption-object) for which the process is only a means and in which it terminates. But action is infinitely more complex in its objectification, in its significance, and in its springs. In the first place, it is linked with speech, which corresponds to human "plurality," to the fact that there is a multiplicity of *unique* men. Together with speech, action is the mode whereby men "appear to each other, not indeed as physical objects, but qua men"—whereby men can express their uniqueness and each can "communicate himself and not merely something." In brief, action is distinct from labor and work because only it can be *revelatory*—revelatory of "who" someone is. And this distinctness is critical. For, says Arendt, a man is still human if he refrains from labor (by having others labor for him) or from work (by merely using things, not producing), but without action a man no longer exists as a man among men—he no longer reveals who he is. And this is because Arendt rejects any human essence: existence—manifest, revealed personal existence—is the key to being a man. Hence action can also be seen to correspond to human "natality"—the "new beginning" inherent in the birth of each unique individual, "the beginning which came into the world when we were born and to which we respond by beginning something new on our own initiative." "To act, in its most general sense, means to take an initiative, to begin [*initium*]." And seen thus, in contrast with the definitive and patterned motions of daily labor and work (which Arendt sometimes calls behavior), action appears miraculous. Prompted by *initiative*, action is the principle of freedom: freedom from the necessity and utility of household (oikia, oeconomica) matters.[53]

New beginnings once again—and again, there is more than one thing involved in it. For by the same token as it is beginning, Arendt insists, action is also *uncertain*. Each actor acts into an "intangible web of relationships," consisting of words and deeds, which overlies the world of objects and men's "object-ive" interests. As the actor interacts with this web, a new process emerges which has two crucial dimensions. First, it becomes the actor's story: who he is emerges only in the reactions of others. And thus uncertainty: the actor is almost never able willfully to reveal "himself" as he desires. Who he is ultimately appears only after he is dead; the full meaning of a man's story (self) emerges only to the story-teller after the story (existence) has ended. Second, the actor's action/story adds to the web, establishing new relationships by subtly (and, by definition, uniquely) affecting all other men who come in contact with it. And here action is uncertain in a second sense. It is "boundless" in its consequences, each reaction to it being a new action which in turn "strikes out and affects others," establishing still more relationships; and thus it is also boundless in its capacity to cut through all boundaries, whether fences, walls, borders, or laws. There is a moral here: "this is why the old virtue of moderation, of keeping within bounds, is indeed one of the political virtues par excellence, just as the political temptation par excellence is indeed *hubris* . . . and not the will to power, as we are inclined to believe."[54]

Action is inherently uncertain; it also inherently establishes relationships among men (qua men)—the two are opposite sides of the same activity. Thus presented, action is a perilous, fragile, and unnerving activity but the only fully human one. The parallel with Camus on rebellion is striking, even to the concern with hubris. But Arendt's conception is not founded on an abstract conception of natural community. It is social rather than metaphysical and refers to concrete (though subtle) relationships. Indeed, Arend herself (though without reference to Camus) puts the difference succinctly: "since action is the political activity par excellence, natality, and not mortality, may be the central category of political, as distinct from metaphysical thought."[55]

But just what *are* the political ramifications of Arendt's conception? The answer emerges from the solution Arendt offers for the uncertainty of action. For her, the Greek polis (not the household) is the model. But the polis must not be understood just as the walled, territorial polity, nor even as its system of laws, for these boundaries are no defense. The polis as political realm must be understood as the public realm. And this *public* is more than the "common" (things and activities which simultaneously relate men and keep them from falling over one another). It is also "public-ity"—"it is the *space of appearance* [my italics] in the widest sense of the term, namely the space where I appear to other men as they appear to me" (as men). It assures men of "the reality that comes from being seen, being heard, and generally appearing before an audience of fellow men," and serves as an "organized remembrance" which collectively replaces the poet or semi-official storyteller by multiplying the occasions for men to distinguish themselves as unique and win "immortal glory," thus "mak[ing] the extraordinary an ordinary occurrence of daily life." Here, with the public realm, action can provide *its own* solution to the problem of its uncertainty. For, Arendt tells us, action is "the one activity which constitutes" the public realm. The public realm arises "directly out of acting together, the 'sharing of words and deeds' "; it arises "wherever men are together in the manner of speech and action."[56]

Yet, what sort of solution is this? Thus understood, the political realm remains fragile. Violence, labor, work—the predominance of any of these can destroy action and hence politics. Arendt stresses that it is only men's *continual* willingness to act and speak together which keeps the public in existence. She aptly notes that violence, being speechless, is the antithesis of action—it can only destroy, not create a public realm. And she reminds us that not all men live in the public realm as defined: menials, slaves, jobholders qua jobholders— all those bound to necessity and utility—do not. Indeed, Arendt terms all labor and fabrication unpolitical. Action is the only activity which "lies altogether outside the category of means and ends," because its end (revelation) lies in the activity itself. Any undertaking that lacks the stress on revelation is not action but mere "achievement." Even legislation is not action but only an activity which serves as a "means." It was only with Plato and Aristotle that "the original, pre-philosophical" notion of action was overridden, and legislation was elevated to the rank of politics. And this was because the philosophers wished to flee action for something certain, substituting eternity for immortality and poiesis for praxis.[57]

In fact, all this makes politics even more fragile than Arendt seems to recog-

nize. Though the web of relationships and the public space are powerful perceptions, they appear to approximate more what we normally would call *social*
than political affairs. Arendtian action is purely the revelation of initiative, of
who someone is—her repeated references to glory, immortality, fame are themselves all too revealing. Arendt is led to this extraordinary position by her reading of her Greek model. Only the distinction between free and slavish activities
makes her usage of politics meaningful, for it allows her to contrast free action
(the citizen's life, the bios politikos) with the balance as slavish social matters.
That there was such a free/slavish distinction in Greece is not in question; but
Arendt's reading of it is. It is by no means obvious that the Greeks initially accepted and then (in philosophy) rejected Arendt's peculiar equation between
politics and action.[58] At all events, by reducing politics to action as revelatory
initiative, any other sort of innovation, even a Camusian focus on positive and
purposeful rebellion, slips away. The connections with structure of authority
(either existing *or* alternative), with creative institutional or normative endeavors, with the criticism, alteration, or implementation of public policy all seem
wholly "intangible." On Arendt's view, politics as action becomes activity in
the polity—but not *of, for,* or *by* it.

This suggests that Arendt's distinctions exhaust neither the types nor the
characteristics of human activities. Ultimately, the difficulties seem to arise
from a category mistake. Arendtian action does not have the same logical status
as do labor and work. Even continued reflection prompts no ready example of
Arendtian action: it has more clear *context* than content. Rather than being a
third, specific type of activity, it seems more an *aspect* of men's relations, which
can enter into various kinds of "doing." (At one point Arendt herself comes
close to seeing this but is blinkered by her terms: "action has the *closest* connection with the human condition of natality; the new beginning inherent in
birth can make itself felt in the world only because the newcomer possesses
the capacity of beginning something new. In *this* sense of initiative, an *element*
of action, and therefore of natality, is inherent in *all* human activities.")[59]

Activities of various kinds—the webbed, public space of relationships is vital
but not a sufficiently distinguishing characteristic when treated as a matter of
mere revelation. Arendt fails to draw some further critical distinctions. Laud-
ably intent on distinguishing action from mere motion, Arendt concludes that
action must have nothing to do with fabrication, with product, end, achievement *of* something. But by this device she blurs some significant lines, between
end as *goal* and as *outcome* and between outcome as *fixed* and as *uncertain.*
Note her equation of legislation with wall building; and the alternative phrases

law *giving* and law *making*. Does not the "making" of a law or policy, or the founding of a body politic or organization, have a dynamic aspect? Do not these activities and their "products" have an uncertainty of outcome, an unforeseeable and continuing impact on men's relationships? In quasi-Arendtian terms, such activities might be called public works or public deeds: rather than fitting into any one of her categories, they manifest more complex characteristics. Indeed, there are vicious ambiguities here in Arendt's discussion of action, legislation, and governmental organization. Generally she presents legislation as *pre*political, preceding action; but she also presents it as *post*political, after a public space (which arises from action) already exists; and at one point she inadvertently presents organization as a product of action — a stance wholly inconsistent with her overall thesis.[60]

Thus, even Arendt's efforts to grapple with politics as action show a familiar erosion. With her, praxis has become even less directed than the pure creativity of Marx's aesthetic utopia or the immediate living and doing of contemporary activism. Politics once more seems to have withered away. New beginnings again seems to vitiate a clear and bounded sense of political creativity. Yet our critique of Arendt helps us see that such a sense of creativity is vital, and some of Arendt's notions can help us capture it. Her contrast between violence and speech is surely a fundamental insight: violence marks the boundaries of politics even in Arendt's sense; it indeed is prepolitical or postpolitical. Equally fundamental is her notion of a public space and the implication that action somehow lies between the poles of violence and mere patterned motion. With some revision these notions can bring together the elements of our discussion. They can lead us to see some positively political action as the idiom of public drama, provoking relationships of a particular kind.

There are many types of activity, many roles and many actors. Even in Aeschylus's *Prometheus Bound*, the figure of Violence is portrayed as muta persona, taking no part in the dialogue or action of the drama of rebellion. In the same way, the chains that Zeus has placed on Prometheus are all that "speak" for Zeus. They are a brooding, restrictive presence and only that; their silence is brutally eloquent but affords no possibilities for interchange. Here is a political corollary to Camus's metaphysical and moralistic concern with violence. And here is another portion of the explanation for the figure of the ultimate étranger, Ch'en. There is a vast gulf between recognizing that violence may at times be necessary, as a last resort to resist or remove obstacles, and believing that it is a sufficient agency: the very notion of obstacles signifies a certain loss of human contact. By itself, violence isolates the violator, preventing meaningful speech with other men. Rather than creating, it purges human contact and initiates the actor into a microcosm which is politically absurd. And it is not Arendtian initiative (revelation of who one is) which is crucial to the contact here. Ch'en all too clearly undertakes an initium, a beginning, and other men (even storytellers) can readily talk *about* him and his fate. That a Ch'en has an impact upon the web of relationships is obvious but hardly sufficient for political creativity. There is more than one sense in which men can be together. In much the same way, purely patterned activity, established roles and expectations, reduces the possibilities of meaningful speech. To behave (behabben) is literally to have oneself, to bear oneself in a certain way, to conduct oneself carefully. It is a matter of demeanor, of being channeled or driven. "*Do* behave (well)." Only that talk which is proper (to task or situation) is allowed or heeded.

Violence and behavior each has its place, but these do not exhaust the possibilities. What precisely is the nature of the other possibilities, of the range of political action and its politically public realm? Erving Goffman reminds us that webs of relationships must be seriously scrutinized: "to call any two individuals a 'two-person group' solely because there is a social relationship between them is to slight what is characteristic of groups and to fail to explore what is uniquely characteristic of relationships." Goffman distinguishes between unfocused gatherings (mere common presence without common undertakings) and encounters —situations where men share a common, single focus of attention and are open to mutual monitoring, forming "an eye-to-eye ecological huddle." Encounters are world building—they generate a world of meanings.[61] In similar manner, we can distinguish between an Arendtian theatrical audience and a truly *political public*: the latter is crucial, for it is more than simply joint presence *and* more than joint watching. Here speech is clearly central. And *innovation* rather than merely Arendtian initiative is involved: innovation requires a public (not just a—perhaps posthumous—audience). To innovate (innovare) is to *renew*; it is to "invent" in the original sense of the term, to come upon, to inventory the resources of the culture rather than to contrive absolutely afresh and seek a total new beginning. The broader the public, the greater the impact of innovation on *public authority*: the greater the possibility of altering men's affairs, their focii of attention, their norms and exemplars, their symbols, their structures of command, advice, gesture, and authorization.[62]

With the notion of coming upon, public innovation, the notion of rebellion as tradition reenters. "We cannot say that [encounter] worlds are created on the spot, because . . . use is usually made of traditional equipment having a social history of its own in the wider society and a wide consensus of understanding regarding the meanings that are to be generated from it."[63] Just so. By working in and out of a culture, finding resources there, the rebel as innovating actor transcends sheer behavior or mere violence—and the resources that nourish his action also provide him with a public, with other men who do not find his action wholly strange or alien. Indeed, a rebel's public *cannot* simply reject him as l'étranger and thus remain purely passive spectators, however startled or angry his action may make them. Understood in this way, rebellion is a form of action that is truly political in that it provokes and capitalizes on concrete communities of men. As a directed activity, it is not mere frenzy or motion; having a public, it is not ethereal. It is a mode of dramatic provocation.

Rebellion is *dramatic*: it operates both in and out of a culture by means of public deeds (the original Greek meaning of drama). An example is necessary for us to grasp all that this involves. Consider Leszek Kolakowski's words:

The antagonism between a philosophy that perpetuates the absolute and a philosophy that questions absolutes seems incurable, as incurable as that which exists between conservatism and radicalism in all aspects of human life. This is the antagonism between the priest and the jester. . . . The priest is the guardian of the absolute. . . . The jester is he who moves in good society without belonging to it, and treats it with impertinence. . . . He could not do this if he belonged to good society; he would then be a salon scandal-monger . . .; yet he must frequent good society so as to know what it holds sacred and to have the opportunity to address it impertinently. . . . In every era the jester's philosophy exposes as doubtful what seems most unshakeable, reveals the contradictions in what appears obvious and incontrovertible, derides common sense and reads sense into the absurd.[64]

Kolakowski suggests the full dimensions of rebellion as political action and the full nature of our mutation of Arendtian notions. For the word jester derives from what would seem its absolute antithesis, the Roman gesta—great deeds, famous doings, heroic exploits. The revelation is not so much of who a hero was but of the publicly exemplary nature of his deeds and of the hero as "the doer of (these) deeds." And the jester shows that publics and exemplars can be worked ironically. Originally the professional reciter of gesta, thus taking the name for himself, the jester became their mocker, jeering at fabled exploits, fame, glory, immortality; jest(er) and prank(ster).

Already we have a hint of a fascinating progression—and of a critical form of rebellion. The jester can play two quite different roles. To make this clearer, look at the jester's ancestor, the fool. The fool makes his appearance in very ancient times, in the old world-cycle reenactments, gradually intruding into the once potent and solemn figures of Antagonist and Learned Doctor, finding a fuller role in such popular dramas as the Greek satyr plays and the Roman *Atellanae Fabulae*. He reappears in the medieval "Feast of Fools," the parodies of the awesome mysteries of the mass, and more generally in "Lords of Misrule" in royal courts, legal inns of court, and universities. His appearance, like the transformation of the jester, signifies that things have been turned upside down, the formerly authoritative or sacred having become a source of *mock* heroics or *mock* ritual. Of course, the mockery may be only temporary or limited, itself indicating the fundamental assurance and social certainty of its target. Thus the clercs of the University of Paris defended their Feast of Fools against the authorities: "Barrels of wine will burst, if one does not sometimes open the bung or the tap, to give them air. Now we are of old vessels and barrels poorly bound, which the wine of *sagesse* will rupture, if we let it boil thus by a continual devotion to Divine service. . . . It is for that reason that we give several days to play and buffooneries [bouffonneries], thus to return with more joy and fervor to the study and exercises of Religion."[65] But the very need for defense showed the potential: social security is not assured. Mere play can become something else. And the Church knew this full well: it owed one of its own martyrs and saints to a serious reversal. Philomen, professional fool-mime in the Egyptian city of Antinoe, was employed by a Christian, during Diocletian's persecutions, to take his place in submitting to the mandatory state rites. Philomen began the religious test as surrogate and mocker but then transformed his role. "The prefect, looking into his eyes, was suddenly startled to find there such a gleam of steady and triumphant light as showed him that no longer was he confronted by the buffoonery of a clown."[66] Mockery and parody can become serious and seriously disconcerting. Thus, the Christmas fools' festival of the boy bishop was banned by the Council of Basel in 1431. And when such official bans were extended, lay sociétés joyeuses sprang up to continue the reversals.

To some degree, the same serious potential is evident even in the jester, as official court fool. He feigns the simplicity of the village idiot or divine fool whose words suggest a wisdom beyond that of men who are clever in the ways of the world, the path of learned ignorance, the negative way to truth. The jester was "usually physically deformed and by profession sober, so that while his body stood as a living symbol of imperfection arousing laughter, his words must have stung by pointing satirically to the imperfections of others which had been kept, and it was hoped would remain, better concealed than his own." In all this, the jester, like all comedians, can be called a sort of rebel against conventional works and wisdoms.[67]

The most famous English jester-fool suggests this rebellious aspect, in a typical passage.

Prince Hal: I see a good amendment of life in thee: from praying to purse-snatching.
Falstaff: Why Hal, 'tis my vocation Hal. 'Tis no sin for a man to labour in his vocation.[68]

But there are many vocations and many sins. Praying and preying do not exhaust the possibilities; and Falstaff's own fate sounds a warning. Kolakowski himself notes that the jester can be either an aristocrat's toy and mere entertainer or one whose "antics have played a part in earthquakes." But he fails to develop the distinction; and he uses the term tradition in the sadly familiar manner— indeed, in terms almost identical with Camus's, as "the cult of the final and the absolute."[69] To make the connection with rebellion explicit and to distinguish it from entertainment, I shall replace Kolakowski's jester with two figures— the Buffoon and the Harlequin.

The Buffoon is the simplest sort of fool. He is a noisy fellow, full of sheer motion and wind. (The etymology of fool and buffoon seem identical: follem/ follis, bellows, hence windbag; buffare, puff, hence buffone and buffo.) Today this type is rampant, his frenzy widespread. Whatever his intentions, when he is not a mere annoyance he is readily *used* for entertainment—he becomes a commodity for consumption by the media. (Similarly, speaking of encounters, Goffman comments that an offender against the common focus of attention can be dealt with by "redefining the situation around the plight of the offender, but treating him now *not as a participant but as a mere focus of attention*—in fact, as an involuntary performer."[70])

But the Harlequin is a more complex and very different figure. He redirects attention, using rather than being used. He moves between theatrical and social drama. His origins are obscure; he is developed in the Commedia dell'arte as outwitter of the clever and challenger of the prevailing ethos, a mischievous and shrewd intriguer, with something unsettling about him. In Paris, playing, within a play, at being a commissaire, he announces "I'm a rascal" and proceeds to trick the pleaders, so outraging one honest citizen, a M. Lefrançois, that he leaves the theater to complain to the police — "what will happen to their offices, so important both for the service of the king and for that of the public?"[71] In London, he so mocks Sir Robert Walpole's intended Excise Act that Walpole descends on him backstage, beats him, and obtains the Lord Chancellor's control over future performances of Royal Companies.[72] He reverses poverty and wealth, freedom and slavery, telling the theater: "you are poverty stricken, since you limit your wealth to money or deviltries of that kind. . . . You are the slaves of your possessions, that you value above your liberty and your fellow men."[73]

But Harlequin stands for more than this sort of satire. Says one of his classic persona: "I am as impudent as a devil."[74] Indeed, Harlequin has to do with more than "wealth or money or deviltries of *that* kind." His name and original, sinister hairy mask ultimately may be derived from demonic lore and legend. His ancestor figures in the late medieval danse macabre, where drama takes to the streets in a time of social turmoil, with birth and death, social and ultimate authority gyrating in figure; the green in his motley dress originally may have symbolized eternal youth. Certainly, Harlequin is fool and jester at their most serious and potent. Of him can truly be said what commentators have sometimes suggested of the fool but is only partly intimated there. He truly possesses a sort of "omnipotence . . . inherited from the omnipotence of the demon. The uncanny and the comic are similar, as we may see in the derivation of many Europeans words which can mean both (as drôle in French and Komisch in German). Comedy is double-edged."[75] Harlequin, not the fool, is truly "not all there" in the sense that "the rest of him is away in dim communion with Unknown Powers, or worse still, that part of him has been pushed out to make room for an alien spirit." He truly is the "foe of fact" as defined by the puritan or businessman; he is a menace to the world.[76] He can be, not merely, but *profoundly* unsettling.

Second Justice: I think this Harlequin comes within the Statue of Incorrigible Rogue—He's an Old Offender. . . .

First Justice: This Fellow is a Vagabond; 'tis true; but he is Son to No-body—Servant to No-body—Belongs to No-Body. Comes from No-where, and is going to No-where. And we none of us, no none of us, know nothing at all about him.

Constable: I wish we were well rid of him, for under favour—I don't think he's of this world. He is certainly something as I may say of the Magic Order about him.[77]

Harlequin is not of this world—the customary, established human world, seemingly fixed and given. His world has been called grotesque, the estranged world where familiar objects become unfamiliar, unreliable, and strangely ominous; as with the fool, he inverts the world, but he does so chillingly, in a frightening manner.[78] By extension from theater to society, Harlequin's invasion upsets men precisely because he works a kind of magic on their normal patterns of thought and life. He truly lives in without being a part of Kolakowski's "good society." And (in Kolakowski's phrase) he *both* "derides common sense" and "reads some sense into the absurd." He is not l'étranger but the opposite. He acts in and on a public, provoking men to unnerving visions of their customary doings, building a world rather than entertaining or merely (negatively) disrupting. And to do this, Harlequin must know and use the alternative resources of the cultural tradition of his society.

Harlequinade thus emerges as a model for rebellion: a form of innovating activity (action), directed at and occurring in a public, touching on public authority. To speak of action and roles in this way is to revive the dramatic metaphor, too often buried beneath systemic or behavioral jargon. Indeed, in a critical sense, harlequinade captures *drama* aside from *theater.* " 'Theater' is largely concerned with *communication* between actors and audience: 'drama' is largely concerned with *experience* by the participants, irrespective of any function of communication to an audience."[79] This comes close but misses the fundamental point. The two terms have different axes and directions of attention; in somewhat special senses, one is a practice, the other a theory word. For while *drama* stresses action, doing, deeds, *theater* stresses being a watcher, a spectator, beholding, with connotations of passivity (its Greek cognates are of course theoria and theoric fund; in archaic English, books could still be titled theaters — view or perspectives — of a subject). Harlequinade as drama does not depend on an audience of theatrical spectators but upon the *joint* experience of a public. True, the democratization and sheer complexity of modern society have undermined older theatrical emphasis on the individual, heroic character's great deeds and replaced that figure with everyman.[80] But socially and politically, this simply shows another way in which a public, rather than an audience is crucial: The Harlequin is not The Hero (not Achilles or even Che) but depends upon and works within his public for his action. His epics are not his alone, but everyman's, truly in the public domain.

Nowhere do these distinctions assume more importance than in positive rebellion: epic may still make (remake) epoch. One American critic-producer speaks of theater as trying to "reconstitute the perceptions and conceptions" of its audience; but adds — "This may not happen." More systematically, Jerzy Grotowski calls theater an enterprise in "challenging" the audience by "violating accepted stereotypes," as did medieval "sacred parody." But he adds, "The audience — all Creons — may well side with Antigone through the performance, but this does not prevent each of us from behaving like Creon once out of the theater." And he thus concentrates on educating only actors, not the audience, for the latter cannot be educated.[81] The logic here, by its very impeccability, shows the gap between stage performance and Harlequin's drama. Ironically, even Brecht's efforts to devise an epic theater through a Verfremdungs (aliena-tion, estrangement) effect foundered on the gap between audience and public, theatrical and political action. It is Harlequin who reverses the effect—puts it right side up: not *lack* of identification by audience with actor, stage, and action (and by actor with character) but identification by the public with a political world become strange and alien. Not Harlequin but the public world appears (politically) absurd. The same cannot always be said of theater. Especially in rebellion, one begins to suspect that theater must be understood from politics, not vice versa.[82] As with the danse macabre, theatrical drama generally may well emerge from social transformation[83] —but the reversal, the emergence of social transformation from political drama, is more "significant," in both senses of the word.

Harlequinade emerges as a model of rebellion, reviving dramatic action. In so doing, it also prompts a sense that there are different types of drama, of which only some are truly (affirmatively) political. The "Surrealist Revolution," wrote Antonin Artaud, "aims to break up logic and disqualify it. . . . It aims to reclassify things spontaneously." Here the mystique of revolution as life (together with a frustrated rejection of language) was connected with a burning desire to revive theater, to thrust it back into life, and thus to revive life as well. The theater has its double. And Artaud's notions, like so many others, have found distorted echoes in contemporary activism.[84] All too often, recent events have seemed a too fleshly enactment of Artaud's Theater of Cruelty. Terms like "creative disorder" or "psychological guerrilla warfare" have tended to mask, at best, buffoonery; at worst, mere disruption, mere frenzy rather than publicly innovating action. (Again: rejection is not enough; and a cult is not a culture.) To be sure, much of the cruelty has occurred because the audience has participated—with a vengeance. But this in itself should indicate the absence of that *public* which is so vital for innovation of a truly political kind to occur.

The human world is a human creation. . . . I have tried to suggest that there is sense in the old phrase—but that no simple activity, no single or final act, no unbridled innocence, and no absolutely novel forging can be the key for politics. Political action is a form of meaningful activity—I have tried to show that the theoretical perspective here can also be practically important, vital for political actors no less than analysts. Harlequin's deeds make public works. His action is seriously symbolic; his acts and words are modes for the reconstruction of political worlds. The trope of language, so often invoked by Camus,[85] does have a potent and positive content, in method and in deed. Politi-cal action has its boundaries—hence the need for it is constant and continual.

Its positive thrust is never complete. And, as with all innovation, its practice has an element of uncertainty. Figure, trope, symbol; turn, reversal, identification — revolving and beginning, the double always doubles. Behind all harlequinade looms the primordial Harlequin: Death in life, symbol of irremediable motley, limit of all achievement. In Camus's phrase, "The real is not entirely rational, nor is the rational entirely real."[86] Indeed, to identify the nature of rebellion, even of harlequinade, as I have tried to do, is neither to call for it from all sectors (it can serve many and opposing aims) nor to assert that it is always possible. For better or for worse, we live now in Dionysian rather than Apollonian times. It may be that all publics are too far destroyed, fear and impatience too great in some places for anything but frenzy or static motion to occur. A polar night of icy darkness may yet lie before us. Will men be bitter or banausic? Will they dully accept their established roles? Or will they escape into Heraclitean spasms? In any of these cases, politics as action will have disappeared — and with it, meaningful and positive rebellion.

IX

How People Change Themselves: The Relationship between Critical Theory and Its Audience[1]

Brian Fay

I

Max Weber was certainly correct in characterizing modern life in terms of the self-conscious spread of zweckrational action. The relationship between theory and practice has assumed in industrial society a distinctly instrumentalist nature, and engineering has come to embody our conception of how knowledge can guide our actions, not only in the natural world but also in our medical practices, political institutions, and dealings with the psychological states of others and even ourselves. And no matter what the causes of this process are, living as we do in a world which depends on, and is dedicated to promoting, our ability to control natural and social processes, it is extremely difficult to conceive of scientific knowledge as useful in any other way except in providing the means by which we can manipulate one state of affairs to produce another, desired state of affairs. A result of the way we live is that we have come to identify this *one* form of rational activity with the whole class of rationally informed and justified action.

This is a most unfortunate situation because it blinds us to alternative ways that knowledge may be relevant to our lives: it leads us to formulate and value only one kind of theoretical knowledge; and it encourages a kind of domination.

Note. This essay was written while on a Joint Research Grant from the National Endowment for the Humanities, RO-22106-75-139. The argument presented here does not necessarily represent the views of the NEH.

in our social lives which has a crippling and enslaving effect on those to whom science had promised an increase in power and freedom.

These are large claims which I cannot justify here. I make them to provide a setting for what follows in this essay. A great deal of what is important in our lives is at stake in this discussion. Certain epistemological ideas about theory and practice are not only philosophically curious but also intellectually damaging, because they foreclose the possibility of alternative types of social theory, and politically dangerous, because they help to support such ordinary social practices as "behavior modification" and "thought reform" and to rationalize the propaganda and mass murder which have become so common in the revolutionary movements of the the Left and the Right in the twentieth century.

The aim of this paper is to present an alternative model of the relationship between theory and practice (I shall call it the "educative model") with the hope that it will serve as a corrective to the dominant model in our time (which I shall call the "instrumentalist model"). In Part II I shall present a simplified version of the educative model in which an absolute distinction is drawn between it and its instrumentalist counterpart. Then in Parts III, IV, and V I shall gradually modify and amend this original statement of the educative model by posing and answering three objections to it, objections whose force is the claim that the educative model is really just a form of instrumentalism after all. One result of this analysis will be to enrich and clarify the educative model; another will be to blur the distinction between the educative and the instrumentalist models. Nevertheless, this distinction remains crucial; for, as I shall show in Part VI, the educative model is still capable of showing how a social theory can be used to bring about social change in a nonelitist and nonmanipulative manner, and in this it provides a stark contrast to the idea of social change that the instrumentalist advances. I will conclude with a few remarks on what further needs to be done to complete the educative model before it can be considered fully satisfactory (Part VII).

The central question of the essay is whether there is a way in which our theoretical thinking about man and society may be employed to guide our actions (and especially actions designed to change social practices) without at the same time encouraging a manipulative role for those in possession of this theory.[2]

II

Of what practical use is social theory? An instrumentalist would give something like the following answer. Theoretical knowledge is useful because of the *power* it confers on those who learn its truths; this power is rooted in a certain kind of knowledge which gives people the capacity to *control* their social environment or the behavior, feelings, and thoughts of others by being able either to produce a particular event or to prevent its occurrence.

How this is possible becomes clear when one realizes the form that the instrumentalist believes social theories will assume. Just as in the natural sciences, social theories will consist of universal, well-confirmed empirical hypotheses of conditional form which state that under certain specified conditions, if the state of affairs C_n occurs, a state of affairs of the type E will also occur or will occur with a probability P. Because social theories assume this form, their explanations of social and psychological phenomena are structurally identical with predictions about the occurrence of these phenomena. With explanation, an event is known to have occurred, and the general laws and statements about particular facts from which a description of it can be deduced are sought; with prediction, statements of the relevant general laws and the particular facts are given, and the statement describing a particular event not yet known to have occurred is deduced from them. A prediction is thus simply the obverse of an explanation.

Now its ability to predict is the key to the power of any social theory, for this ability allows one to know that if one alters one state of affairs, another state of affairs will be correspondingly altered; and this means that one can bring about states of affairs that one desires or prevent the occurrence of other states of affairs that one dislikes by manipulating the conditions that produce or prevent them. By knowing what conditions are responsible for what events and by altering these conditions in the prescribed manner, one has the power to control events. As Comte put it epigrammatically one hundred and fifty years ago: "From Science comes Prevision, from Prevision comes Control."

The instrumentalist conception depends on a naturalist metatheory of social science, i.e., a metatheory which asserts that there is no difference in principle between the logical form that knowledge assumes in both the natural and the social sciences. Essentially, this naturalist perspective is a nomological one because it insists that an explanation of an event requires a knowledge of those laws in virtue of which a particular event occurred; explanations must show precisely how a puzzling event is part of a regularly recurring lawful process, and hypotheses adduced as possible explanations must consequently be such that one can predict future events. It is thus no accident that philosophers whose epistemology is essentially a philosophy of natural science also put forward an instrumentalist conception of theory and practice when they discuss the usefulness and point of achieving knowledge;[3] Hobbes is a good example:

Science is the Knowledge of Consequences, and the dependence of one fact upon another: by which, out of what we can presently do, we know how to do something else when we will, or the like, another time: Because when we see how anything comes about, upon what causes and by what manner: when the like causes come into our power, we see how to make it produce the like effects. (*Leviathan*, Part I, Chap. 5)

The instrumentalist conception of theory and practice is clearly a manipulative conception because it is rooted in the conviction that there are certain sets of naturally recurring general regularities which can be used to achieve one's purposes by altering one set of conditions to effect another. Social theory provides the basis for a social engineering with which one can rationally control objective processes through the manipulation of independent variables.

Not only is the instrumentalist conception a manipulative one, but it is ordinarily (though not necessarily) an authoritarian one as well. This is true for at least two reasons. First, it requires that those who employ theoretical knowledge possess the requisite expertise and skills, and, since acquiring these calls for a specialized education, this encourages the emergence of a knowledgeable elite. Second, it presupposes that those who are knowledgeable are in positions of power so that they can alter social conditions to control social and psychological processes.

The particular political and psychological theories of social control that have incorporated this instrumentalist model are many and diffuse, but all are characterized by a basic manipulative elitism of the kind I have been discussing. Given a larger format, I think it could easily be shown that among the doctrines sharing an instrumentalist conception of theory and practice are Lenin's theory of revolution, Skinner's theory of behavior modification, Mannheim's (and Saint-Simon's and Comte's) vision of a scientific politics, Keynes's general theory of employment, Robert Owen's conceptions of socialism, as well as the more mundane (and perhaps more dangerous) set of beliefs underlying and legitimizing normal bureacratic practices of economic planning, much mental-hospital administration, treatments of delinquents and prisoners, and so on. All of these conceive of social theory as revealing those conditions which must be altered to produce a desired state of affairs, and all reveal an underlying assumption that, because of their expertise, some members of the social order should control others.

Today it is difficult to think of an alternative to this instrumentalist position. "What other way can genuinely scientific knowledge be practical?" is often a reaction to being asked to reconsider the instrumentalist case. Not only is this an indication of how deep the rationalization, which Weber said characterized the modern world, has progressed, but it is also a symptom of the impoverishment of thought which this process causes. For there are many alternatives to instrumentalism which have been given throughout human history.[4] Here I intend to offer as an alternative what I will call the educative model: I think, for reasons too complicated for the compass of this essay, that a certain form of it, and it alone, offers the only plausible option to the instrumentalist model, given the structures and attitudes of contemporary life.

According to the educative model, theoretical knowledge is useful to the extent that it informs people what their needs are and how a particular way of living is frustrating these needs, thereby causing them to suffer; its goal is to enlighten people about how they can change their lives so that, having arrived at a new self-understanding, they may reduce their suffering by creating another way of life that is more fulfilling. In the instrumentalist model, social theories increase power by providing appropriate knowledge in terms of which one can manipulate the causal mechanisms that characterize a certain social order so that a desired end state is produced; in the educative model, social theories are the means by which people can liberate themselves from the particular causal processes that victimize them precisely because they are ignorant of who they are.

Perhaps a good place to begin filling in the background without which this thumbnail sketch would be totally inadequate is by seeing how the educative model is committed to a belief in the causal efficacy of ideas in producing and sustaining forms of human behavior. It is so committed in an obvious and a not-so-obvious way. The educationist obviously believes that his analysis can be effective insofar as it leads to a new self-understanding by the audience to which it is directed. In other words, the educative model is predicated on the notion that changing people's basic understanding of themselves and their world is a first step in their radically altering the self-destructive patterns of interaction that characterize their social relationships.

But this leads directly into the not-so-obvious way that the educative model is committed to the causal role of ideas; this can be seen in what its holders must assume about the causes of people's suffering in a given social order, if indeed their hopes of eliminating it in the way just outlined can be justified. For to think that enlightenment can be the beginning of liberation, the educationist must assume that frustrating and repressive forms of social interaction can continue to wreak their havoc on the people who engage in them partly because these people, systematically ignorant of their own needs, unwittingly participate in sustaining these forms of interaction. Certain causal chains between particular sorts of social structure and particular sorts of behavior that are unfulfilling have as one of their elements certain general self- (mis)understandings of the actors; hence, alter these self-understandings by presenting to people an alternative conceptualization of their situation, and one has taken the first step toward breaking the causal chains which are frustrating people and in which they are unwitting accomplices.

Of course, such an analysis is always liable to degenerate into a naive idealist theory which fails to take into account that the kind of ignorance it is seeking to overcome itself plays a role in the forms of social interaction that are producing the suffering.[5] In other words, particular social forms not only presuppose a kind of ignorance (as I said above), but they also give rise to it in the first place and sustain it as long as a person participates in this form. Thus it is no accident that a certain social order that is repressive and that causes unhappiness can continue to operate with the unwitting collusion of those whom it frustrates, for this order produces in its members just the sort of false consciousness required for them to continue to participate in their own misfortune. (Usually this is not a deliberate conspiracy by those who control the system but is instead the end of result of a process of internalization by which the systematic ignorance of one generation, incorporated into its basic values, norms, and beliefs, becomes part of the new generation's self-understanding—and even the basis for its institutional innovations and reforms.)

I will return to this question of the embeddedness of self- (mis)understandings in concrete social structures when I discuss the problem of resistance in Part IV. But at this point it is important to recognize that there exists a version of the educative model that tries to steer a middle course between the idealism of some of its versions, which claims that ideas are the determinants of social structure but not vice versa, and the epiphenomenalism of traditional materialism, which claims that social structure determines ideas but not vice versa. The educative model attempts to synthesize these positions by claiming that ideas are a function of social conditions but also that they do in turn play a causal role in creating and sustaining particular social structures; it tries to see the relationship of conditions and ideas as a dialectical one. But how this synthesis actually works out in what is today called critical theory will only become clear as I move through the arguments of Parts III-V.

It is crucial to realize at this point that the assumption of the educationist about the causal efficacy of ideas is not arbitrary. Such an assumption can be rationally supported by drawing attention to the by now well-known conceptual distinction between action and movement. To identify an action (like voting) as opposed to a mere bodily movement (like a person's arm rising), the intention embodied in the action and the meaning which the agent attaches to it must be understood. It is not enough in identifying and describing an action to know the physical movements that comprise it, since no set of physical movements is ever a sufficient condition for performing a particular action; only in certain circumstances and when people are in certain mental states can particular movements count as an action of a certain sort. (One may pull the voting-machine handle and thereby vote for a candidate, or one may perform the same movements and still not be voting—one may be acting in a movie or fixing the machine, for instance.) Furthermore, an agent's intentions are logically inseparable from his beliefs; thus the action of voting presupposes a whole web of beliefs about the political process and how one particpates in it. The upshot of these considerations is that *some self-interpretation will be at least implicit in all the actions a person performs.*[6] Apart from a person's conceptions of himself and his society, his beliefs about his role, the meaning of particular movements, the norms governing particular situations, and his understanding of what his needs are and what will satisfy his desires, there is literally no action that a person can be said to have performed. It is on the basis of considerations like these that the educative model grounds its assumption that altering basic action-guiding beliefs by criticizing them may lead to altering the behavior they produce.

The educative model is rooted in the idea that repressive and frustrating social conditions exist at least partly because people are systematically unclear about their needs and the nature of their social relationships. By helping to remove this unclarity by revealing to people how their own false pictures of themselves and of society are a contributory cause of their own unhappiness, the educationist intends to be the catalytic agent who sparks these people into changing the way they live and react to others. In this account, knowledge plays a role in the lives of people which is fundamentally different from that which it plays in the instrumentalist model: it doesn't increase power by informing people how to achieve their ends by getting certain causal relationships to work for them; rather, it is intended to free these people from certain causal relationships. No longer must some people be the unwitting dupes of certain causal processes which result in their suffering only because they are ignorant of their real needs and, because of this ignorance, participate in these repressive processes; instead, by increasing their self-knowledge and rethinking the meaning that certain practices have for them, they have taken the first step in transcending these causal processes.[7]

Both the instrumentalist and the educative models promise freedom; but in the former it is the freedom that results from knowing how to achieve what one wants, whereas in the latter it is the freedom to be self-determining in the sense of being able to decide for oneself, on the basis of a lucid, critical self-awareness, the manner in which one wishes to live. In the educative model, the practical result of social theory is not the means for greater manipulative power but rather the self-understanding that allows one's own rational thinking to be the cause of one's actions; i.e., social theory is a means toward increased *autonomy*.

For theoretical knowledge to be practical in a way that conforms to the educative model and that does not degenerate into a naive idealism, a metatheory different from the naturalist one I mentioned in connection with the instrumentalist model must come to serve as an account of the nature of social science. One such metatheory is called critical theory; I am most interested in it because, while it claims that social theory can be efficacious by enlightening its audience, it also seeks to overcome the obvious moralism of other (idealist) metatheories which are also committed to the educative model of theory changing practice but which fail to appreciate that ideas are themselves a function of external conditions. This is why I subtitled the paper "The Relationship between *Critical Social Theory* and Its Audience" and not "An Examination of the Educative Model of Theory and Practice." In trying to show that social theory can be revolutionary without being manipulative and elitist, I really mean social theory of a particular sort, namely, critical theory. In the rest of the paper, therefore, I will be examining only one version of the educative model.

In this essay I cannot elaborate on this alternative metatheory, though I have tried to do so elsewhere.[8] But based on what I have said so far, as well as some remarks I will make later, I think it would be useful to enumerate those features which distinguish it from the naturalist metatheory. Critical theory insists that social science is in fact a science (in the sense of offering systematic theories to explain the underlying interconnections between social institutions and the behavior, feelings, and beliefs of their members, theories which can be tested against intersubjectively verifiable empirical evidence); however, it also maintains that: first, social theory must try to explain the *sufferings* of a class of people; second, drawing on the distinction between action and movement, a social theory will contain an *interpretative account* of the meanings of actions and practices; third, recognizing the causal role of beliefs, motives, desires, and other psychological states and processes, social theory will provide *quasi-causal* accounts of the relationships between social structures and kinds of behavior;[9]

fourth, believing that the suffering of people results from the inability of their form of life to satisfy their real desires, such theory must give a *historical account* of how the relevant social actors came to be what they are, i.e., having certain needs (about which they are ignorant) they are trying to satisfy but cannot, given the forms of social interaction in which they engage; fifth, rooted in the assumption that frustrating and repressive social practices can continue to exist at least partly because of the false consciousness of those who engage in them, a social theory must be built around an *ideology-critique* which seeks to show that the basic categories in terms of which the relevant people think of themselves are incoherent or inadequate and therefore doomed to lead to unhappiness as long as they guide these people's lives; sixth, assuming that ideas can change people's lives only under certain social conditions, a social theory must offer a *theory of crises* as a way of explaining why the dissatisfaction of the people will have become such that they will be ready to listen to the ideology-critique and to change their social order on the basis of this critique; seventh, it must provide *a theory of communication* that explains how people can come to have a false consciousness and that lays out the conditions necessary to satisfy for them to be disabused of their illusions;[10] and eighth, it must furnish an *action-plan* that seeks to show social actors how to act differently and therefore achieve the satisfactions for which they so yearn.

A number of social theories of the past hundred years meet all or most of these conditions: I am thinking of Marx's theory of capitalism, Freud's theory of neurosis, Habermas's theory of late capitalism,[11] and Laing's theory of schizophrenia. All of these are today regarded by the mainstream university social scientists as either on the weird fringe of "real" social science or as patent pseudoscience. I mention them as concrete instances of another conception of social science, not because I think they are all true (I don't) but as a way of demonstrating that there are ongoing research programs that ostensibly meet criteria radically different from those found in the naturalist tradition.

Now one of the strongest rationales for continuing to think of social science in a purely naturalist way is the belief that the only viable conception of theory and practice is the instrumentalist one;[12] it is for this reason I said in my introduction that the instrumentalism that marks our culture blinds us to alternative ways of thinking about social theory. Coming to appreciate that an alternative educative model exists may well be one way of *coming to rethink what a good social theory should look like* (which involves having a different metatheory of social science and, perhaps more important, different heroes). From my point of view this would be a liberating move, not only because it would lead to better theories but also because — in this rationalistic age when people seek to order their social arrangements on the basis of their knowledge—it may ultimately result in the purposeful creation of social practices free of the domination and repression that today characterizes not only our social life but, ironically, most of our attempts to free ourselves from this miserable condition as well.

III

To all of this an instrumentalist might well reply that the distinctiveness of the educative model is only apparent but not real. The basis for such a reply would probably be this: when the educationist claims that appropriate social theories can enlighten the subjects of these theories about how they can free themselves from the power of certain causal mechanisms which are responsible for their suffering, the educationist just means he hopes to provide information to the agents about the external conditions that produce their misery so that by manipulating these external conditions, the relevant psychological states will not be forthcoming. And this is, after all, a use of scientific knowledge which is fully accounted for by the instrumentalist model of theory and practice.[13]

The instrumentalist may point to Stuart Hampshire's little book, *Freedom of the Individual*,[14] as an instance of just the point he is trying to make. For in a book that tries to give an essentially noninstrumentalist and nonnaturalist account of the relationship among knowledge, beliefs, action, and freedom are found the following remarks:

The felt needs, impulses, the cravings, the moods, the sudden passions which descend upon me, cannot be reliably anticipated when their causes are unknown. But if their causes are understood within some systematic theory of the mind's working, and their incidence reliably predictable, new decisions are called for. Now knowing that allowing oneself to be in a certain physical state will lead to a certain mental state, one will be said to have allowed this state of mind to occur. (p. 89).

In fact, Hampshire claims that such a "systematic theory" will allow us to control our own inner states indirectly:

The kind of psychological knowledge that gives us systematic understanding of the causes of desires, attitudes, and other states of mind can be put to use, either in manipulation and control of others, or in self-control, that is, in a man's contriving by some technique that his state of mind and disposition should in future be as he wants them to be. (p. 93).

Here we have a clear statement of an engineering conception of knowledge and feeling/action. The scientifically informed person treats himself (as well as others) as an object that operates according to naturally recurring general pat-terns, and produces feelings and subsequent actions by altering the antecedent conditions that, his theory has told him, cause them. And so Hampshire gives the example of ridding oneself of certain irrational and upsetting fears by learn-ing what situations cause them and either altering or avoiding these situations (p. 84), and he claims that we should cope with a self-defeating disposition to be vacillating and weak-willed in the same mannter (pp. 90-91).[15]

Now the educationist would surely disagree that this is an adequate portrayal of the role he hopes his theories will play in the lives of those for whom he is writing. For he intends that the discovery of certain regularities between exter-nal conditions and actors' feelings and behavior will be a prolegomenon to their *elimination*, not the basis of a technique by which these actors can *accommo-date* themselves to them. The point of a critical theory is to free people from causal mechanisms that had heretofore determined their existence in some important way, by revealing both the existence and precise nature of these mechanisms and thereby depriving them of their power. This is what is meant by the often heard remark that critical theory seeks to aid people who are ob-jects in the world in transforming themselves into active subjects who are self-determining.

These aspirations are founded on the fact that external conditions are always mediated by a person's ideas and values, as well as on the fact that what a per-son wants is at least partly a function of his own self-understanding. By mediate I mean that how an external condition will affect a particular person will de-pend on the meaning that this situation has for the person, so in a sense the very identity of the external conditions for the person is in part a result of his interpretations of it. For this reason, how one conceives of his situation and understands himself in relation to it is of fundamental importance in the causal process linking particular conditions and particular actions.

This of course does not entail the obviously false claim that for people to act they must be able to articulate just which of their self-conceptions are re-sponsible for their behavior. One would only think this claim follows from what I have said if one equated ideas with self-consciously articulated ideas, and, after the work of Freud and Wittgenstein, there is no need to make such a mistake ever again. Indeed, just this distinction lies at the heart of the educa-tive model, for it is rooted in the belief that our ignorance of ourselves is respon-sible for the situation in which, in a certain sense (i.e., unconsciously), we per-mit certain conditions to make us feel and act in ways that are self-destructive or anxiety producing, and yet, in another sense (i.e., consciously), we are victims of these conditions and their causal force just because we do not know how to relieve ourselves of our suffering. In other words, certain causal processes that produce suffering in a person can continue to operate even though their efficacy depends on the beliefs and values of this same person just because he is unaware that some of his (mis)conceptions about himself give a situation its causal force.

Perhaps a crude example will help show how changing one's self-understanding can liberate one from social processes that cause one to suffer; I will use the example of self-knowledge helping a person free himself from the power of advertising. Let us take the case of a person who devotes a great deal of his energy to acquiring more and better consumer goods. He is constantly planning to buy some item or other; he spends much of his time either working for money to purchase these items or shopping for them, his daydreams and fantasies revolve around winning the lottery and the new houses and boats which his winning would enable him to buy; and so on. Now it is on such a person that advertising gimmicks and propaganda are phenomenally successful. By using certain techniques, manufacturers can make this person want and buy their goods.

For the sake of argument, assume that this person is unhappy and dissatisfied with his existence. Life seems empty; the short-lived pleasure of acquiring a new object affords no lasting contentment; his career seems to be a treadmill. Also assume that his misery reaches such a point that he goes to an analyst for help. There, through a series of discussions informed by a particular social theory—a process not without its own pain—this person comes to the insight that his buying of consumer goods is really only an attempt to reach sexual satisfaction and to cope with his lack of it. Moreover, he also comes to understand that his rampant consumerism could never satisfy his need for sexual fulfillment; for that, he is going to have to relate to people in different ways, and to do this a much deeper and more systematic understanding of why he is sexually frustrated and of what sexual satisfaction consists, and of his illusions and why he has those illusions, will be necessary. He consequently must embark on the long educative process of psychoanalysis.

Now how can such a process of enlightenment free him from the causal power of advertising? It can do so precisely because this power is itself dependent upon the ignorance of the person in question. The advertisers are successful because they are able to tap the sexual needs of the consumer, and they are able to tap these needs just because the consumer has unconsciously been associating the satisfaction of these needs with the acquisition of consumer goods.

Indeed, the consumer is not just ignorant of his needs; he actually subscribes to an altogether different account of what he is after—he thinks that all he wants is a better stereo, or whatever—and this belief helps blind him to the real meaning of his activity. Of course, the advertisers are not so ignorant; they know exactly what they are doing, for their ads contain a heavy, if disguised, sexual content. When the consumer comes to see advertising for what it is—a process which could get him to act just because it tacitly promised a certain kind of satisfaction—and when he adopts a new self-understanding and attendant way of life which precludes his ever again infusing consumer goods with the power to satisfy his sexual needs, he will have freed himself from the advertisers' power because he no longer will be seeking sexual satisfaction in such a surrogate manner.

Here we have an instance of knowledge freeing someone from a causal process that contributed to his suffering. The causal process was an advertisement with a hidden message (which said, "buy this product and you will be sexually satisfied") making a person want to buy the relevant product. Knowledge undermined this process by allowing the person to recognize both the hidden message in the advertisement as well as the total irrationality of his response to it, because such a response could never bring him the satisfaction he sought. By subjecting this causal process to rational analysis and assessment, the person is thereby able to prevent this process from automatically producing in him certain inevitably unsatisfying behaviors.

Before going on, it is important to note that the educative model as I have outlined it does not entail the claim that a critical theory offers people the means to their freedom in the sense of lifting them out of the causal realm altogether, thereby making their feelings and actions in some sense uncaused. This is an old (and unfortunate) position based on the incompatablist argument that determinism and freedom are antithetical, but it is not one to which the educationist is committed. In fact, according to what I have written, an action is unfree (as in the case of the consumer's compulsive behavior) when it is outside the agent's own rational self-control, which is to say, when it is not undertaken on the basis of the agent's own deliberation. And for this it is not enough that the action simply be caused but rather that its causes be such that they do not include the agent's rational reflection and/or that they are immune to his attempts to comprehend and alter them accordingly. Now this is just the situation with the consumer who was a slave to the advertisers; they caused him to act in ways that were not his own because their power depended on processes of which he was unaware and which he was unable to comprehend given his own resources, processes which worked independently of his conscious thoughts and desires. Introducing the relevant considerations that made him understand what the advertising meant to him increased his freedom, because he was now able to cease being a victim by taking control of this own responses; now the causes of his behavior included reasoning processes which were truly his own, and freedom consists of exactly this. To uphold the educative ideal of theory and practice, one need not be an antideterminist.[16]

Of course, the example I have given is simple and naive; its deficiency as a general case becomes apparent when one tries to extend its lessons to situations in which certain fundamental needs and purposes of a person, or (more typically) a group of persons, are actively frustrated by a certain set of social relationships and forms of behavior. For surely it rarely happens that simply by correcting the beliefs of certain people, they will thereby automatically gain their freedom from the conditions and actions producing their misery. It is not simply changing the *ideas* of a group of people that will free them from oppressive social institutions—they must change *these conditions and forms of behavior themselves* on the basis of their new understandings of themselves.

To this point the critical theorist would readily accede. He will point out, however, that enlightening people about the processes that determine their existence is a necessary first step in their self-liberation and that, indeed, this must occur if this "liberation" is not to be produced by an elite for the rest who are ignorant. Critical enlightenment can lead to liberation because (as in the case of the consumer) the causal force of the social conditions is dependent upon the subjects' holding certain ideas and values. When the people come to understand the precise ways in which they have been implicated in the causal processes that oppress them, a group of social actors can learn what needs to be changed and how to change it. Without such a group-wide understanding, any theorist can attempt only to implement social change in which one set of causal processes which operate over the heads of a particular group is replaced by different processes which act in a similar manner; in both cases, the relationship between the theorist and his audience is that between the leaders and the blindly led, i.e., a relationship of domination.

IV

At this point the instrumentalist might feel constrained to admit that the notion of an educative transformation—by which people, who were victims of causal processes which had their power because these people were ignorant of them, subvert these processes by learning the theory and acting in terms of it—is not a use of scientific knowledge which he had envisioned. Nevertheless, he might well claim that this educative transformation can itself occur only along strictly instrumentalist lines. His argument would take the following form.

A problem arises for the critical theorist when he begins to spell out how his knowledge can be emancipating. Clearly, for his theories to change people and their social orders in the manner he claims they will, he must confront the problem of people's inability to see and accept his analysis of their situation. He must face the problem of *resistance*.

One reason why the critical theorist must expect resistance from his audience concerns the kind of ignorance he is trying to eliminate. When discussing the kind of ignorance that underlies repressive social practices, the critical theorist means more than simply a number of false beliefs; he is talking about something far more systematic and pervasive than this. By false consciousness or systematic self-misunderstandings the critical theorist means a set of interrelated illusions about human needs, about the nature of happiness, about what is good and of value, and about how one should act in one's relations with others to achieve these things. These illusions are usually shared by a whole group of persons whose roles in society are the same, or even by a whole community; they constitute an important element of the conceptual scheme in terms of which these people talk about themselves and their social world. Furthermore, they are illusions and not merely false ideas, and this means, as Freud noted, that "a wish-fulfillment is a prominent factor in their motivation."[17] In other words, these false beliefs are attempts to satisfy certain important needs and desires of the people who hold them, and this means they will have a great power in the psychological economy of their believers.

Both these facts about illusions—their systematic, shared, and deep nature, as well as their being rooted in their holders' needs—combine to make any attempt at dislodging them extremely difficult. This is because giving up such illusions requires abandoning one's self-conceptions and the social practices that they engender and support, things people cling to because they provide direction and meaning in their lives. It involves acquiring a new self-identity.

This last consideration leads to another reason why the critical theorist must face the problem of resistance; this reason is internal to the very nature of critical theory. For this metatheory is explicitly founded on the assumption that certain conditions can cause certain beliefs, and it is thus eminently qualified to recognize that the illusions people have about themselves are produced in them by their social order. Consequently, a critical social scientist must be prepared for a situation in which the people to whom his theories are directed are unable to genuinely consider his novel and strange-sounding interpretations, given the kind of social arrangements under which they live and the kind of social experience they have had.

Now the instrumentalist might well be aware that critical theorists have given a number of answers in order to solve this problem:[18] ideology-critique must be made accessible to the oppressed by grounding it in their own self-understandings; ideology-critique must try to demonstrate just how the illusions of the oppressed latently indicate their real needs; critical theory must develop a theory of crisis which attempts to show that the social order, based on ideas that are illusions, will be marked by contradictions which exacerbate tensions and increase suffering and thus ultimately undermine the appropriateness of the ideologies that the actors in these situations presently possess. Nevertheless, none of these answers meets the following instrumentalist claim: since people can become open to a rational analysis only when certain causal conditions are present, these conditions must be established *before* a critical analysis can become truly practical. This can only happen when someone who knows these causal laws has enough power to manipulate the relevant variables to ensure the existence of these conditions. And, of course, this is a return to the instrumentalist account of the relation of thought to action, and it undermines what is supposedly distinctive about critical theory.

Nor should anyone think that this return to instrumentalism is merely an imaginary possibility, for this very line of argument has occurred *within the thinking of critical theorists themselves.* Both Lukács and Marcuse are examples. In parts of *History and Class Consciousness*[19] Lukács developed an analysis of the proletarian revolution which fits the educative model (especially in his insistence on seeing reification as the source of the power and the inadequacy of capitalism and his consequent emphasis on the development of class consciousness and the capacity for self-determination as the essential goal of revolutionary activity). However, Lukacs also claimed that even when bourgeois society is in extreme crisis, the proletariat will fail to develop the appropriate ideological self-understanding; instead, the Communist party must separate itself from the rest of the working class and ultimately assume the power of the state on behalf of the workers and alter the economic and social structure, thereby bringing about the change in proletarian consciousness necessary for the emergence of the truly communist society. This constituted his basic opposition to the theory of revolution developed by Rosa Luxemburg as well as his basic support of the (essentially instrumentalist) theories and practices of Lenin. In so doing, Lukács undermined what is distinctive about critical revolutionary theory and returned to an essentially manipulative political practice.

Marcuse, especially in his confused and unsatisfying book *An Essay on Liberation*, claims that even though there is enormous potential for human liberation present in advanced technological societies, almost all members of this society —including the working class—are so conditioned by it that in what he calls their very "biological nature" they desire and support this irrational system.[20] Indeed, he even thinks that the deadening associated with the process of one-dimensionalization has progressed so far that this society has actually induced long-range contentment and satisfaction (p. 13) so that people voluntarily enter into servitude. This produces the central dilemma for the revolutionary:

This is the vicious circle: the rupture with the self-propelling conservative continuum of needs must *precede* the revolution which is to usher in a free society, but such rupture itself can be envisioned only in a revolution . . . (p. 18)

Here Marcuse states exactly the difficulty with critical theory which the instrumentalist critic has raised. Unfortunately, even after reading the rest of the book, it remains a mystery how Marcuse plans to get out of this dilemma. But the general point seems to be the claim that the relevant consciousness will emerge in groups marginal to industrial society and that they will revolt and impose the revolution on those who have unwittingly and self-destructively become slaves of the social system.[21] Here again is an essentially manipulative and authoritarian theory of revolution emerging from what was once a critical-theory perspective because of the apparent inability of this perspective to deal with the problem of resistance.

But is this the only possible response by a critical theorist to the fact that those to whom a critical analysis has been addressed often do reject such an analysis, and that they do so on irrational grounds (refusing to entertain the theory even as a possibility or resisting it out of hand for purely emotional reasons)? Does the explanation of this fact—that certain causal conditions must be established before any attempt is made to alter peoples's self-understanding —inevitably lead back to an instrumentalist account of theory and practice à la Lukács and Marcuse?

I think not, though in meeting this objection some alteration in my account of the educative model will have to be made. The return to a purely instrumentalist conception can be resisted by making the crucial logical distinction between *necessary* and *sufficient* conditions. For although it must be admitted that there are certain conditions to be met before rational reflection and behavior can occur, there is clearly something contradictory in arguing that there are causal conditions sufficient to produce such reflection but that these conditions do not include persuasion through discourse itself. The unpacking and defense of this claim will take up the rest of this section and the next one as well.

That there are external condtions to be met before a critical theory can influence people's behavior is an obvious truth. For example, the critical theorist must have access to the relevant people. And in certain circumstances — for instance, in a totalitarian state or in a state governed by martial law — this may be an absolutely crucial point: for one of the major difficulties encountered by those who wish to overthrow such social orders is getting their critical analysis to the people whom it is supposed to liberate. There are any number of other conditions which any ordinary person knows have to be met if the self-understandings of people and their behavior are to be the result of critical self-reflection: they must not be starving; they must be able to understand the language that the analysis of their situation is being expressed in; and so on.

Morevoer, one of the jobs of social science is to investigate other, more recondite causal conditions of a social, psychological, or physiological kind which are necessary for people to open themselves to critiques that try to account for the unhappiness of their lives. Such factors as the amount of sugar in the blood (and the practice of insulin treatment to regulate it) and the amount of anxiety a person is experiencing (and the practice of chemotherapy to reduce it) are examples of two relatively new discoveries of psychology which are not obvious but are relevant to the question at hand and which have led to the development of new techniques in psychotherapy.

Furthermore, instituting the conditions necessary for rational reflection to occur, and ensuring that they are maintained, is clearly a translation of theory into practice that is instrumental in nature. And this means that no account of the educative model that draws an *absolute* distinction between it and its instrumentalist counterpart is going to be adequate. For any critical theory to be translated into action may well require some kind of manipulation of variables to ensure that the conditions within which enlightenment can occur indeed exist.

In fact, it is not as if the discovery of these necessary conditions is a matter which critical theorists can ignore. On the contrary, it is absolutely essential for a critical theorist to develop as part of his general theory an analysis of the conditions under which people can become clear to themselves. This is so for three reasons.

First, since a critical theory is one whose whole point is to be translated into enlightened action, then such a theory must develop an account of the conditions that must be met if people are going to be in a position to actually consider it as a possible account of their lives.

There is a second and rather more subtle reason why a critical theorist must work out a theory about the empirical conditions under which people will let rational considerations bear on their lives. One test of the truth of a critical theory is the considered reaction by those for whom it is supposed to be emancipating. This is because a critical theory is one that offers an interpretation of a person's actions, feelings, and needs, and interpretations must be tested against the responses that those being interpreted make to them. When a person does not, under any condition, accept a social theorists's account as giving the meaning of his behavior, providing an accurate description of what he feels, or revealing his "real" purpose or desires, then this is prima facie evidence against the correctness of the account.

Now a theory of the conditions that must be satisfied for a critical theory to be even possibly accepted by its audience is necessary to keep this criterion of truth operational. Otherwise, the critical theorist has no way of distinguishing between, on the one hand, reasoned rejections of his analysis — rejections which are disconfirming instances of this analysis — and, on the other, the ignorant and unthinking responses of irrational people — responses which can be discounted when assessing the worth of the theory. In this situation, no matter what the responses of his audience to his analysis, the critical theorist could continue to assume it was true. Without a theory that specifies when people are in a situation to respond rationally to a critique of their ideology, any negative response which would count as evidence against the theory could be ignored; and one doesn't have to be a Popperian to recognize the inadequacy of this situation for any theory that claims to be scientific.

Moreover, this leads to the third reason why a theory of necessary conditions of rational response is crucial: to prevent a critical theory from degenerating into pure instrumentalism in just the way that Lukács's and Marcuse's theories have. For if one is unable to distinguish between legitimate and illegitimate rejections of one's theory, *any* rejection of the theory by its audience can then be interpreted as indicating that its rejecters must continue to be manipulated in an instrumentalist manner (read: drugged; coerced by imposed laws; kept in prison; etc.) until they are supposedly "rational enough" to respond to the theory in a reflective and coherent way (read: until they accept the critical theorist's analysis of their situation).

One major danger for anyone who aspires to alter the way people think, feel, and act is dogmatism. One way that critical theory distinguishes itself from mere dogmatism is its setting out of conditions which, if met, would show the theory to be false. The discovery of conditions under which people can rationally consider a particular analysis of their situation is an important ingredient in this task.

And it is heartening to note that a number of what I take to be critical theorists have developed empirical theories (and, in some cases, practices) which try to specify the ways in which rational self-understanding is systematically prevented and the conditions that must prevail for this systematic distortion to be overcome. A vigorous literature does exist which attempts to flesh out the educative model of theory and practice with concrete empirical analysis. A brief mention of some of this literature will not only indicate where to look for a corrective to the dominant instrumentalist thinking of our day, but it will also provide me with the analysis I will need for discussing, in Part VI, the relationship between critical theory and broad-based social change.

The first name that comes to mind in this context is Freud. Freud developed a theory of therapy that was consistent with his own understanding of neurosis and that tried to account for the practical efficacy of psychoanalysis in the face of his patients' obvious resistances to the therapeutic process—resistances which were themselves further instances of the repression involved in the patients' neurosis in the first place. The critical element which Freud invoked in this regard was *transference*. Transference is the displacement of feelings (especially hostile ones) onto the analyst. Through transference the patient constructs an "artifical neurosis" within which he reenacts basic conflicts around the person of the analyst. This means that in the analysis the patient is actually "acting out," and by a series of interpretations of this presently occurring drama, the analyst is able to intervene directly in the neurotic processes of the patient, giving him the opportunity to make conscious the various impulses that were originally unconsciousness and closed to view. On the basis of this theory, Freud concluded that a necessary condition for the effectiveness of therapy is the creation and maintenance of a certain sort of relationship between therpist and patient, namely, one in which transference can occur.

In our own day a quite different theory of therapy has been developed by R. D. Laing and his cohorts which is rooted in a quite different theory of so-called mental illness. Laing has tried to show that the conditions of people labeled by psychiatrists as schizophrenic have been produced by essentially distorted communication (especially in the family) which has put these people into binds placing inconsistent demands on them but about which they can know nothing and from which they cannot escape. Laing has tried to show that schizophrenia is a response to such an intolerable situation and a potentially positive one at that, i.e., it is a move out of the "normal" world of alienation into the "abnormal" world of integration and autonomy. In light of his general theory, Laing tries to show that the positive energy of the illness can be tapped only in an environment in which the kind of distorted communication he has so brilliantly characterized is absent. In the creation of antihospitals and the therapeutic communities of the Philadelphia Association, the conditions that foster and reinforce the self-destructive confusions of ordinary life are eliminated and replaced with an environment that encourages the full expression of feelings and ideas in an atmosphere of mutual trust and respect and in an institutional setting of collective decision making.[22]

Critical theories about the conditions necessary for an ideology-critique to be even possibly effective have not been confined to so-called mentally disturbed people, moreover. In the educational writings of Paulo Freire, for example, a fairly systematic theory of critical education for the illiterate poor of under-developed countries has been articulated with an eye toward developing what Freire calls "conscientizaçao." Conscientizaçao is the development of a radical consciousness that has learned to see that certain social forms are oppressive and they can be altered by exploiting certain social, political, and/or economic contradictions, as well as the utilization of this radicalized consciousness to initiate and guide action against its oppressors.

Freire claims there are two basic facts about the peasants with which any critical educator must come to terms. The first is what he calls their "culture of silence," meaning that these people are submerged in a situation in which they do not possess the capacities for critical awareness and response. They do not see that their situation can be different from what it is; they do not perceive that they have at least the potential power to intervene in the social world and to transform it, making it other than it is. They are passive, fatalistic, dependent, adaptive to almost whatever occurs.

On the basis of these observations Freire argues that the "pedagogy of the oppressed" cannot just aim to fill its students with knowledge about how things work — in fact, such a "banking model" of education would be self-defeating; rather, the educator must try to get them to see their social setting as one which offers problems that can be solved, or "limit-situations" that can be transcended. True education must first aim to persuade the peasants that they have the ability to assess their situation rationally, with a view toward changing it.

True enlightenment starts with the peasants' development of a self-conception in which they are subjects able to determine their situation, not mere objects in it, at the mercy of whatever others happen to do.

The second major fact about the peasants is that they have internalized the values, beliefs, and even world view of their oppressors so that they are unable to see themselves as oppressed and, indeed, so that they willingly cooperate with those who oppress them in maintaining those social practices that result in their oppression. Freire enumerates a variety of ways in which "the oppressor is inside the oppressed" so that they secretly admire him, wish to be like him, accept the legitimacy of his position, and believe in his invulnerability. It is on the basis of these attitudes that resistance is grounded; in fact, as Freire himself says, "as long as the oppressor 'within' the oppressed is stronger than they themselves are, their natural fear of freedom may lead them to denounce the revolutionary leaders instead" (p. 169).

At precisely this juncture a theory of communication is required that will guide educators in overcoming this resistance without at the same time imposing themselves on the peasants so that they undermine the very point of education, namely, the development of conscientizaçao. Freire lays out such a theory with his "problem-posing model" of education. This model is strikingly similar to the one found in psychotherapy. In particular: the relations between students and teachers must be dialogic; the content of the education must be based on the concrete experience of the students themselves;[23] the presentation of this experience must emphasize its historical character, i.e., how it came to be what it is and how it can be changed; the educational process must take place in small intimate cultural circles in which a free and uncoerced exchange of ideas and experiences is encouraged, in which concern is shown for the problems of individuals, and in which they are given emotional support to overcome their own feelings of inadequacy and guilt as they become critics of the social world they inhabit.

With the work of Freire, one moves out of the relatively individualistic world of psychological rehabilitation into the wider public world of concerted social and political action. At this point, however, one discovers a real weakness in the tradition of critical theory, namely, its failure to develop its conception of the necessary conditions of emancipation in a way that is both relevant to, and plausible for, mass social action. Such a weakness is deeply rooted in the history of political theory. Thus, probably the first modern thinker to examine the conditions under which free and uncoerced communication might take place in the political realm was Rousseau in the *Social Contract*; yet it is clear that he had no good idea how such a political order might be instituted, and he had little hope that such an order could be established in an advanced civilization.[24]

Indeed, it was Marx who criticized the utopian and moralistic stance of Rousseau. But even in Marx we find very little thinking on the subject of how the capitalistic system would be overthrown and almost nothing on the role his own theory was supposed to play in this process.[25] This is partly because Marx himself was confused about the place of class consciousness in the revolutionary process: often as not he resorted to a purely materialistic viewpoint which made ideas merely epiphenomenal and which made the evolution of the forces and forms of production subject to purely natural laws which operated "over the heads" of the actors who lived and worked with them (this is most noticeable in *The German Ideology*). But it is also partly because Marx himself never really developed an adequate theory of ideology and ideology-critique.

One result of this confusion was to open the door for the purely instrumentalist conception of Marxian theory and practice found in the life and thought of Lenin. In *What Is To Be Done?* Lenin outlined a theory of revolution in which a vanguard of elite, professional party members (organized hierarchically as an army with the Central Committee as its general and maintaining strict secrecy) directs its energies to "overthrowing the autocracy" and seizing power. In this process the development of class consciousness and a new self-understanding informed by Marxist theory among the broad majority of workers is not a major goal of the party's activity, and this for two reasons: first, such a development is not a prerequisite for the revolutionary take-over of the bourgeois state (all that is necessary is mass discontent directed toward the government, and this is why Lenin confines the educative function of the party to mere political "exposure" and "agitation"); second, Lenin believed the proletariat was essentially reformist in its attitudes and that therefore only an external, revolutionary elite acting in its name could bring about the revolution the working class "really" wanted. This kind of thinking has been responsible for the widely held belief that Marxism involves an essentially instrumentalist conception of theory and practice in which the leaders of the movement act for and on their followers by assuming positions of power from which they can control affairs.

Moreover, I have already shown how such nominally critical thinkers as Lukács and Marcuse have actually resorted to an instrumentalist model once confronted by the problem of organizing a mass political movement among people opposed to Marxist analysis because they are supposedly so corrupted by the oppressive world in which they live.[26] And surely one of the great weaknesses of Habermas's work is that he gives no idea at all how it is that what he says at the level of individual psychology can be made appropriate for someone interested in social reform.

There are those who would claim that such an extension from individual psychology to mass politics is an impossible undertaking just because the conditions under which critical analysis can be effective are such that they must be restricted to the intense personal interchange of therapy and the closed world of certain sorts of therapeutic communities.[27] This may well be so, but if it is, it is bad news indeed. For it would mean not only that liberation is possible just for the few in specialized settings — and, in light of the widespread suffering of people caused and being caused by other people in this century, this would be a deeply pessimistic doctrine — but that this individualistic liberation would be confined to those few who would be able literally to opt out of the social world which comprises the matrix of everyday life. The reasons for this are simple: on the one hand, such liberated people would end up operating on self-understandings and values widely at variance with those of their former society, and so it is hard to see how any kind of real, sustained interaction would be possible; on the other hand, forms of distorted communciation and repressive ideologies exist within a framework of social interaction that extends outward from the family to the wider society, i.e., to forms of economic, social, and political domination,[28] so that it is unrealistic to think that one can achieve liberation by isolating a small part of one's existence but continue to participate in more public institutions. To institute a social setting in which certain kinds of coercion and repression are absent, one would have to cut one's ties with the social practices that have fostered these negative relationships. But how is this possible for those whose lives are enmeshed in, and who must continue to function in, the wider life of a repressive social order?

It is partly on the basis of reflections like these that those who have started communes, kibbutzim, monasteries, utopian societies, etc. have based their activity. Unfortunately, such a radical split offers little hope to the great mass of sufferers in the world, and the question arises, is there some form of revolutionary political and social activity that is in accord with the educative model but that does not require an immediate and total rejection of the normal everyday world, i.e., a form of activity that seeks to transform this world from within?

I will take up this very question in Part VI. However, before I can do so I must turn my attention from the necessary conditions of enlightenment to its sufficient conditions. I said earlier that one could not give a purely instrumentalist account of conditions that are *sufficient* to bring about the kind of enlightenment the educative model calls for; I now want to examine whether this is really so.

V

In our own century momentous social and political revolutions have occurred at least partly as a result of the changes of consciousness of a mass of people; but the interesting thing is that these changes were produced in people by an elite using essentially manipulative techniques which ensured that the relevant changes in self-understanding would occur among the masses. I am thinking of the rise to mass leadership of the Nazi party in Germany as well as the so-called cultural revolutions which have periodically swept through China since the Communists captured power in 1949. The occurrence of these two historical examples seems to undermine the claim that the educative model, which bases social change on the enlightenment of a group of people, provides a clear alternative to the instrumentalist model—for here we have the requisite "enlightenment" produced in a purely instrumentalist way.

Moreover, these examples are even more damaging to the educative model than this, for they seem to show that its whole idea of liberation is an unsound one. These examples seem to have this force because they are concrete instances of profound social change deriving from, at least in part, the new self-understandings of a group of people responding to what is clearly an ideology-critique, and yet it would seem strange indeed to claim that such changes were a movement toward increasing these people's freedom. It would be paradoxical in the extreme to claim that those propagandized and manipulated masses in the stadium at Nuremburg were actually partaking in their own emancipation or that the victims of Chinese brainwashing were now "truly free." In what sense, therefore, can the educative model actually prevent domination and increase personal autonomy?

In answering these instrumentalist counterclaims and questions I must amend further the original, simplified account of the educative model that I gave in Part II. There I made it sound as if the really crucial element for the educative approach were getting a mass of people to accept a particular critical analysis of their situation and to act on the basis of this new self-conception. And even in Part IV I concentrated on the question of how to establish the conditions necessary for this change in self-conception to occur, as if the only distinctive feature of the educative model were the oppressed coming to view themselves differently. But it ought to be clear from the counterexamples of the Nazis and the Chinese Communists that a solution to these problems is not enough to distinguish the educative model from the instrumenalist model. *What matters is not only the fact that people come to have a particular self-understanding, and that this new self-understanding provides the basis for alter-*

ing social arrangements, but also the manner in which they come to adopt this
new "guiding idea." In fact, rational discourse must be the cause of the op-
pressed's change in basic self-conception.

The educative model is based on the claim that its method of translating
theory into practice brings genuine liberation to people who have been acting
in irrational and self-destructive ways, by helping them free themselves from
the willy-nilly causal processes that have determined the direction and shape
of their lives and that are responsible for their suffering and anxiety. It enables
them to free themselves just because it gives them the knowledge whereby they
can understand their lives; hence they can now act on the basis of their informed reflection rather than being determined by conditions about which they
had no knowledge and over which they had no control. By his analysis a critical
theorist seeks to provide rationally compelling arguments to the oppressed
people (or person), with the hope that these people will now be able to subject
their own existence to their own reasoned self-control. This is what is meant
by self-determination and increased autonomy.

Now as I had occasion to remark in Part II, the kind of freedom to which
the educative model points does not require that its possessor somehow remove
himself from the realm of causality; it does require that the causes of his behavior cease being factors that are purely external to him because he has no
knowledge or control over them, and that they come to include his own conscious, rationally informed self-reflection. The point is that this clearly cannot
happen when people's new self-conceptions are produced by manipulating their
external conditions so that they "just have" these self-conceptions: this is in
fact the description of their *original* state from which critical theory is meant
to liberate them. Freedom does not arise when one moves from a state of following one blind dogma to a state of following another dogma.

It is ironic that the Chinese Communists at least (but not the Nazis) would
probably accept this argument, for they would want to maintain that they in
fact were giving freedom to their followers; they would recognize that the creation of a mass of manipulated and blindly following automatons would hardly
fit with any conception of freedom worthy of the name. At least partly for
this reason, I believe, the Chinese include among their techniques of persuasion
the presentation and elaboration of their own particular theory of man and
society.[29] In other words, precisely because they have wanted to argue that
by getting people to follow the party they have given these people freedom,
the Chinese leaders have felt compelled to present and to disseminate an elaborate and sophisticated social theory to act as a rational justification for their

assuming power, and have insisted that the people come to describe and explain their social experience in terms of the theory.

Unfortunately, this just won't do. For although the party leaders did offer their audience a theoretical account of their historical position partly to preclude the charge that they were enslaving their followers by forcing or duping them into following the "correct path," these rational justifications were always accompanied by brute force, psychological pressure, intimidation, new forms of propaganda, and assorted techniques of mass indoctrination. Moreover, those who failed to adopt the correct ideological position were subject to the worst kind of threats, removed from their position in society, often imprisoned, and sometimes summarily executed. In this kind of situation it is hardly possible to claim that just because a great many of the people came to act on the basis of new self-understandings, they were consequently free: for they clearly did not come to hold these new understandings because of reasoned argument and rational persuasion. One set of external causal conditions, which produced one sort of self-conception independent of any rational reflection by the people, was simply replaced by a different external set which produced another such conception in essentially the same manner.[30]

This is an obvious point, and so it makes one wonder what else the Chinese Communists might have believed which would support their claim that, by literally forcing people to agree with their analysis of their historical situation, they were giving these people their freedom. I suspect that such a claim is supported by the further conviction that people can only be free when they live according to a theory that is in fact true. Here we have a version of the doctrine that "the truth shall set you free"; on this view, what is ultimately important for freedom is not the reasons why people believe as they do, or how they come to adopt a particular view, but rather that what they believe is correct. If this is indeed so, then it won't do either; for such a claim rests on a conceptual confusion between the notions of rationality and truth.

The concept true is predicated of what is believed, namely, statements, whereas the concept rational applies to actions, dispositions, attitudes, beliefs, and other states of people. For a statement to be true it must fulfill certain conditions, viz., actually represent what is the case; however, for a belief to be rational it must fulfill other criteria, viz., it must be believed on the basis of available relevant procedures for obtaining and weighing evidence, and it must not be inconsistent with other beliefs held simultaneously. Thus the concepts true and rational do not have the same referent, nor are their criteria of application identical. For these reasons a situation may arise in which a person is irrational for holding a true belief: for example, he may believe it simply because he wants it to be true; or he may believe it even though he has no grounds defensible in his own terms for doing so. Similarly, a person may be rational in holding a false belief, for he may be employing the best canons and information available to him in maintaining this belief (so that it may have been rational at one time for someone to have believed the world to be flat).

The basic difficulty in the case of the Chinese Communists as I have presented it is its philosophical mistake in taking as one of the criteria for ascribing rationality (and hence freedom) to the beliefs and actions of people, the assent to the truth of particular propositions which they themselves happen to affirm. In doing so, they obliterate the distinction between truth and rationality. One cannot claim that people are emancipating themselves from conditions that have enslaved them by revealing to them how they can act according to rationally adopted beliefs and attitudes, and at the same time maintain that how they came to adopt these beliefs and attitudes is immaterial so long as their content is true. For rationality refers precisely to the grounds on which beliefs, attitudes, and courses of action are adopted and maintained.

What is required to get people to change their basic beliefs by rational reflection? Not only must a particular theory be offered as the reason why people should change their self-understandings, *but this must be done in an environment in which these people can reject this reason.* For the very essence of rational assent to a proposition is that it is ultimately the force of the argument and not some extraneous factor that leads a person to adopt a new viewpoint. One cannot impose on another person a new attitude or belief, or create a situation in which the person has no choice but to accept this new belief, and at the same time claim that his acceptance is due to critical reflection. This is just a straightforward contradiction between objective and method.

These basically conceptual distinctions can be used to explain certain empirical evidence; I take it that this is the case with Goffman's work on "total institutions," for example.[31] One chief characteristic of these institutions is the insistence of those in power that all the inmates accept the view of reality and self-characterizations that those in power happen to believe. This insistence, together with the sanctions and inducements associated with it, not only gets the inmates to adopt these basic conceptualizations, but it also produces a passive and uncritical population which has lost the capacity for critical self-reflection and the ability to act in terms of this reflection. And as Goffman shows, this happens even with those institutions like mental hospitals in which the adoption of a new self-conception is thought to be in the best interests of the inmates, because even in these places the process of adopting a new self-interpretation is accompanied by rituals of debasement, regimentation, discounting, mortification, and other witting and unwitting techniques whereby the patients are made to believe they have lost the capacity to have any command over their world. These processes are reinforced by "confessional periods" and "therapy sessions" in which the self-conceptions of the patients are systematically discredited, and their statements are themselves discounted as mere symptoms. The end result of this whole process (although it is always mitigated somewhat by countervailing factors in the social life of the inmates themselves) is that the change in what Goffman calls the "moral careers" of patients is accompanied by the destruction of the patients' capacity for self-direction. Here we see that convincing people to adopt a new picture of themselves and their relation to their social world is not sufficient to bring about their freedom; and this is so even if these new pictures are in fact true pictures.

We learn from Goffman's work that although there can be no set of purely external conditions sufficient to produce the kind of rational reflection I have been discussing which did not include the offering of arguments in a free and open environment, there can be such a set of conditions sufficient to promote nonrational thoughts and actions. It is possible to create situations in which adducing and inquiring into logically relevant considerations is institutionally forbidden (as in totalitarian regimes) or is systematically omitted in the process of getting people to hold beliefs (as in the techniques of mass propaganda). Such situations are enough to make autonomy impossible.

The distinctions I have been drawing are deeply rooted in human reflection about how to get people to change their ideas—indeed, they are the very heart of the argument in the *Gorgias*. In the dialogue Socrates points to the difference between rhetoric and philosophy; philosophy (or dialectic or education) attempts to persuade people to agree or to change their minds through rational discourse in which the giving and examining of logically relevant considerations is the major causal element in producing the desired change; rhetoric, on the other hand, produces beliefs by techniques which do not include the invoking of reasons or relevant information as the element responsble for the change. The issue I am addressing is as old as that between Socrates and Gorgias: whether there is a crucially important distinction to be drawn between the different ways beliefs can be changed, and whether effecting such changes by mere rhetoric is reprehensible (because it enslaves those on whom it works) regardless of whether the new beliefs are true or false.

Critical theory looks to the elimination of socially caused misery by the emergence of people who are conscious of themselves as active and deciding beings, bearing responsibility for their choices and able to explain them by referring to their own purposes, ideals, and beliefs. Such a theory is rooted in the belief that a great deal of suffering is the result of people unwittingly cooperating to produce it because they do not know their true needs and are unable to discover them, of structures of authority which have their power only because their unhappy victims are unaware of the ways in which they are participating in their own victimization.[32]

In other words, this kind of social theory is rooted in the belief that when people come to act on the basis of rational reflection, and not as the result of causes that are, as it were, external to them, they can alleviate those elements of frustration, anxiety, boredom, and terror that are the result of some people's actions toward them. And it is because of its insistence on the developing of critically aware people—able to reflect on their situation, to express their desires and opinions, to demand consideration in the way in which their affairs are structured and conducted—that a critical theory must emphasize not only its particular substantive interpretation of the social world but the manner in which this view (may or will) come to be held by the audience to whom it is directed.

Persuasion, argumentation, debate, criticism, analysis, education: these activities—in all the countless institutional settings in which they may occur, in all the various aesthetic forms they may take, in an environment in which the educator may be rejected—are the heart of the educative model of theory and practice. True, they may not be enough in themselves to bring about enlightenment and its consequent altered behavior (because certain necessary conditions must be instituted for them even to be possibly effective), but they must provide the core of the critical theorist's approach to the dangerous task of fomenting social change.

VI

The arguments in Parts IV and V help, I think, undermine the critical theorist's hopes for broad-based social change following the educative model. Indeed, the kinds of restrictions that I have had to put on any attempt to translate a critical theory into practice may well make such a theoretically informed and enlightened revolution seem impossible. I do not think such an extremely negative conclusion is warranted; however, I do think those who hope to change basic social structures in a nonmanipulative way are going to have to develop strategies of social change that are radically opposed to the notion of revolution so unfortunately ingrained in the Left, namely, that which envisages an avant-garde acting in the name of some group, seizing control of the governmental apparatus amid a mass upheaval, and undertaking to make basic social change. This is an inadequate (and, given the history of such revolutions, a hazardous) notion, because it does not allow for the creation of those conditions necessary and sufficient to bring about rational enlightenment of a mass of actors, at least on any theory that is at all plausible regarding the ways that enlightenment occurs and the kinds of strategies that such a vanguard would have to employ to keep itself in power.

Placing the burden for social change on rational enlightenment resulting from a process of interpretation and analysis and, moreover, recognizing what we have learned about the dynamics of such enlightenment, I think it is unlikely that the sorts of change envisaged by the educative model can occur outside of certain sorts of institutional settings. These settings are groups that are relatively small, relatively egalitarian (in the sense that no member has command over another without the other's approval), relatively free of recrimination between members, relatively committed to rationally discussing its members' situations and experiences. and relatively insistent that its members take responsibility for whatever claims, decisions, or actions they undertake to make. Only within settings like these can "consciousness raising" based on rational reflection apparently take place.

We are all, of course, familiar with these sorts of arrangements—usually tucked away in the interstices of our society—in halfway houses, drug clinics, certain prison-reform programs, in some types of family therapy sessions, and in other essentially individualistic enterprises.[33] The question is, are there any examples of such enterprises devoted to basic social change conducted along the lines I have been discussing? I think there are (some, of course, more promising than others), and I would like to discuss briefly just one of them, the Women's Liberation Movement.[34]

One of the lessons the Women's Liberation Movement has taught us is the inadequacy of any view of revolutionary social change that equates itself with the narrowly political. Marx should have been corrective enough of such a view, but given the actual course that so-called Marxist revolutions have historically taken, revolution has all too often been equated with the seizure of the governmental apparatus. Such a view is inadequate because it overemphasizes the role of government in our lives and, more important, because it fails to appreciate the ways in which changes in government can often follow changes in the other spheres of social life.[35]

The Women's Liberation Movement was guilty of just this narrow focus for much of its recent history, but since World War II (no doubt as a result of structural changes in the society at large) it has broadened to include the wider (and more experientially relevant) questions of economic opportunities, domestic roles, sexual relationships, psychological independence, and so on. And as it has broadened and gained followers, the movement has begun to affect in deep and unpredictible ways whole areas of social life, fundamentally altering the methods by which people raise their children, divide family responsbilities, relate to members of the opposite sex, view marriage, and carve out their careers. What other social changes might be forthcoming from this social movement — whether it will lead to socialism, as some of its followers predict, for example — remains to be seen; but even at this point it seems quite clear that a genuine revolution is occurring all around us.

From the perspective of someone interested in the relationship of theory to practice, there are at least two things interesting about the Women's Movement. The first is the role of social theory in its development. One of the most striking facts in this social movement has been the extreme importance of social analysis in guiding it. Analysis of all sorts — the detailed, concrete accounts of contemporary women found in novels and social histories; the manifestos articulating goals and forms of organization; the elaborate social scientific theories of the current situation; the legal briefs; the autobiographical accounts of liberated women; the vast literature on the psychology of women, on psychoanalysis, on the question of women's unique needs (if any); the historical surveys of past treatment of, and thought about, women; the philosophical works that have tried to provide a new conceptual scheme in terms of which people should talk about the roles and relations of the sexes — these and numerous other categories of analysis have played a vital role in instigating this movement, giving it its impetus, providing it with a vocabulary with which to describe itself and explain its relationship to contemporary society, and focusing and directing its energies.

Moreover, all this theorizing has not served to increase instrumental power but to emancipate, i.e., its primary usefulness has been educative. Thus it has been useful insofar as it has provided a critique of the ideology that characterized women's thinking about themselves and their world, and insofar as it has provided a concrete social analysis that explained the power of the movement and showed the direction it must take. Its function has been to enlighten a particular class of people, whose suffering is partly the result of their being nescient cooperators in maintaining social practices and relations that caused them to think, feel, and act in self-defeating ways, so that they could come to subject these processes to scrutiny and ultimately to undermine them. Knowledge has led to "consciousness raising," i.e., appreciating the irrationality of particular actions and self-understandings, and learning the appropriate further steps to take in light of rationally supported argument and information.

The second interesting feature of the Women's Movement for my purposes has been the role of so-called consciousness-raising groups. One major institutional arrangement by which the movement has been fostered has been the establishment of thousands of small groups throughout the country composed of women seeking to exchange with other women their thoughts, experiences, and feelings. It seems that the emergence of this social form was spontaneous in the sense that it was not done because some explicit theory called for it. Nevertheless, its institution is perfectly understandable given the kinds of conceptual distinctions and empirical evidence I have mentioned in this paper. Coming to a radical new self-conception is hardly ever a process that occurs simply by reading some theoretical work; rather, it requires an environment of trust, openness, and support in which one's own perceptions and feelings can be made properly conscious to oneself, in which one can feel free to express and examine one's fears and aspirations, in which one can think through one's experiences in terms of a radically new vocabulary which expresses a fundamentally different conceptualization of the world, in which one can see the particular and concrete ways that one unwittingly collaborates in producing one's own misery, and in which one can gain the emotional strength to accept and act on one's new insights.

The experience of the Women's Movement confirms that radical social changes through rational enlightenment requires some mechanism for ensuring that those conditions necessary for such enlightenment will be established and maintained. But it also shows, I think, that given these conditions, as well as the existence of a critical analysis and the social crises which such an analysis predicts, mass social upheaval resulting from rational enlightenment is possible.

VII

Someone may object at this point by saying that the kind of "revolution by enlightenment" outlined in discussing the Women's Movement is only possible because this movement hasn't really had much opposition. But this is simply untrue; throughout its history — and at no time more than now — women seeking liberation have had to confront enormous legal, political, economic, social, and psychological pressures seeking to prevent them from doing what they thought necessary. Or again, someone might say that this isn't a "real" revolution because it has involved little physical violence, bloodshed, and murder. This is true, but irrelevant; it calls into question our quite common identification of violence with revolution, whereas in fact neither is a necessary condition for the other. History is full of movements that were revolutionary by any standard but that did not involve the armed clash of opposing armies or the systematic performance of wanton terrorist activity, and a study of them (of the spread of Christianity throughout the Roman Empire, for example) might prove salutary to those who wish to maintain that critical knowledge and the ensuing enlightenment of large numbers of people cannot be truly revolutionary.

Nevertheless, these objections do point to a weakness in the educative model as I have adumbrated it so far, namely, its silence on the question of the opposition, not of those whom it is supposed to emancipate, but of those in power who stand against these newly enlightened oppressed. It is obvious, but crucial, to remember that critical theorizing is essentially a subversive activity, for it is directed against those who are benefitting from social arrangements that cause others to suffer. A critical theory seeks to show how certain forms of misery can be eliminated by changing the social world in some specified way; but just as some people suffer in the present world, so also some people benefit from its arrangements: and it is more than likely that these people will strongly and often violently oppose any attempt to undermine their positions.[36]

Two basic problems emerge for a critical theory that has to deal with this kind of opposition. First, how can it be properly disseminated, since those in power will probably try to stamp out all traces of a doctrine that calls for their deposition?[37] Second, how can it be implemented, for how are the newly enlightened going to be able to act if what they do and refuse to do runs directly contrary to those who are in charge? Both these problems reveal a basic truth, namely, that no discussion of the educative model is fully adequate as long as it fails to provide some understanding of the ways in which those enlightened by the theory can overcome the opposition of those in power. The problem of resistance, which provided the basic difficulty for any attempt to characterize sufficiently the relationship between critical theorist and audience, returns at a higher stage to sow doubts about the practical efficacy of such a theory.

The question arises, therefore, if there could be a theory of revolutionary change within a critical theoretic approach. In other words, can one elaborate an account of how radical social change can occur given the conceptual resources of the educative model? These questions must be answered if, in the end, the viewpoint of critical theory is going to provide us with a model of how social theory can inform social practice that is distinctive, realizable, and truly liberating. To my knowledge, no such account presently exists.

Notes

Notes

Editor's Introduction
Terence Ball

1. Sheldon S. Wolin, "Political Theory as a Vocation," *American Political Science Review*, 63 (December 1969), pp. 1062-1082, at 1078.

2. Plato, *Republic*, 518 b - d.

3. Max Horkheimer, "Traditional and Critical Theory," in Horkheimer, *Critical Theory: Selected Essays*, trans. M. J. O'Connell et al. (New York: Herder & Herder, 1972). If the contributors to the present volume have little to say about the critical theory of the Frankfurt School, this is because the earlier and later critical theorists—Horkheimer, Adorno, Marcuse, Habermas, et al.—speak well enough for themselves; and their writings are now readily available in translation. For a critical and historical overview of critical theory see Martin Jay, *The Dialectical Imagination* (Boston: Little, Brown, 1973) and William Leiss, "Critical Theory and Its Future," *Political Theory* 2 (August 1974), pp. 330-349.

4. See the majesterial survey by Nicholas Lobkowicz, *Theory and Practice: History of a Concept From Aristotle to Marx* (Notre Dame, Ind.: University of Notre Dame Press, 1967) and his essay in the present volume.

5. Jürgen Habermas, *Theory and Practice*, trans. John Viertel (Boston: Beacon Press, 1973).

6. Cf. Stephen Toulmin, "From Logical Analysis to Conceptual History," in Peter Achinstein and S. F. Barker, eds., *The Legacy of Logical Positivism* (Baltimore: Johns Hopkins Press, 1969).

7. "But," he adds, "in and through all this they retain a kind of homesickness for the scenes of their childhood." Soren Kirkegaard, *The Concept of Irony*, trans. L. M. Capel (London: Collins, 1966), p. 47.

8. Lobkowicz, this volume, p. 13.

9. See Max Weber, *The Theory of Social and Economic Organization*, trans. Talcott Parsons (New York: Free Press, 1964), p. 115. Weber's concept of action (das Handeln) does not correspond at all to the Greek notion of action (praxis), although there are over-tones of the latter in Weber's concept of wertrational action, viz., action that is absolute, i.e., not a means to an end.

10. The instrumentalist view that a theory is to be judged by its "fruitfulness" may be traced to Francis Bacon's *Novum Organum* (1620); see Lobkowicz, *Theory and Practice*, Chap. 7.

11. See Robert A. Dahl, "Political Theory: Truth and Consequences," *World Politics* 11 (October 1958), pp. 89-102.

12. Euben, this volume, p. 32.

13. Cf. Raymond Plant, *Hegel* (London: Allen & Unwin, 1973), pp. 15-25.

14. Karl Marx, *Critique of Hegel's 'Philosophy of Right'*, trans. Joseph O'Malley, (Cambridge: Cambridge University Press, 1972), pp. 136-138; and Shlomò Avineri, *The Social and Political Thought of Karl Marx* (Cambridge: Cambridge University Press, 1970), pp. 134-149.

15. Fuss, this volume, p. 97.

16. Hannah Arendt, *The Human Condition* (Chicago: University of Chicago Press, 1958), pp. 7-11 and Chaps 3-5 *passim*.

17. *Ibid.*, p. 192.

18. Arendt, *Between Past and Future* (Cleveland & New York: Meridian Books, 1963), Chap. 4.

19. See Arendt's Preface to *Between Past and Future* and "Civil Disobedience" in her *Crises of the Republic* (New York: Harcourt Brace Jovanovich, 1972).

20. Nichols, this volume, p. 197.

21. Insofar as the English word education has instrumentalist overtones, it is misleading. What Fay means by education is perhaps better expressed by the Greek *paideia* or the German *Bildung*, with their noninstrumentalist connotations of growth, maturation, and self-development.

22. Fay, this volume, p. 204.

I. On the History of Theory and Praxis
Nicholas Lobkowicz

1. Cicero, *Tusculan Disputations*, V, 3, 8-9.

2. Cf. *ibid.*, V, 35, 101; Aristotle, *Magna Moralia*, II (1204 a 31 - 1204 b 3).

3. *Nichomachean Ethics*, X, 9 (1180 a - 1181 b).

4. This is particularly clear in Aristotle's discussion of the primacy of the noetic over the dianoetic virtues: *Nichomachean Ethics*, X, 2 (1172 b 3 - 1173 a 2).

5. *Ibid.*, I, 2 (1094 b 11-28).

6. Aristotle, *Metaphysics*, 1062 a; Aristotle, *Prior Analytics*, 53 b 9.

7. In his "existentialist conception of science" Heidegger characterizes science as a "manner of conduct" (Verhaltensweise), a "mode of being" (Seinsart), a "way of existence" (Weise der Existenz), and a "mode of being-in-the-world" (Modus des In-der-Welt-seins). Martin Heidegger, *Sein und Zeit* (Tübingen: Niemeyer Verlag, 1953), pp. 357-361.

8. *Nichomachean Ethics*, VI, 3 (1139 b 18-25).

9. *Patrologia Graeca*, ed. J.-P. Migne (Paris, 1844), XLIV, 1,000 C - D.

10. St. Luke, X, 32-42; Origen, *In Lucam Fragmentum* 171, in *Die Homilien zu Lukas*, ed. M. Rauer (Berlin: Akademie Verlag, 1959), p. 298.

11. See St. Augustine, *Sermones* 103, 104, and 179, in *Patrologia Latina*, ed. J.-P. Migne (Paris, 1857), pp. 615-618, 963.

12. *Oeuvres de Descartes*, Vol. X, pp. 359-361.

13. The following examples are of course merely illustrative. For a fuller discussion see Nicholas Lobkowicz, *Theory and Practice: History of a Concept from Aristotle to Marx* (Notre Dame, Ind.: University of Notre Dame Press, 1967), Chaps. 5 and 6.

14. This view is more properly associated with Engels and some latter-day Marxists than with Marx himself. See also Benjamin Farrington, *Greek Science* (Harmondsworth Middlesex: Penguin Books, 1963); J. D. Bernal, *The Social Functions of Science* (London: Routledge & Sons, 1939); and *Science and Industry in the Nineteenth Century* (London: Routledge & Paul, 1953).

15. Locke, *Essays*, IV, 3, 18; Locke, *Philosophical Works*, ed. J. A. S. John (London, 1892), II, p. 154.

16. Rüdiger Bubner, *Theorie und Praxis als nachhegelsche Abstraktion* (Frankfurt: Kohlhammer Verlag, 1972).

17. Jürgen Habermas, *Erkenntnis und Interesse* (Frankfurt am Main: Suhrkamp Verlag, 1968), esp. Chap. 3, and the journal *Praxis*, the recently suppressed organ of the Yugoslav Praxis group.

II. Creatures of a Day: Thought and Action in Thucydides
J. Peter Euben

1. Grant McConnell, *Private Power and American Democracy* (New York: Knopf, 1966), pp. 22-23 and *passim*.

2. "Historical materialism aims at achieving an explanation of social evolution which is so comprehensive that it embraces the interrelationships of the theory's own origins and application. The theory specifies the conditions under which reflection on the history of our species by members of this species themselves has become objectively possible; and at the same time it names those to whom this theory is addressed, who then with its aid can gain enlightenment about their emancipatory role in the process of history. The theory occupies itself with reflection on the interrelationships of its origin and with anticipation of those of its application, and thus sees itself as a necessary catalytic moment within the social complex of life which it analyzes; and this complex it analyzes as integral interconnections of compulsions, from the viewpoint of the possible sublation — resolution and abolition — of all this." Jürgen Habermas, *Theory and Practice*, trans. John Viertal (Boston: Beacon Press, 1973), p. 2.

3. Ergon can also mean "function, work, or duty" (see H. R. Immerwahr, "Ergon: History as Monument in Herodotus and Thucydides," *American Journal of Philology*, 81 (1960), pp. 261-290; and William Arrowsmith, "A Greek Theatre of Ideas," *Arion*, 2 (1963), pp. 32-56). Logos is an enormously rich word which changes dimensions in meaning throughout the development of Greek thought. See the discussion of logos in W. K. C. Guthrie, *A History of Greek Philosophy*, Vol. I (Cambridge: Cambridge University Press, 1962), pp. 410-426; and the analysis of logos and ergon in Adam Milman Parry, "Logos and Ergon in Thucydides," Department of Classics Doctoral Dissertation, Harvard University, Cambridge, Mass., 1957, pp. 10-89. I had not read Parry's thesis until I had begun this essay, but I have found it very helpful. His general view of the *History* can be found in "Thucydides' Historical Perspective," in *Yale Classical Studies*, Vol. XXII (Cambridge: Cambridge University Press, 1972), pp. 47-61; "The Language of Thucydides' Description of the Plague," University of London, *Institute of Classical Studies Bulletin*,

16 (1969), pp. 106-114; and "Thucydides' Use of Abstract Language," *Yale French Studies*, 45 (1970), pp. 3-20.

4. See Richard Braxton Onians, *The Origins of European Thought* (Cambridge: Cambridge University Press, 1951), pp. 442-444.

5. All my quotations of pre-Socratic fragments are from Kathleen Freeman, *Ancilla to the Presocratic Philosophers* (Oxford: Blackwell, 1948). Frag. 44 of Heraclitus is at page 27, Frag. 2 of Alcmaeon, at p. 40.

6. See Philip Wheelwright, *Heraclitus* (Princeton: Princeton University Press, 1959), pp. 99-101.

7. Werner Jaeger, *Paideia: The Ideals of Greek Culture*, Vol. I, 2nd ed. (New York: Oxford University Press, 1945), p. 151.

8. See H. F. Cherniss, "The Characteristics and Effects of Presocratic Philosophy," in David J. Furley and R. E. Allen, *Studies in Presocratic Philosophy*, Vol. I (New York: Humanities Press, 1970), pp. 1-28; S. Philip, *Pythagoras and Early Phythagoreans* (Toronto: University of Toronto Press, 1966); and M. L. West, *Early Greek Philosophy and the Orient* (New York: Oxford University Press, 1971), Chaps. 4-6, who makes some strong criticisms of the usual presentations of the pre-Socratics in histories of philosophy.

9. Werner Jaeger, "On the Origin and Cycle of the Philosophic Ideal of Life," in his *Aristotle*, 2nd ed. (New York: Oxford University Press, 1962), p. 426. But see the argument in Alister Cameron, *The Pythagorean Background of the Theory of Recollection* (Menasha, Wisc.: George Banta, 1938), Chap. III.

10. It does not follow of course that they were in fact doing political philosophy or political theory. The general argument for the polis as paradigmatic in this regard was made in a series of essays by Gregory Vlastos. See, for instance, his review of Cornford's *Principium Sapientiae* in *Gnomon*, 27 (1955), pp. 65-76; "Equality and Justice in Early Greek Cosmologies," in *Classical Philology*, 42 (1947), pp. 156-178; and "Isonomia," in the *American Journal of Philology*, 74 (1953), pp. 337-366. The first two essays are reprinted in Furley and Allen, *Presocratic Philosophy*.

11. I do not mean to deny that something new emerged in Ionia in the sixth century B.C. For the first time, nature was considered an autonomous realm whose unity, order, and necessity was intelligible to human reason. Though still influenced by mythical conceptions of nature, these new men offered a theoretical causal inquiry into the myths of creation and the nature of the visible world; they sought to discover what the nature of things were, how they came to be that way, and how it was possible for them to come to be and pass away. "In its full sense Ionian *historia* was a systematic concern with the constitution and meaning of existence without specialization of compartmentalization; it was universal in scope, largely free of anthropocentrism, and insistent that an impersonal causal nexus held all the objects and events in the world together." Cherniss, *Presocratic Philosophy*. See also Max Pohlenz, "Nomos und Physis," *Hermes*, 81 (1953), pp. 418-438.

12. It is of course possible to argue that the Greeks are in some broad sense a philosophical people as Bruno Snell does in his interesting comparative remarks on Greece, India, and China in the chapter "Theorie und Praxis" in *Die Entdeckung Des Geistes* (Hamburg: Claassen Verlag, 1955); except for untranslated chapters I will refer to the English translation, *The Discovery of Mind* trans. Thomas G. Rosenmeyer (New York: Harper & Row, 1960).

13. The word comes from thea meaning "spectacle" and horan meaning "to see." On the etymology see C. Kerenyi, *The Religion of the Greeks and Romans*, trans. Christopher Holme (New York: Dutton, 1962), Chap. IV; and Nicholas Lobkowicz, *Theory and Practice: History of a Concept from Aristotle to Marx* (Notre Dame, Ind.: University of Notre Dame Press, 1967), Chaps. 1-4.

14. Snell, *Discovery of Mind*, p. 4.

15. Cf. John Finley, *Four Stages of Greek Thought* (Stanford, Calif.: Stanford University Press, 1966), Chap. I; Eric Voegelin, *The World of the Polis* (Baton Rouge: Louisiana State University Press, 1957), Parts I and II; and Snell, *Die Entdeckung Des Geistes*, Chap. 17.

16. Thus Theognis 805: "It is necessary that the theoros be straighter than the interpreter of the compass and chalkline, being a guardian, to whom the voice of the Priestess declares an answer from the rich inner sanctuary. For neither by adding can you find a remedy nor in the taking from the god escape offence." See Maurice Bowra, "Two Poems of Theognis," *Philologus*, 103 (1959), pp. 157-166.

17. Because the god Apollo travels great distances to see his people he is called a theorios and thearios. The word theoria would not be used for a spectacle in one's own city. It was necessary that the viewer come from afar. Thus Aeschylus uses the word when the daughters of Oceanus come from a great distance to view the sufferings of Prometheus (118, 302). On this see Kerenyi, *Religion*; and Walter F. Otto, *The Homeric Gods*, trans. Moses Hadas (Boston: Beacon Press, 1964), Chap. III.

18. See Herodotus on Anarcharsis IV 75 and Lobkowicz, *Theory and Practice*, Chap. 1.

19. Snell writes that already with the Seven Sages "das Theoretische sich abzuspalten von der praktischen Weisheit" (*Die Entdeckung Des Geistes*, p. 404) and sees Solon (on too little evidence) as the first who went out into the world *solely* for the sake of theory, just to see the world.

20. Cicero (in *Tusculan Disputations*, V, 3, 8-9) retells a story of Plato's student Heraclitus of Ponticus in which Pythagoras supposedly offered a simile to enlighten others regarding what it meant to be a philosopher. Some men, Pythagoras says, come to the Olympic games to see and make money, otheres to compete for fame and glory, others to admire the beautiful works of art, fine performances and excellent speeches. The philosophers of course are likened to the latter. On the simile, its significance, and the controversy surrounding it see John Burnet, *Early Greek Philosophy* (Cleveland & New York: World Publishing, 1963), p. 98; Guthrie, *History*, pp. 164, 204; Lobkowicz, *Theory and Practice*, pp. 5-7; and Jaeger, "Philosophical Ideal."

21. "The eyes and ears are bad witnesses for men if they have barbarian souls"; that is, if they are childish, asleep, or like animals. See Frags. 107, 40, 81.

22. Frag. 2, 17. Cf. Jaeger, *Paideia*, Chap. 9; and his *The Theology of the Early Greek Philosophers* (New York: Oxford University Press, 1967), Chap. 9.

23. There is no end to this search. "You could not in your going find the ends of the soul, though you traveled the whole way; so deep is the logos." (Frag. 45.)

24. Heraclitus's teaching is a moral critique of human existence insofar as conduct fails to understand or imitate logos. Philosophy for him must find a natural, rational foundation for law, life, and action. (Cf. Solon, Elegiac Poems 16 and Jaeger's discussion of it in *Paideia*, Vol. I, pp. 149, 453.) It is Heraclitus who connects knowledge of Being with insight into human values and conduct to make the former include the latter. See Jaeger in *Paideia* and "Philosophical Ideal."

25. Parmenides's Prologue in Freeman, *Ancilla*, pp. 41-42.

26. Hannah Arendt, *The Human Condition* (New York: Doubleday, Anchor, 1959), pp. 16-17.

27. Cf. C. Mugler, "Sur la Méthode de Thucydide," in *Lettres d'humanité*, 10 (1951), pp. 20-51. There is a lively controversy about the degree to which the medical tradition influenced Thucydides and the extent to which he is a sophist. On the former see Adam Milman Parry, "Description of the Plague." On the latter consult Lowell Edmunds's dis-

cussion of techne and gnome in his *Chance and Intelligence in Thucydides* (Cambridge, Mass.: Harvard University Press, 1975), Chap. III. John Finley, Jr. (in his *Thucydides* [Ann Arbor: University of Michigan Press, 1963], Chap. 2; and his *Three Essays on Thucydides* [Cambridge, Mass.: Harvard University Press, 1967], Chap. II) shows how the sophists influenced Thucydides's style. This does not, of course, entail that Thucydides shared a "sophistic" solution to a shared sense of problems (if there is such a thing as a single sophistic doctrine.)

28. Thucydides's *History of the Pelopennesian War*, Crawley translation (New York: Random House, Modern Library, 1951), p. 453, where the historian is concluding his discussion of the Athenian defeat at Syracuse. Thucydides is, however, deeply impressed with Athens's ability to fight on even after this devastating defeat. (Except when otherwise noted, I will rely on this translation and put the page references after the quote. When I use another, I will note it. Where only book paragraph and sentence appear, the translation includes my own emendations.)

29. What the Corinthians say of Athens, p. 40.

30. In *Thucydides' Mythistoricus* (London: Routledge & Kegan Paul, 1965) Cornford makes an elaborately detailed case for its tragic structure.

31. Alcibiades speaking in the debate on the Sicilian expedition, p. 349.

32. Cornford, *The Unwritten Philosophy* (London: Cambridge University Press, 1950), p. 54.

33. There is a unity of speech and deed that is traditional and Spartan. I shall have little to say about it because I think Thucydides has little to say about it, in part because he regards Sparta as reactive and inferior to Athens in power, daring, and vision (see note 40), in part because of the laconic Spartan manner. William Scott Ferguson (in his *Greek Imperialism* [Boston: Houghton Mifflin, 1913], p. 43) reports that in Sparta a gravestone simply had a man's name on it unless he had died for his country in which case "in war," expressing "with laconic brevity his ground of distinction." Perhaps it is wise to extend Thucydides's warning that the lack of impressive physical remains would blind future historians of Spartan power to its speech as well.

34. All quotes are from Thucydides, pp. 77-78; cf. his comments on Antiphon, p. 490.

35. Quoted in Maurice Bowra, *Periclean Athens* (New York: Dial Press, 1971), p. 73.

36. Arnold Wycombe Gomme, *More Essays in Greek History and Literature* (Oxford: Blackwell, 1962), pp. 92-121. See also Finley, *Thucydides*; and Jacqueline de Romilly, *Thucydides and Athenian Imperialism*, trans. Philip Thody (Oxford: Blackwell, 1963), Part II.

37. Given Socrates's relation to Alcibiades, there is special irony in Plato's criticisms of Pericles in the *Protogoras* and *Gorgias*.

38. It is not simply a matter of Athens having changed such that the political condition for Periclean leadership no longer existed. As usually put that is a tautology, a post hoc judgment, whereby the absence of a Pericles proves there could have been none.

39. Compare Pericles's defense of himself in his third speech with Alcibiades's defense of himself in the Sicilian debate. See especially the concluding paragraph of Alcibiades's speech on Sicily, p. 350.

40. It is of great significance that Sparta is only successful when counseled by an Athenian (Alcibiades), in alliance with the most Athenian-like power (Syracuse) and with a fleet. Sparta wins the war but the Athenian spirit triumphs, which is another way of saying that both Sparta *and* Athens lose the war.

41. Arthur W. H. Adkins, *Merit and Responsibility* (Oxford: Clarendon Press, 1960), p. 238; and Alasdair MacIntyre, *A Short History of Ethics* (New York: Macmillan, 1966), p. 17.

42. Edmunds (*Chance and Intelligence*, p. 109) calls Nicias an "Athenian with a Spartan heart."

43. That it was not Pericles alone who understood the Athenian achievement is made clear by Thucydides's device of having some Athenian merchants defend their native city against Corinthian criticism at Sparta.

44. Edmunds, *Chance and Intelligence*, pp. 82-83. Guthrie (*History*, pp. 205-206) says that the dominant idea in sixth and fifth century literature was "if excess is to be avoided and limit observed . . . then this for man means that he must recognize his mortality and content himself with a mortal's life. Between mortals and immortals, gods and men, a barrier was fixed, and it was hybris to cross it."

45. Freeman, *Ancilla*, Frag. 1, p. 125.

46. R. G. Collingwood, *An Autobiography* (London: Oxford University Press, 1970), p. 146 and Chap. X.

47. Speaking of Pericles, M. I. Finley writes, "While his influence was at its height, he could hope for continual approval of his policies, expressed in the people's vote in the Assembly, but his proposals were submitted to the Assembly week in and week out, alternative views were before them, and the Assembly always could, and on occasion did, abandon him and his policies. The *decision* was theirs, not his or any other leader's; recognition of the need for leadership was not accompanied by a surrender of the power of decision. And he knew it." (*Democracy Ancient and Modern* [New Brunswick, N.J.: Rutgers University Press, 1973], pp. 24-25.)

48. There is some tantalizing philological evidence relevant to this point. Ta theorica, which has a common root with theory, was the money given to poor Athenians to enable them to live a more public life (whether that entailed attending dramas or participating in juries and assemblies). This innovation was probably introduced by Pericles, and it is tempting, concrete political reasons aside, to see this as a democratization of theory.

49. The description of the Plague should be compared in detail with the Funeral Oration (as well as the portrait of the Revolution in Corcyrea).

50. *Ibid.*, pp. 113, 119; and Parry, "Description of the Plague."

51. Plutarch, but not Thucydides, informs us that the Melian expedition was Alcibiades's idea.

52. I have altered the Crawley translation, p. 334. See the translation of the passage in W. K. C. Guthrie, *The Sophists* (Cambridge: Cambridge University Press, 1971), p. 86; and Cornford, *Thucydides*, p. 179.

53. The Melians are right. "It was night when the Paralus reached Athens with her evil tidings, and a bitter wail of woe broke forth. From Piraeus, following the line of the long walls up to the heart of the city, it swept and welled as each man to his neighbour passed on the news. On that night no man slept. There was mourning and sorrow for those that were lost, but the lamentation for the dead was merged with an even deeper sorrow for themselves, as they pictured the evils they were about to suffer, the like of which they had themselves inflicted upon the men of Melos. . . ." (Xenophon *Hellenica*, Book II, Chap. 2.3, 2.17.) But so are the Athenians, since Sparta, despite the pleas of its allies, does indeed save Athens from destruction.

54. Pericles and the Athenians balance contradictory principles—such as intelligence and tradition. This is clear from the introduction to the Funeral Oration where Pericles speaks critically of the custom that provides the occasion for his speech and emphasizes his duty to obey the laws that rightly command the deepest respect and reverence. Though he disparages the innovation, he carries it further by neglecting its conventional form and content. (See Edmunds, *Chance and Intelligence*, p. 33.) And despite his praising of ancestors

who made the present constitution possible, his real praise is for the role of intelligence and mind rather than institutions and laws vouchsafed by the gods. His concern then is with the present uniqueness of Athens.

55. See the discussion of Salamis in Bowra, *Periclean Athens*; and Alvin Gouldner, *Enter Plato* (New York: Basic Books, 1965), pp. 65-66.

56. Thucydides, vi, iii, 3; and Cornford, *Thucydides*, p. 103.

57. *Athenian Imperialism*, Parts II and III, Chap. 2.

58. Jaeger, in *Paideia*, Vol. I, p. 401.

59. Cf. Thucydides, pp. 389-392. Alcibiades does render notable service: afterward. (Pericles too had a dual standard for internal and international politics, but he understood their interdependence in a way Alcibiades does not.)

60. The realism of Melos and Thucydides is stressed by Jaeger, *Paideia*; Paul Shorey, "Implicit Ethics and Psychology of Thucydides," in *Transactions of the American Philological Association* (1893), pp. 68-88; and G. E. M. Ste. Croix, *The Origins of the Peloponnesian War* (Ithaca, N.Y.: Cornell University Press, 1972), pp. 5-34. For discussions of the relation between Athens's policy at Melos and its domestic discords, see David Grene, *Man in His Pride: A Study in the Political Philosophy of Thucydides and Plato* (Chicago & London: University of Chicago Press, 1950).

61. Though I think this conclusion fair, a conclusive argument would require showing in detail how both the realism and hope differ from that expressed by Pericles and the Athenians earlier in the *History*. It is Pericles after all who celebrates decisive daring and speaks (in his third speech) of the world as something for use.

62. The theme of necessity and compulsion does not suddenly appear at Melos and in the Melian Dialogue. Most generally it informs the *History* as a whole, providing much of its tragic structure. In the "Archeology," Thucydides makes it clear that the Peloponnesian War is part of a historical process that goes far back in time. (See Daniel P. Tompkins "The Problem of Power in Thucydides," in *Arion*, New Series 1-2 (1973-1974), pp. 401-416.) More particularly one can find references to being compelled, constrained, or forced to do or not to do certain things in almost every speech. At Melos what had been background becomes foreground and we become directed back over the *History* to ask increasingly general questions: Would Athens have acted differently at Melos or decided differently in the Sicilian debate were Pericles alive (and would he have been elected)? At *any point*, could Athens have done other than it did? And finally, Is political freedom and political choice the delusion of men ignorant of their situation and condition?

63. For discussions of the role of chance, see Cornford's discussion of Pylos in *Thucydides*; A. W. Gomme's alternative interpretation in *A Historical Commentary on Thucydides*, Vol. III (Oxford: Clarendon Press, 1956), pp. 488-489; and Edmunds's assessment, *Chance and Intelligence*, passim.

64. Cf. Wheelwright, *Heraclitus*, pp. 35, 121.

65. But not completely; Pericles after all is killed by the Plague.

66. Hanna Pitkin, *Wittgenstein and Justice* (Berkeley & Los Angeles: University of California Press, 1973), p. 323. See also Hannah Arendt, "What is Freedom?" in *Between Past and Future* (New York: Viking Compass Books, 1968), esp. pp. 143-145.

67. Herodotus, V, 78. See the discussion of this passage in T. A. Sinclair, *A History of Greek Political Thought* (London: Routledge & Kegan Paul, 1959), p. 39.

68. See R. C. Jebb, "The Speeches of Thucydides," in E. A. Abbott, ed., *Hellenica: A Collection of Essays on Greek Poetry, Philosophy, and Religion* (London: Rivingtons, 1882), pp. 266-323.

69. Cleon's tyrannical behavior becomes much clearer in this context, for he is the

most violent man in Athens and the only one (except Sthenelaides) who attacks speech.

70. Four speeches are made by Syracusians, the most Athenian of all cities. They are usefully contrasted with both the earlier speeches by Athenians and the Sicilian debate.

71. Thucydides, *History*, pp. 346-347, 400. Adam Parry (in "Logos and Ergon") argues that from Book IV Athens is driven by chance and hope—hope is the logos (speech concept) farthest removed from reality, while chance (tyche) is external reality at its most incalculable, the most inaccessible to logos.

72. *Ibid.*, p. 363. Thucydides agrees that Athens is increasingly corrupt. He may even agree that past a certain point no new Pericles could emerge. But that need not alter his perception of either Pericles or Periclean Athens. Thus the criticism is right only if one grants that Thucydides shared the values of his critic.

73. In *Four Stages*, p. 64.

74. Thucydides created the twenty-seven-year "Peloponnesian War" (though he never used the phrase), for his contemporaries knew of two wars, the Archidamian or Ten Years War (431-421) and the Decelean War (414-404). The memory of the war and of Athenian greatness during it exists because of the man who wrote its history. See Voegelin's comments, *World of the Polis*, p. 350.

75. Parry, "Logos and Ergon"; and the Loeb Classical Library's Thucydides, trans. Charles Forster Smith, Vol. I, p. 41.

76. Finley, *Thucydides*, p. 19. Others have argued that the *History* is an attempt to understand, predict, and control the uncertainties of politics. "Thucydides, we may say, was strongly influenced by the methods of the Hippocratic school. He used the medical conception of disease as a model in conceiving his kinesis; he was in search of an eidos or idea of the kinesis as well as of its causes; he wanted to explore and define this essence in order to furnish a basis for prediction (prohasis) in the future. . . ." Voegelin, *World of the Polis*, p. 354. For similar views see C. N. Cochrane, *Thucydides and the Sciences of History* (London: Oxford University Press, 1929); and J. P. Wallace, "Thucydides," *Phoenix*, 18 (1964), pp. 251-261. An overstated but I think correct critique of this view can be found in Parry, "Description of the Plague," p. 116.

77. Parry, "Logos and Ergon"; de Romilly, "L'Utilité de l'histoire selon Thucydide," in *Histoire et historiens dans l'antiquité* (Entretien sur l'antiquité, classique IV) (Vandoeuvres/Geneva, 1956), pp. 39-66; and H. P. Stahl, *Thukydides: Die Stellung des Menschen im geschichtlichen Prozess* (Zetemata Heft 40) (Munich, 1966).

78. See Edmunds's discussion of the relations between sophes and acribeia, *Chance and Intelligence*, pp. 155-156; and Jacqueline de Romilly's comment in *Histoire et Raison Chez Thucydide* (Paris: Collection d'Etudes Anciennes, 1956) that "rien ne l'a guidé que son intelligence, reinne lui a servi de critère que sa raison," pp. 12-13.

79. What I mean is clear if one contrasts Thucydides with the methodological preoccupations of much modern behavioral sciences.

80. Collingwood, *Autobiography*, p. 106. "If the function of history was to inform people about the past where the past was understood as a dead past, it could do very little towards helping them to act; but if its function was to inform them about the present, insofar as the past, its ostensible subject matter, was encapsulated in the present and constituted as part of it not at once obvious to the untrained eye, then history stood in the closest possible relation to practical life." Cf. pp. 112-115.

81. See the introductory remarks of Bertrand De Jouvenel to the Hobbes translation of *Thucydides* (Ann Arbor: University of Michigan Press, 1959), pp. v-xiv.

82. This is an overstatement as Edmunds argues in *Chance and Intelligence*, *passim*. At times Thucydides does seem to suggest a political techne. It was this latent technicism

that was part of Thucydides's attraction for Hobbes, who, as Habermas has stated, regards the translation of knowledge into practice as a technical problem. (*Theory and Practice*, p. 43.)

83. Cf. Finley's *Four Stages*, *passim*.

84. Pitkin, *Wittgenstein*, p. 326; Arendt, *Between Past and Future*, p. 77.

III. Plato and Aristotle: The Unity versus the Autonomy of Theory and Practice
Terence Ball

Author's note: An earlier version of the present essay was published in the *Western Political Quarterly*, 15 (September 1972), pp. 534-545.

1. See, e.g., Robert A. Dahl, *Modern Political Analysis* (Englewood Cliffs, N.J.: Prentice-Hall, 1963), p. 24, where Plato's "characteristic preference for imaginative and somewhat rigid theoretical notions drawn from brilliant fancy rather than hard fact" is contrasted with Aristotle's "solid good sense." Aristotle is even credited with being "the first great behavioral scientist"; see Bernard Berelson and Gary Steiner, *Human Behavior: An Inventory of Scientific Findings* (New York: Harcourt, Brace & World, 1964), p. 13.

2. Throughout this essay I shall use theory and philosophy interchangeably, not because they are entirely synonymous but because the distinctions between them do not concern me here. Etymologically, however, the two are closely related; but nowhere are they simply contrasted with praxis. On the etymology of these concepts, see Ernst Kapp, "Theorie und Praxis bei Aristoteles und Platon," *Mnemosyne*, 5 (1937), pp. 179-194; Georg Picht, "Der Sinn der Unterscheidung von Theorie und Praxis in der Griechischen Philosophie," *Evangelische Ethik*, 8 (1964); Nicholas Lobkowicz, *Theory and Practice: History of a Concept From Aristotle to Marx* (Notre Dame, Ind.: University of Notre Dame Press, 1967), pp. 3-57, and his essay in this volume.

3. There are some revealing parallels between the structure of Greek drama and the political theorist's place in the polis. The polis is like a stage, where men display their talents and distinguish themselves publicly; the theater, too, was a public space of sorts. The chorus was in a position to see what ordinary spectators could not see; yet the chorus was neither wholly on nor off the stage, neither a part of the action nor yet wholly aloof. The chorus—like the theorist—brings out the universal in particular events and actions on the stage, sees the extraordinary in the ordinary and commonplace, and so on. It is perhaps significant that the actors on the stage rarely heard, much less heeded, the entreaties, advice, and predictions of the chorus.

4. *Republic*, Cornford translation, 474 B - 478. I have also relied extensively though indirectly upon Allan Bloom's recent translation of the *Republic* (New York: Basic Books, 1968).

5. *Letters*, Post translation, VII, 342 b - 343 c.

6. See Sheldon S. Wolin, *Politics and Vision* (Boston: Little, Brown, 1960), Chap. II.

7. Hannah Arendt, *The Human Condition* (New York: Doubleday, Anchor, 1959), pp. 25-26.

8. Bertrand de Jouvenel, *Sovereignty: An Inquiry Into the Political Good*, trans. J. F. Huntington (Chicago: University of Chicago Press, 1963), p. 304.

9. *Republic*, 431. Plato's myth (pseudos) of metals is one of the instruments of temperance (*ibid.*, pp. 414-415). I do not, however, entirely concur with Cornford's easy accommodation of such myths as "mere allegories," for such a view appears to obscure and underestimate their deceptive and manipulative character. Cf. *ibid.*, p. 106, n. 1. On the place of fear in the Platonic scheme, see *Letter* VII, 336 e-337 b; and *Laws*, XII.

10. See Thucydides, *History of the Pelopennesian War*, Crawley translation (New York: Random House, Modern Library, 1951), p. 79.

11. *Statesman*, Skemp translation, 276 d - e.

12. *Ibid.*, 296 b.

13. *Ibid.*, 293 a.

14. It might be objected that Plato in his later dialogues, especially the *Laws*, rescinded or overcame his earlier objections to a jurisprudential approach to governance. This certainly appears to be a plausible reading of the *Laws* — until one comes to Book XII, where Plato the erstwhile jurist reverts to Plato the perfectionist philosopher. For in the end he cannot trust governance wholly to codified law, any more than the philosopher can rely entirely upon the spoken or written word in his pursuit of truth. Plato's most perceptive critic noted his reversion in the *Laws* to the earlier ideals and institutions of the *Republic*; Aristotle, *Politics*, II, 6, § 4.

15. *Republic*, 514 - 21; *Statesman*, 294 a - d.

16. As a canvas must be "scraped clean" to be fit for the touch of the artist (*Republic*, 500).

17. Most notably, perhaps, by Wolin, *Politics and Vision*, p. 66.

18. *Republic*, 473.

19. *Ibid.*, 485.

20. Arendt, *Human Condition*, p. 173.

21. *Republic*, 540; *Statesman*, 305 d; *Nichomachean Ethics*, X, 7; *Politics*, II, vii, § 12.

22. *Apology*, Tredennick translation, 31 D.

23. *Sophist*, 216 c - d.

24. See Arendt's criticism in *Human Condition*, p. 20.

25. *Republic*, 496.

26. *Politics*, VII, ii, § 3.

27. *Republic*, 488-495. Plato may have been suggesting that Alcibiades's philosophical talents had been corrupted by Athenian society.

28. *Nichomachean Ethics*, Thompson translation, X, 9, p. 314.

29. *Ibid.*, p. 315.

30. *Ibid.*, X, 7, pp. 303-305.

31. *Ibid*. Compare I, 9; also *Politics*, VII, ii, § 14.

32. *Nichomachean Ethics*, X, 9, p. 310.

33. *Ibid.*, VI, 6, p. 178.

34. *Ibid.*, VI, 8, p. 181. It is instructive to contrast Aristotle's understanding of political science, as the paradigmatic "practical science," with that of a modern observer who, despite his frequent favorable references to Aristotle, can nevertheless write: "At the very outset . . . we must distinguish political science as the systematic *study* of politics from the *practice* of politics." And again: "I want to emphasize that actually engaging in politics is not at all the same thing as studying politics in order to develop principles of general relevance. Political science means the study, not the practice, of politics." (Robert A. Dahl, "What is Political Science?" in *American Politics and Government: Essays in Essentials*, ed. Stephen K. Bailey [New York: Basic Books, 1965], pp. 1, 3.) As for "develop[ing] principles of general relevance," Aristotle would doubtless ask: relevant *to* what? His answer would, one suspects, differ from Professor Dahl's.

35. *Nichomachean Ethics*, VI, 7, p. 180.

36. *Ibid.*, III, 3, pp. 85-87. See *Politics*, VII, ix, on deliberation as the proper function of mature citizens.

37. *Nichomachean Ethics*, X, 7, p. 304.

38. *Ibid.*, X, 9, pp. 314-315.

39. This analogy suggests a crucial question: Who then is the *composer?* At the risk of pushing the analogy too far, I should say that Plato is both a critic of traditional music and the composer of a new and flawless symphony. Aristotle, by contrast, is less a composer than a critic who compares and judges those musical forms which have been passed down from other times and places.

40. Cf. Barker's edition of Aristotle's *Politics*, Appendix V, p. 386.

41. *Rhetoric*, I, ii § 7 (1356 a 25 - 30).

42. *Nichomachean Ethics*, I, *passim.*

43. *Politics*, VII, ii, § 16.

44. *Ibid.*, VII, iii, §§ 7 - 8.

45. *Republic*, 518.

46. *Politics*, II, v, § 16.

47. See note 1.

48. "The philosophers have heretofore only attempted to understand the world; the point is, however, to *change* it."

IV. Kant on Theory and Practice
Carl Raschke

1. G. W. F. Hegel, *The Phenomenolgy of Mind*, trans. J. B. Baillie (London: Macmillan, 1931), p. 616.

2. Cf. "It is impossible to conceive anything at all in the world, or even out of it, which can be taken as good without qualification, except a *good will.*" *The Groundwork of the Metaphysic of Morals*, trans. H. J. Paton (New York: Harper & Row, 1964), p. 61. Immanuel Kant, *Gesammelte Schriften* (Berlin: Georg-Reimer Verlag, 1911), iv, p. 393. Hereafter referred to as *Schriften.*

3. "Theory and Practice," in Hans Reiss, ed., *Kant's Political Writings* (Cambridge: Cambridge University Press, 1970), pp. 81-83. *Schriften*, viii, pp. 15-31.

4. See "The Metaphysics of Morals," in Reiss, *Kant's Political Writings*, p. 147; see also n. 94. *Schriften*, vi, p. 323.

5. See "The Contest of the Faculties," in Reiss, *Kant's Political Writings*, p. 183. *Schriften*, vii, p. 85.

6. *Critique of Practical Reason*, trans. Lewis W. Beck (New York: Bobbs-Merrill, 1956), p. 23. *Schriften*, v, p. 24.

7. The main Marxist criticisms of Kant's formalism that I have in mind are found in Nicholas Lobkowicz, *Theory and Practice: History of a Concept from Aristotle to Marx* (Notre Dame, Ind.: University of Notre Dame Press, 1967); Herbert Marcuse, *Studies in Critical Philosophy*, trans. Joris de Bres (London: New Left Books, 1972); Lucien Goldman, *Immanuel Kant*, trans. Robert Black (London: New Left Books, 1971).

8. "Theory and Practice," p. 61. *Schriften*, viii, p. 275.

9. *Critique of Practical Reason*, p. 15. *Schriften*, v, p. 15.

10. *Critique of Pure Reason*, trans. J. M. D. Meiklejohn (New York: Everyman's Library, 1964), p. 452. See also p. 457, as well as the discussion of Kant's theory of knowledge in Peter Strawson, *The Bounds of Sense* (London: Methuen, 1966). *Schriften*, iii, p. 517.

11. *Critique of Practical Reason*, p. 15. *Schriften*, v, p. 15.

12. *Critique of Pure Reason*, pp. 452-454. See also *Critique of Practical Reason*, pp. 3-5. *Schriften*, iii, p. 517 and v, p. 3.

13. P. 18. *Schriften*, iii, p. 19.

14. See "On the Failure of All Theodicies," trans. Michael Despland, unpublished typescript, Harvard University. The German edition is found in *Schriften*, viii.

15. Kant's notion that every moral agent must hold certain necessary beliefs concerning the ultimate reconcilability of his aspirations with the general nature of things may be compared with William James's contention that the existence of God must be assumed as a "live option," even if He cannot be scientifically demonstrated, to make personal virtue practicable.

16. *Critique of Practical Reason*, p. 4. *Schriften*, v, pp. 4-5.

17. I have offered my own translation and in the following quoted passage instead of relying on the standard English editions, which do not capture the subtle twists of meaning in this section of the first *Critique*. The German passage here is found in Kant, *Schriften*, iii, p. 371.

18. *Ibid.*, p. 372.

19. For Hume's discussion see his *Treatise of Human Nature*, Part III, Section III; also *An Inquiry Concerning Human Understanding*, Secion VI.

20. *Critique of Pure Reason*, p. 326. *Schriften*, iii, p. 374.

21. *Critique of Pure Reason*, p. 328. *Schriften*, iii, p. 376.

22. *Groundwork*, p. 74. *Schriften*, iv, p. 407.

23. Cf. *Critique of Pure Reason*, p. 326. *Schriften*, iii, p. 374.

24. See E. C. Ballard, "The Kantian Solution to the Problem of Man," *Tulane Studies in Philosophy* 3 (1954), p. 35.

25. For more intricate discussions of the kinds of situations in which intentional language can justifiably be construed as causal, see A. R. Louch, *Explanation and Human Action* (Berkeley: University of California Press, 1966), Chap. vi; Daniel Taylor, *Explanation and Meaning* (Cambridge: Cambridge University Press, 1970), Chap. vi; P. H. Nowell-Smith, *Ethics* (Baltimore: Penguin Books, 1954), pp. 298-331. It should be noted that these authors, as is implied in Kant's coining of the term *causa noumenon*, do not make the rather fashionable, yet arbitrary, distinction between reasons and causes, where the former are considered purely subjective forms of action-explanation and the latter regarded as the general or more scientific types of accounting.

26. See G. N. A. Vesey, "Agent and Spectator," in *The Human Agent* (London: Macmillan, 1967), pp. 139-140.

27. See Gilbert Ryle, *The Concept of Mind* (New York: Barnes & Noble, 1949).

28. See Louch, *Explanation and Human Action*, pp. 95-98.

29. Cf. *Groundwork*, pp. 124-125. *Schriften*, iv, p. 456.

30. *Groundwork*, p. 118. *Schriften*, iv, p. 450.

31. *Groundwork*, p. 89. *Schriften*, iv, p. 421.

32. See *Critique of Practical Reason*, p. 25. *Schriften*, v, p. 26.

33. See John Rawls, *A Theory of Justice* (Cambridge: Harvard University Press, 1971), p. 27.

34. *Ibid.*, p. 32.

35. "Theory and Practice," p. 72. *Schriften*, viii, pp. 288-289.

36. Thomas Hobbes, *Leviathan*, ed. C. B. Macpherson (Baltimore: Penguin Books, 1968), p. 191.

37. Cf. ". . . it is a precept, or generall rule of Reason, *That every man, ought to endeavour Peace, as farre as he has hope of obtaining it; and when he cannot obtain it, that he may seek, and use, all helps, and advantages of Warre*. The first branch of which Rule, containeth the first, and Fundamentall Law of Nature, by which men are commanded to endeavour Peace, is derived this second Law; *That a man be willing . . . to lay down this*

right to all things; and be contented with so much liberty against other men, as he would allow other men against himselfe." *ibid.*, p. 190. Cf. also Thomas Hobbes, *De Cive*, ed. Sterling Lamprecht (New York: Appleton-Century-Crofts, 1949), pp. 33-34.

38. *Leviathan*, pp. 215-216.

39. *Ibid.*, p. 216. Cf. also Hobbes, *De Cive*, p. 57.

40. "Theory and Practice," p. 79. *Schriften*, viii, p. 297.

41. "Theory and Practice," p. 79.

42. *Ibid.*, Cf. also "The Metaphysics of Morals," p. 162. *Schriften*, vi, p. 340.

43. "The Metaphysics of Morals," p. 133. *Schriften*, vi, p. 230.

44. "The Metaphysics of Morals," p. 134. *Schriften*, vi, p. 231.

45. "Theory and Practice," p. 86. *Schriften*, viii, p. 306.

46. *Leviathan*, p. 189.

47. *Leviathan*, p. 228.

48. "Theory and Practice," pp. 74-75. *Schriften*, viii, p. 291.

49. "Theory and Practice," p. 74. *Schriften*, viii, p. 291.

50. *Religion within the Limits of Reason Alone*, trans. Theodore Greene and Hoyt Hudson (La Salle: Open Court, 1934), p. 87. *Schriften*, vi, p. 95.

51. *Ibid.*, p. 85. *Schriften*, vi, p. 94.

52. Rawls, *Justice*, p. 15. For a more careful treatment of how the fairness doctrine derives from Kantian moral principles, see Paul Taylor, "Universalizability and Justice," in Howard E. Kiefer and Milton K. Munitz, eds., *Ethics and Social Justice* (Albany: State University of New York Press, 1968), pp. 142-163.

53. Loyd D. Easton and Kurt H. Guddat, *Writings of the Young Marx on Philosophy and Society* (New York: Doubleday, 1967), p. 431.

54. "Idea for a Universal History with a Cosmopolitan Purpose," in Reiss, *Kant's Political Writings*, p. 50. *Schriften*, viii, p. 27.

55. "Idea for a Universal History," p. 43. *Schriften*, viii, p. 19.

56. "Idea for a Universal History," p. 42. *Schriften*, viii, p. 18.

57. "Idea for a Universal History," p. 45. *Schriften*, viii, p. 22.

58. "Idea for a Universal History," p. 45. Italics mine. Passages like these go far to alter the common misunderstanding that Kant did not have any genuine *social* conception of humanity or of any notion of natural law underwriting his ideal form of community. One of the more noteworthy examples of this erroneous interpretation of Kant is found in Otto Gierke, *Natural Law and the Theory of Society*, trans. Ernest Barker (Boston: Beacon Press, 1957), pp. 102-103. Gierke claims that Kant's insistence on the priority of moral autonomy abstracts from the natural conditions of human association and thus renders the formation of an authentic society based on a unity of purpose impossible. An interesting constructive piece of philosophy refuting the legitimacy of social constraints upon the individual and inspired by this misreading of Kant's conception of autonomy appears in Robert P. Wolff, *In Defense of Anarchism* (New York: Harper & Row, 1970).

59. Cf. "If a *popular revolution* is to coincide with the *emancipation of a particular class* of civil society, if *one* class is to stand for the whole of society, all the defects of society must conversely be concentrated in another class." Easton and Guddat, *Writings of the Young Marx*, p. 261.

60. "Idea for a Universal History," p. 45. *Schriften*, viii, p. 21.

61. "Idea for a Universal History," p. 44. *Schriften*, viii, p. 20.

62. "Idea for a Universal History," p. 45. *Schriften*, viii, p. 21.

63. "Such a spectacle would force us to turn away in revulsion, and, by making us despair of ever finding any completed rational aim behind it, would reduce us to hoping

for it only in some other world." "Idea for a Universal History," p. 53. *Schriften*, viii, p. 30.

64. "Idea for a Universal History," pp. 52-53. *Schriften*, viii, p. 30.

65. See Herbert Marcuse, "The Concept of Essence," in *Negations* (Boston: Beacon Press, 1968), p. 75.

66. *Ibid.*, p. 76.

67. Revolution motivated by passing outrage, Kant also believes, precludes the search for consistent political theory: "If we therefore consider the *welfare* of the people, theory is not in fact valid, for everything depends on practice derived from experience." "Theory and Practice," p. 86. *Schriften*, viii, p. 306.

68. "Theory and Practice," p. 83. *Schriften*, viii, p. 302. For some brief but excellent discussions of Kant's ideas on revolution, see Lewis W. Beck, "Kant and the Right of Revolution," *Journal of the History of Ideas* 32 (July-September 1971), pp. 411-422, and Sidney Axinn, "Kant, Authority, and the French Revolution," *Journal of the History of Ideas* 32 (July-September 1971), pp. 423-432.

69. "The Metaphysics of Morals," p. 147. *Schriften*, vi, p. 323. Kant in not consistently sanguine about the events of 1789. In a letter to J. E. Biester (Oct. 5, 1793), he talks about "the ever increasingly repulsive French Revolution, in which the actual freedom of reason and morality and all wisdom in statecraft and legislation are being more shamefully trampled under foot . . ."

70. See Hans Reiss's introduction to *Kant's Political Writings*, p. 7.

71. "Perpetual Peace," in Reiss, *Kant's Political Writings*, p. 118n. *Schriften*, viii, p. 373n.

72. "Perpetual Peace," p. 119. *Schriften*, viii, p. 373n.

73. "Contest of the Faculties," pp. 184-185. *Schriften*, vii, p. 88.

74. "What is Enlightenment?" in Reiss, *Kant's Political Writings*, p. 55. *Schriften*, viii, p. 36.

75. Kant uses the words contract and constitution interchangeably. By contract he does not mean an actual agreement between subjects and sovereign, as we have seen, but an a priori rubric of justice that logically meets the requirements of universalizability and fairness (cf. Rawls) and which may either be formally drawn up in a document or rationally assumed to govern relations in a society.

76. "Theory and Practice," p. 85. *Schriften*, viii, p. 305.

77. "Theory and Practice," p. 87. *Schriften*, viii, p. 306.

V. Theory and Practice in Hegel and Marx: An Unfinished Dialogue
Peter Fuss

1. *Karl Marx: Early Writings*, trans. and ed. T. B. Bottomore (New York: McGraw Hill, 1964), e.g., pp. 8, 10, 15, 31, 55, 59, and, in slightly variant terminology, 167.

2. I am indebted to Jacob Taubès who first taught me how to read this passage some twenty ago and to the work of Alexandre Kojève for helping me understand it from a Marxian perspective. The responsibility for the interpretation advanced here is, of course, my own.

3. G. W. F. Hegel, *Phänomenologie des Geistes*, ed. J. Hoffmeister (Hamburg: Felix Meiner, 1952), p. 32; cf. Hegel's *Phenomenology of Mind*, trans. J. B. Baillie (New York: Harper & Row, 1967), p. 96. Hereafter referred to as Hoffmeister and Baillie respectively.

4. A more Sartreian way of putting this: "the look" of the other initially disintegrates my self-assurance, i.e., unmasks my lack of integrity as an autonomous person, although subsequently it may confirm the presence of that integrity in its properly interpersonal frame of reference.

5. Hoffmeister, pp. 141-143; Baillie, pp. 229-231.

6. Hoffmeister, pp. 143-145; Baillie, pp. 231-234.

7. Hoffmeister, pp. 145-148; Baillie, pp. 234-237.

8. Hoffmeister, pp. 148-150; Baillie, pp. 237-240.

9. The turnings of intellectual history being what they are, it is not inappropriate to call this the Marxian moment in Hegel's thought — just as the stress on sublimation in this seminal passage is a recognizably Freudian one. And although the terminology is exactly reversed, Hegel's sharp contrast between absolute fear (Furcht) and a measure of mere anxiety (einige Angst) is vintage existentialism.

10. This distinction strikingly parallels Rousseau's almost despairing and generally ill-fated one between amour propre and amour de soi; cf. *Emile* (Paris: Armand-Aubree, 1829), Vol. I, p. 106. Rousseau's distinction has not survived in modern French, any more than has Hegel's in German.

11. Thus, for instance, the airiness of Stoic self-containment, the childish self-deception of full-blown skepticism, and the self-dichotomized character of the "Unhappy (Judeo-Christian) Consciousness" (Chapter four, B); the perplexities of rational self-consciousness as it alternately seeks to "find" itself in the world through scientific observation and "make" its presence felt through a series of fragmentary modes of individualism: hedonic, Romantic, virtuous, atomistically social, and (as it were from on high) morally legislative (Chapter five); and the trials of an immature spirit as it first seeks positive embodiment in the unreflective ethical community, in the tragic agonal conflict, and in abstract legal personhood; then finds itself estranged from institutionally congealed forms of its own political and moral authority, wealth, and deeper meaning as an autonomous end in itself; and finally reaches the threshold of concrete actualization by reconciling the bifurcated moments of its abstract Kantian universalism and its Romantic individualism (Chapter six).

12. I have translated this and subsequent passages from Karl Marx, *Texte zu Methode und Praxis* II (Pariser Manuscripte, 1844), ed. Günther Hillmann (Hamburg: Rowohlt, 1968), p. 113. For variant renditions see Raja Dunayevskaya, *Marxism and Freedom* (New York: Bookman, 1958), pp. 309-310; Bottomore, *Karl Marx*, pp. 202-203; and *Karl Marx: Early Texts*, trans. and ed. David McLellan (Oxford: Blackwell, 1971), p. 164.

13. *Ibid.*, p. 116; cf. Bottomore, *Karl Marx*, p. 206; McLellan, *Karl Marx*, p. 167.

14. *Ibid.*, p. 116; cf. Bottomore, *Karl Marx*, p. 206; McLellan, *Karl Marx*, p. 167.

15. *Ibid.*, p. 120; cf. Bottomore, *Karl Marx*, p. 210; McLellan, *Karl Marx*, p. 170.

16. *Ibid.*, cf. McLellan, *Karl Marx*, p. 171.

17. *Ibid.*, pp. 123-124; cf. Bottomore, *Karl Marx*, p. 214; McLellan, *Karl Marx*, p. 174.

18. It is at once epistemological and ethical, hence nothing short of ontological.

19. There are recurrent references in the *Philsosphy of Right* to a "universal class," which Hegel seems on occasion to identify with the civil service — very likely having in mind the generation of cultivated and enlightened administrators (Hardenberg, Stein, etc.) whom Hegel had just cause to admire in his own time. See Shlomo Avineri's discussion of this in *Hegel's Theory of the Modern State* (Cambridge: Cambridge University Press, 1972), pp. 158-160 and *passim*. I return to this "universal class" in Section four of this essay.

20. "Who built Thebes with its seven gates? In all the books its says kings." — Bertold Brecht.

21. I use Bottomore's translation here (*Karl Marx*, pp. 56-58).

22. *Ibid.*, p. 56.

23. Catalyst is quite another matter.

24. Bottomore, *Karl Marx*, p. 59.

25. Compare the analysis that follows with Hannah Arendt's treatment of these and related matters in a much fuller historical setting in her excellent and far too neglected magnum opus, *The Human Condition* (Chicago: University of Chicago Press, 1958; paperback version, New York: Doubleday, Anchor, 1959), especially her concluding chapter.

26. See pages 103-104 of this essay.

27. For a searching discussion of this see Avineri, *Hegel's Theory*, Chapters five and seven. See also my review article on this book in the *Journal of the History of Philosophy*, 13, no. 2 (April 1975), pp. 235-246. Because of these other sources, my summary here is only skeletal.

28. At this point the term is to be taken in both its philosophical and nonphilosophical sense.

29. Cf. Theodor W. Adorno, *Negative Dialektik* (Frankfurt am Main: Suhrkamp, 1966), pp. 305-320. Adorno's work has already done much to revitalize critical social theory on the Continent, in part, I think, because although it is representative of the critical humanist wing of the neo-Marxist controversy, it is less impacted within this controversy just because it has worked its way back to that controversy's historical and conceptual roots.

30. *Hegel's Philosophy of Right*, trans. T. M. Knox (New York: Oxford University Press, 1973), p. 193.

31. Feuerbach in his turn had found inspiration for the idea in Hegel, whose "universal class" was supposed to embody it.

32. Marx was by no means unique in this respect. For a most impressive effort to draw such a distinction and to project the many-sided historical consequences of failing to observe it, see Hannah Arendt's *The Human Condition*. At this point in an already rather lengthy essay I must presuppose not only the general validity of her contentions but the reader's familiarity with them.

33. Understood in these terms, there is of course nothing distinctively Marxian about the dilemma in question.

34. I.e., Marxian theorists and tacticians, the "revolutionary vanguard," etc., more often than not straylings from what their own rigid class analysis has no choice but to stamp "middle."

35. This remark is aimed at certain Marxists, not at Marx himself, who seems never to have lost sight of the central place of the humanist moment of *self*-emancipation in any revolutionary theory or praxis worthy of the name. See Brian Fay's essay in this volume.

36. By now everyone is a little weary of talk about "alienation." I should therefore apologize for dredging up yet another form of it, viz., the estrangement of critical thought itself from precisely those whose action is most in need of being animated by it.

37. One could say that "class" is precisely what it lacks. I don't mean to pun; I think our language is suggestive here. Some aristocracies had class, and the same is true of various groupings of the poor and the not so poor. It is not, in the end, a question of what you have or lack but of what you are, or can become, in confrontation with the world around you. There can be nobility in the exercise of a paternalistic social role, just as there can be dignity in patience and resignation—especially in a world where scarcity, want, and other natural misfortunes are (or in good faith are thought to be) inescapable. The irony of our present situation is that the so-called middle class, forever pretending to itself that it is the hapless victim of a world it was largely instrumental in making, has for some time now lacked the social cohesiveness that is traditionally the first, if not the most important, mark of a class; whereas those who were supposed to have long since been rendered obsolete by technological and social progress—i.e., the poor—continue to be the only ones who on occasion have or show class.

VI. The Unity of Theory and Practice: The Science of Marx and Nietzsche
Edward Andrew

1. Parts of this paper are similar to sections of two of my articles hitherto published: "A Note on the Unity of Theory and Practice in Marx and Nietzsche" *Political Theory*, 3, no. 3 (August 1975) pp. 305-316; and "Marx's Theory of Classes: Science and Ideology" *Canadian Journal of Political Science*, 8, no. 3, (September 1975), pp. 454-466.

2. R. Hilferding, *Das Finanzkapital* (Frankfurt: Europaeische Verlagsanstalt, 1968), pp. 20-21; S. Hook, *Towards the Understanding of Karl Marx* (London: Victor Gollancz, 1933), pp. 17-19; S. Ossowski, *Class Structure in the Social Consciousness* (London: Routledge & Kegan Paul, 1967), p. 75; R. Dahrendorf, *Class and Class Conflict in Industrial Society* (Stanford: Stanford University Press, 1963), pp. 8-35.

3. *The Will to Power*, ed. W. Kaufmann (New York: Random House, Vintage, 1968), pp. 77-78.

4. *The Use and Abuse of History*, trans. A. Collins (New York: Bobbs-Merrill, 1957), p. 3.

5. *On the Genealogy of Morals*, in *On the Genealogy of Morals and Ecce Homo*, ed. W. Kaufmann (New York: Random House, Vintage, 1969), pp. 157-158.

6. E. Fromm, *Marx's Concept of Man* (New York, Ungar, 1963), p. 257.

7. *Ecce Homo*, in Kaufmann, *On the Genealogy of Morals and Ecce Homo*, pp. 231-232, 242.

8. *Contribution to the Critique of Hegel's Philosophy of Right: Introduction*, in *The Marx-Engels Reader*, ed. R. C. Tucker (New York: Norton, 1972), pp. 13, 23; *The Will to Power*, p. 488; *Twilight of the Idols*, in *Twilight of the Idols and the Anti-Christ* (London: Penguin, 1968), p. 32; *Human, All-Too-Human*, Part 1, in *Complete Works*, ed. O. Levy (London: Russell & Russell, 1924), Vol. 6, pp. 57-58.

9. *The Use and Abuse of History*, p. 37.

10. *Theses on Feuerbach*, in *The German Ideology*, trans. W. Lough (London: Lawrence & Wisehart, 1965), p. 645.

11. *The Dawn of Day*, in *Complete Works*, Vol. 9, p. 47.

12. *Contribution to the Critique of Hegel's Philosophy of Right: Introduction*, pp. 11-23.

13. *Theses on Feuerbach*, p. 647.

14. *The Will to Power*, p. 318.

15. *Ibid.*, p. 322.

16. *The German Ideology*, p. 58.

17. *Private Property and Communism*, in Tucker, *The Marx-Engels Reader*, p. 76.

18. *The Will to Power*, pp. 266, 272, 278, 326; *Joyful Wisdom*, trans. T. Common (New York: Ungar, 1968), pp. 154-155; *Human, All-Too-Human*, Part 1, pp. 18-19; *Beyond Good and Evil*, in Levy, *Complete Works*, Vol. 12, pp. 9-11.

19. *The Will to Power*, p. 275.

20. *On the Genealogy of Morals*, p. 119.

21. *Ibid.*; *Thus Spoke Zarathustra*, trans. J. R. Hollingdale (London: Penguin, 1961), pp. 144-145.

22. *The Will to Power*, p. 227.

23. *Human, All-Too-Human*, Part 1, p. 236.

24. *The Dawn of Day*, p. 168; cf. p. 185.

25. *The Will to Power*, p. 150.

26. *Thus Spoke Zarathustra*, p. 229.

27. *The Dawn of Day*, p. 325.

28. *Ibid.*, p. 315.

29. *Human, All-Too-Human*, Part 2, in Levy, *Complete Works*, Vol. 7, p. 347.

30. *Human, All-Too-Human*, Part 1, p. 7; *The Dawn of Day*, pp. 349-350; *Joyful Wisdom*, pp. 219-220.

31. *Theses on Feuerbach*, p. 645.

32. *Ibid.*, p. 647; cf. *Private Property and Communism*, p. 75.

33. In Tucker, *The Marx-Engels Reader*, p. 405.

34. *The Poverty of Philosophy* (Moscow: Foreign Languages Publishing House, n.d.), p. 59.

35. *Capital* (Moscow: Foreign Languages Publishing House, 1962), Vol. 3, pp. 862-863.

36. *Die Moralisierende Kritik und die Kritisierende Moral*, in *Werke* (Berlin: Dietz Verlag, 1959), Vol. 4, p. 349. My translation.

37. *The Eighteenth Brumaire of Louis Bonaparte*, in Tucker, *The Marx-Engels Reader*, p. 516.

38. *The German Ideology*, p. 78.

39. *Ibid.*, pp. 68-69, 77; *The Communist Manifesto*, in Tucker, *The Marx-Engels Reader*, p. 343.

40. *The Communist Manifesto*, p. 342.

41. *The German Ideology*, pp. 76-77; *The Communist Manifesto*, pp. 340-343.

42. *The German Ideology*, p. 78; *The Communist Manifesto*, pp. 342-343.

43. *The Poverty of Philosophy*, pp. 167-168.

44. *Werke*, Vol. 31, p. 446. My translation.

45. *The German Ideology*, pp. 31-32.

46. *Estranged Labour*, in Tucker, *The Marx-Engels Reader*, pp. 57-67; *The German Ideology*, p. 83; *Grundrisse der Kritik der Politischen Oekonomie* (Berlin: Europaeische Verlagsanstalt, 1953), p. 505; *Capital*, Vol. 3, p. 800; *Inaugural Address of the Working Men's International Association*, in Tucker, *The Marx-Engels Reader*, p. 380.

47. *Critique of the Gotha Program*, in Tucker, *The Marx-Engels Reader*, p. 388.

48. *The Will to Power*, p. 251.

49. *Joyful Wisdom*, p. 235.

50. *Ibid.*, pp. 154-155; *Thus Spoke Zarathustra*, pp. 136, 144-145; *The Will to Power*, pp. 60, 202-203, 227, 266, 272; *Human, All-Too-Human*, Part 1, pp. 18-19; *The Dawn of Day*, p. 365; *Beyond Good and Evil*, pp. 8-11, 14; *Private Property and Communism*, pp. 75-76; *Critique of the Hegelian Dialectic and Philosophy as a Whole*, in Tucker, *The Marx-Engels Reader*, pp. 87-103; *The German Ideology*, p. 645.

51. *The Use and Abuse of History*, p. 69.

52. *Critique of the Hegelian Dialectic and Philosophy as a Whole*, pp. 90, 91, 93.

53. *Science of Logic* (London: Allen & Unwin, 1929), Vol. 1, p. 43.

54. *Human, All-Too-Human*, Part 2, p. 141.

55. *Estranged Labour*, p. 61.

56. *Critique of the Hegelian Dialectic and Philosophy as a Whole*, p. 94.

57. *Thus Spoke Zarathustra*, p. 111.

58. *The German Ideology*, p. 58.

59. *The Will to Power*, p. 272; cf. *Private Property and Communism*, pp. 72-79; *The German Ideology*, pp. 55-59.

60. *Joyful Wisdom*, pp. 235-236.

61. *Thus Spoke Zarathustra*, pp. 41, 65, 75, 104, 138, 215-216, 297.

62. *The German Ideology*, pp. 86, 646; cf. *Werke*, Vol. 8, p. 598.

63. *Thus Spoke Zarathustra*, p. 220.

64. *The Will to Power*, p. 503.

65. *Joyful Wisdom*, pp. 219-220.

66. *Beyond Good and Evil*, p. 152.

67. Article written on September 12, 1947 in L. S. Feuer's edition of *Marx and Engels: Basic Writings on Politics and Philosophy* (New York: Doubleday, 1959), p. 269.

68. *The German Ideology*, p. 86.

69. *Ibid.*, p. 646.

70. *Ibid.*

71. *The Dawn of Day*, pp. 362-363.

72. *Werke*, Vol. 8, p. 598. My translation.

73. The Chinese revolution provides the most instructive example of Marx's hope for a revolutionary alteration of men on a mass scale although it was not proletarian based, nor internationalist in inspiration, nor has it as yet culminated in "the self-government of the immediate producers."

74. *Thus Spoke Zarathustra*, pp. 79, 152-155, 168; *The Dawn of Day*, pp. 351-352; *Beyond Good and Evil*, p. 255.

75. *Contribution to the Critique of Hegel's Philosophy of Right: Introduction*, p. 18.

76. *The Will to Power*, p. 327.

77. *Thus Spoke Zarathustra*, p. 74.

VII. Hannah Arendt: The Ambiguities of Theory and Practice
Richard J. Bernstein

1. *The Human Condition* (New York: Doublday, Anchor, 1959), p. 40.

2. See "Lying in Politics," *Crises of the Republic* (New York: Harvest Books, 1972), pp. 3-57.

3. *The Human Condition*, p. 157.

4. *Ibid.*

5. "What is Freedom?" *Between Past and Future* (New York: Viking Compass Books, 1968), p. 153.

6. *The Human Condition*, p. 157.

7. *Ibid.*, p. 158.

8. See *On Revolution* (New York: Viking Compass Books, 1965).

9. "Eichmann in Jerusalem," An Exchange of Letters between Gershon Scholem and Hannah Arendt, *Encounter* (January 1964), p. 53.

10. For an exploration of the movements of this dialectic, see my discussion of Kierkegaard in *Praxis and Action* (Philadelphia: University of Pennsylvania Press, 1971), Part II.

11. *The Human Condition*, p. 159.

12. *Ibid.*, p. 158.

13. *Ibid.*, pp. 9-10.

14. *Ibid.*, pp. 178-179.

15. For a conceptual analysis of the distinctions, see *The Human Condition*, pp. 178-186; and "On Violence," in *Crises of the Republic*.

16. *The Human Condition*, p. 185. A full-scale analysis of the systematic web of concepts tied to action would also have to take account of the distinctive cognitive functions appropriate to action, especially judgment and opinion.

17. This is not the place to analyze and evaluate the vehement attacks on her Eichmann

book, although I believe that Arendt's scholarly mistakes have been grossly exaggerated. Reading much of the polemic that her book stirred up, I am struck by the willful misreading of her study — a misreading that in a curious way proves Arendt's point of how — especially on matters of vital concern — we cling to precedent and a conventional "wisdom" which can blind us from grasping what is novel. To illustrate my claim that throughout her work Arendt has engaged in that type of independent thinking which attempts to forge new categories and concepts required for understanding what is genuinely novel, I think it is worth quoting at length what *is* the main conclusion of her report (a conclusion ignored by so many):

Eichmann, it will be remembered, had steadfastly insisted that he was guilty only of "aiding and abetting" in the commission of the crimes with which he was charged, that he himself had never committed an overt act. The judgment, to one's great relief, in a way recognized that the prosecution had not succeeded in proving him wrong on this point. For it was an important point; it touched upon the very essence of this crime, which was no ordinary crime, and the very nature of this criminal, who was no common criminal, by implication, it also took cognizance of the weird fact that in the death camps it was usually the inmates and the victims who had actually wielded "the fatal instrument with [their] own hands." What the judgment had to say on this point was more than correct, it was the truth: "Expressing his activities in terms of Section 23 of our Criminal Code Ordinance, we should say that they were mainly those of a person soliciting by giving counsel or advice to others and of one who enabled and aided others in [the criminal] act." But "in such an enormous and complicated crime as the one we are now considering, wherein many people participated, on various levels and in various modes of activity — the planners, the organizers, and those executing the deeds, according to their various ranks — there is not much point in using ordinary concepts of counseling and soliciting to commit a crime. For these crimes were committed en masse, not only in regard to the number of victims, but also in regard to the numbers of those who perpetuated the crime, and the extent to which any one of the many criminals were close to or remote from the actual killer of the victim means nothing, as far as the measure of his responsibility is concerned. On the contrary, in general the *degree of responsibility increases as we draw further away from the man who uses the fatal instrument with his own hands.*" (*Eichmann in Jerusalem* [New York: Viking Compass Books, 1965], pp. 246-247; Arendt's italics.)

18. *The Origins of Totalitarianism* (New York: Meridian Books, 1958), pp. 478-479.

19. *On Revolution*, p. 222.

20. *Ibid*.

21. For an alternative interpretation of Hegel and Marx to Arendt's reading, see my discussion of Marx in *Praxis and Action*, Part I.

22. These quotations are from Marx's letters to Ruge written in 1843. They are translated in *Writings of the Young Marx on Philosophy and Society*, ed. Loyd D. Easton and Kurt H. Guddat (New York: Doubleday, Anchor, 1967), pp. 212, 214.

23. For a systematic attempt both to recover and develop this conception of critique or critical theory, see the work of Jürgen Habermas, especially *Knowledge and Human Interests* (Boston: Beacon Press, 1971).

VIII. Rebels, Beginners, and Buffoons
Raymond L. Nichols

1. Albert Camus, *The Rebel* [*L'Homme révolté*], trans. A. Bower (New York: Vintage, 1958), p. 4. Versions of this paper were originally presented to the Monash University

Politics Colloquium and to the Melbourne chapter of the Conference on Political Theory. I am indebted to the stimulation provided by my colleagues – especially to a series of exchanges with Carolyn Elliott (University of California, Santa Cruz) from which many of these ideas had their initial, inchoate germination, and to the penetrating comments made on an early draft by Harry Redner and Rufus Davis (Monash University).

2. I have deliberately excluded any reference to the extensive contemporary linguistic philosophical literature on action (e.g., Melden, Hampshire, Strawson, Peters, MacIntyre, Taylor, Louch). I do not wish to deny its own potentials; but its incorporation here would be premature at best, misleading at worst. For the purposes of this essay, rebellion makes the political focus far clearer than the more familiar "paradigms." At all events, any full-blown theory must come later. (See notes 62 and 63.)

3. Camus, *The Rebel*, pp. 13, 14. A hint of Camus's archetypal status is his invocation by the Columbia University "rebels" of 1968, in J. Avorn *et al.*, *Up Against the Ivy Wall* (New York: Atheneum, 1969), p. 223.

4. The Sartre review is quoted from the translation by P. Thody in *Albert Camus: Lyrical and Critical* (London: Hamish Hamilton, 1967), p. 147; the *Combat* article from the translation by J. O'Brien in *Resistance, Rebellion and Death* (New York, Knopf, 1961), p. 59.

5. Camus, *The Myth of Sisyphus*, trans. J. O'Brien (London: Hamish Hamilton, 1971), pp. 16, 18-20 (on intimations) and pp. 11-13, 29-43, 47-52, 57-63, 75, 96-99 (on the three responses).

6. *Myth of Sisyphus*, pp. 24, 30.

7. *Ibid.*, p. 7 (new preface) and pp. 31, 56.

8. *The Rebel*, pp. 5-11, 21. On the "existential contradiction" of absurdism, which Camus so succinctly identifies and transcends in his text here, see the fine study by R. W. K. Paterson, *The Nihilistic Egoist: Max Stirner* (London: Oxford University Press for the University of Hull, 1971), especially pp. 171-172, 187-188, 227-228, 242-243, 249.

9. *The Rebel*, p. 136.

10. *Ibid.*, pp. 13-19, 22. On Spartacus, see pp. 25-27 and 108-110; on human nature, see also pp. 134, 250, 300, 302.

11. *Ibid.*, pp. 3-4, 16-19, 23-28, 58, 101-109, 177, 249. On bourgeois, Stalinist, and Fascist revolutions, see pp. 112-120, 178-183, 188-198. Camus is partly involved here in settling philosophical accounts with existentialism as he knew it in France; and here is the center of his famous quarrel with Sartre over revolution. See *ibid.*, pp. 6 and 249; and cf. M. Merleau-Ponty, *Humanisme et terreur: essai sur le probleme communiste* (Paris: Gallimard, 1947), for a view of revolutionary violence directly opposed to Camus's.

12. *The Rebel*, p. 22.

13. *Ibid.*, pp. 281-282, 287-289, 291-292, 296-298 (and cf. pp. 166-172). On art as a form of rebellion, see pp. 252-272, 276; on limits, moderation, and tension, see also pp. 11, 20, 101, 166-172, 248, 301-302. Camus is consistent in applying his thesis to both French and FLN terrorism in the Algerian struggle: see especially *Actuelles III: Chroniques Algeriennes, 1939-1958* (Paris: Gallimard, 1958), pp. 16-20. The "sap" metaphor of efficacy which Camus employs in *The Rebel* is obviously ambiguous – does it suggest gradualism or simply life? It may indeed suggest a belief in spreading a revised consciousness: see *The Rebel*, pp. 14 and 20 (awareness rather than value), p. 136 (on Hegel), and pp. 273-277 (on a renaissance).

14. *The Rebel*, pp. 21, 303-304; cf. p. 17.

15. See *ibid.*, pp. 169-172; and Camus's play, *Les Justes.*

16. *The Rebel*, p. 16, note 2. After all, Camus dealt in his dissertation in Algiers with

Neoplatonism in Plotinus and Augustine. See Camus's references to the radical syndicalist tradition, *The Rebel*, pp. 217, 230, 297-300; and "Entretien sur la revolte," *Actuelles* II, especially p. 57.

17. *The Rebel*, p. 4. (Cf. p. 252.)

18. *Ibid.*, p. 302. Cf. *ibid.*, pp. 4 and 19. For Camus's pessimism even regarding rebellion, see pp. 292-293.

19. Peter Euben has aptly characterized the nature of this more general reaction: "Political Science and Political Silence," in P. Green and S. Levinson, eds., *Politics and Community: Dissenting Essays in Political Science* (New York: Vintage, 1970), especially pp. 10-14.

20. See André Malraux, *Man's Fate* (*La Condition humaine*), trans. H. M. Chevalier (New York: Modern Library, 1933), pp. 9-19.

21. On Charriére, see J. Weightman, "Moth Myth," *New York Review*, 8 October 1970. Something like my notion of tradition has been suggested by Michael Oakeshott, speaking of "voices in conversation" (*Rationalism in Politics and Other Essays* [London: Methuen, 1962]). But Oakeshott's treatment is savagely vitiated by his orthodox political conservatism, albeit philosophically enshrined: for Oakeshott, the real *is* the rational. Much better is the discussion by J. G. A. Pocock, "Time, Institutions, and Action: An Essay on Traditions and Their Understanding," in P. King and C. Parekh, eds., *Politics and Experience* (Cambridge: Cambridge University Press, 1968), pp. 212-217, 223-223, 237. Cf. also Sheldon Wolin's "radicalization" of Oakeshott, especially his view of culture (albeit less philosophically based), in "Political Theory as a Vocation," *American Political Science Review*, 63 (December 1969), pp. 1062-1082. Perhaps more familiar (though less complete) is L. and S. Rudolph, *The Modernity of Tradition* (Chicago: University of Chicago Press, 1967).

22. See *The Rebel*, pp. 10-11.

23. *Ibid.*, pp. 20-21 and 159.

24. On Rousseau, see *The Rebel*, pp. 114-115, 117; and Insard, *Observations sur le principe qui a produit les révolutions de France, de Genève, et d'Amerique dans le dix-huitième siècle* (Paris: de l'imprimerie de la veuve malassis, du Roi, et de Monseigneur l'Evêque, October 1789), pp. 3-6, 23-28, and *passim*.

25. C. Brinton, *The Anatomy of Revolution* (New York: Vintage, 1958 [1938]), pp. 16-18; Thucydides, *History of the Peloponnesian War*, especially II.52-54 and III.70-84; Burckhardt, *Force and Freedom*, ed. J. H. Nichols (New York: Meridian Books, 1965), pp. 71 and 239-258.

26. Arendt, *On Revolution* (New York: Viking, 1965), pp. 14-16, 21-28, 95-97, 108, 146-149, 152, 199-204. Compare the different view of D. W. Brogan, *The Price of Revolution* (London: Hamish Hamilton, 1951), pp. viii, 1-5, 16-17. On violence, see the ambiguities of Brinton, *Anatomy of Revolution*, pp. vi-vii (1958 preface), 7, 187, 195, 199, 201-207, and pp. 18, 156, 179; L. P. Edwards, *The Natural History of Revolution* (Chicago, University of Chicago Press, 1927), pp. 16-21, 166, and 180; and G. S. Pettee, *The Process of Revolution*, Political Science Associates, Studies in Systematic Political Science and Comparative Government, Vol. V (New York: Harper, 1938), pp. ix, 4-5, 27. On Thermidor see the musings of J. H. Meisel, *Counter-Revolution: How Revolutions Die* (New York: Atherton, 1966), pp. 20-26, 52, 62-63.

27. See T. Kuhn, *The Structure of Scientific Revolutions* (Chicago: University of Chicago Press, 1964), pp. 91-93; and Tom Hayden *et al.*, "The Triple Revolution," in P. Long, ed., *The New Left* (Boston: Porter Sargent, 1969), especially pp. 339-354.

28. On "creative violence," Robert Aron and A. Dandrieu, *La Révolution nécessaire* (Paris: Bernard Grasset, 1933), pp. 7-9, 149-150, 169-170. The clearest call for delimitation

is Harry Eckstein's "Introduction" to *Internal War* (New York: Free Press, 1964), pp. 1-32. Cf. G. S. Pettee, "Revolution, Typology and Process," in C. J. Friedrich, ed., *Nomos VIII: Revolution* (New York: Atherton, 1966), pp. 10-33. The quoted passage on urban violence is from the introductory essay in D. R. Bowen and L. H. Masotti, eds., *Riots and Rebellion: Civil Violence in the Urban Community* (Beverley Hills: Sage Publications, 1968), p. 19.

29. Eugene Kamenka, "The Concept of Political Revolution," in Friedrich, *Nomos VIII*, pp. 122-135. On the general difficulties of building a notion of change around violence, see H. Bienan, *Violence and Social Change: A Review of Current Literature* (Chicago, University of Chicago Press, 1968), pp. 3-11, 21-22, 37-38, 98-99, 103-106.

30. Chalmers Johnson, *Revolutionary Change* (Boston: Little, Brown, 1966), especially pp. 26, 36, 40, 53-60, 153. It is depressing to note that Johnson's three major English-speaking predecessors called (with varying insistence and precision) for something like his model: see Brinton, *Anatomy of Revolution*, pp. 16-18; Edwards, *Revolution*, pp. 7-9, 38-41, 109, 120; Pettee, *The Process of Revolution*, pp. 1-3, 27, 107, 152. Even the notion of a political system is hard to apply with consistency and (political) illumination: see the extraordinary conceptual schizophrenia of Z. Brzezinski and S. P. Huntington, who try to distinguish revolutionary from instrumental political systems, in *Political Power: USA/USSR* (New York: Vintage, 1965), especially pp. 36, 71-77, 91.

31. P. Schrecker, "Revolution as a Problem in the Philsosphy of History," in Friedrich, *Nomos VIII*, pp. 34-52.

32. On rebellion as primitive, see the varying accounts of B. Crozier, *The Rebels* (London: Chatto & Windus, 1960), pp. 9-10, 246; E. J. Hobsbawm, *Primitive Rebels* (Manchester: Manchester University Press, 1959), especially pp. 1-3, 12, 64; Tom Hayden, *Rebellion in Newark* (New York: Vintage/New York Review, 1967), Chap. V and pp. 68-71.

33. E. Wilson, *To the Finland Station* (New York: Doubleday, Anchor, 1940), pp. 6 and 2. On the "Myth of Revolution," cf. the varied interpretations of James Joll, *The Anarchists* (London: Methuen, 1969), Chap. II, pp. 40-58; and Raymond Aron, *The Opium of the Intellectuals*, trans. T. Kilmartin (London: Secker & Warburg, 1957), Chap. 11, pp. 35-65.

34. H. L. Nieburg, *Political Violence: The Behavioral Process* (New York: St. Martin's, 1969), pp. 3 and 4; H. Bourges, "Foreward," *The French Student Revolt*, trans. B. R. Brewster (New York: Hill & Wang, 1968), pp. 1 and 3; Lewis Namier, *1848: The Revolution of the Intellectuals* (New York: Doubleday, Anchor, 1964), p. 5; Bagehot, "Letters on the French Coup d'Etat of 1851" (January 8, 1852), *Bagehot's Historical Essays*, ed. N. St. John-Stevas (New York: Doubleday, Anchor, 1965), pp. 384-385.

35. The translation from the *Iliad* (VI.146) is that of Richmond Lattimore (Chicago: University of Chicago Press, 1951). On mythic rebirth/returning, see M. Eliade, *Cosmos and History* (*The Myth of the Eternal Return*), Bollingen Library (New York: Harper, 1959); Eliade, *Rites and Symbols of Initiation* (*Birth and Rebirth*) (New York: Harper, 1965), *passim*; and Eliade, *Myth and Reality* (New York: Harper, 1968), Chaps. 1-4.

36. See Augustine, *The City of God*, I (preface), XI.6, XII.11 and 20, XIV.13, XV.1 and 21, XVII.24 and 30; *The Confessions*, XI.1, 3-7, 11, 15-20, 24, 26-28.

37. Thucydides, especially III.70 and 82; Plato, *Republic*, 545 d; Aristotle, *Politics*, V, *passim* (and cf. *The Athenian Constitution*, Chap. 41).

38. The reminders from Arendt are in *On Revolution*, pp. 28-32, 35-36, and 38. In contrast, on the emergence of the term revolution from the fourteenth century, see the useful series by Melvin J. Laski in *Encounter*: "The Prometheans" (October 1968), pp. 22-32; "The Metaphysics of Doomsday" (January 1969), pp. 36-47; "The Sweet Dream"

(October 1969), pp. 14-27; and "The Birth of a Metaphor," Parts I and II (February and March 1970), pp. 35-45 and 30-42. Norman Cohn has documented the extension from cosmology to political practice with later medieval millenarialism; but Cohn goes too far in describing the millenarialists as "revolutionary." This seems a reading-back of terms and connotational complexes which commits the reverse error of Arendt's. See *The Pursuit of the Millennium* (New York: Harper, 1961), pp. xiv-xv and 308-309. More apt is his study of the seventeenth century, "The Ranters," *Encounter* (April 1970), pp. 15-25.

39. Compare especially Hobbes's "Introduction" to *Leviathan*, and his repeated condemnation of all figurative (analogical) language, in Chaps. 4, 5, and 8.

40. The translation of the Manifesto is Raymond Postgate's, from *Revolution from 1789 to 1905: Documents Selected and Edited with Notes and Introductions* (New York: Harper, 1962 [1920]), p. 55; the later quotation is from Le R. P. Felix, *Qu'est ce que la revolution?* Collection Saint Michel (Paris: G. Téqui, 1879), pp. 38-47.

41. See *The Rebel*, pp. 189-195, 210-211, 223.

42. Explored more fully in my paper, "Ideology, Theory, and the Problem of Action: Political Controversy and Political Literalism," delivered to the Western Political Science Association Conference, Honolulu, Hawaii, April, 1969; and the subject of a work currently in progress.

43. *The Rebel*, pp. 106, 107.

44. *Leviathan*, Chap. 1. It is interesting to note that Parsons uses action to translate Weber's das Hendeln. As nearly as I can determine, that word comes from die Handlung (deed, performance, transaction, business); it contains the dual, dramatic and material/commercial, connotations of its root, as is indicated by the fact that its most general translation is simply acting—clearly, das Hendeln is by no means unambiguous. Note that Parsons himself says that he chooses action as a translation in order to avoid "the behavioristic connotations of the term behavior" (*The Structure of Social Action* [New York: Free Press, 1949] p. 641, note 4). Parsons, of course, sought to continue Weber's emphasis on finding the meaning of an event or situation to the individuals involved therein, as an alternative to positivistic behaviorism ("external" or mechanistic explanation). But the result, given Parsons's stress on patterns and systems (which he claimed as his major theoretical advance over Weber), was to lose any notion of innovation or creation. Not that this is stressed in Weber's formulation; as I have noted, his own terms were highly ambiguous. But Parsons's treatment seems an ironically justified response to Weber's question, "What is a 'political' association from the sociological point of view?" ("Politics as a Vocation," in L. Gerth and C. Wright Mills, *From Max Weber* [New York: Oxford University Press, 1958], p. 77).

45. See: G. Sorel, *Reflections on Violence* (New York: Collier, 1961), pp. 41-53, 58, 89, 135, 175-191, 211-213, 220-224, 228-232, 242-249; Lenin, *What Is To Be Done?* (New York: International Publishers, n.d.), pp. 14-15, 22-23, 26, 31-49, 54-59, 71-73, 79-89, 167; R. Debray, *Revolution in the Revolution?* (New York: Grove Press, 1967), pp. 15, 20, 27-32, 60, 87-89, 101-106. Also cf. Lenin, *"Left-Wing" Communism, An Infantile Disorder* (New York: International Publishers, 1940), especially pp. 17, 22 ("There are compromises and compromises"), 27-28, 53; and Rosa Luxemburg, *The Russian Revolution (and) Leninism or Marxism?* (Ann Arbor: University of Michigan Press, 1961), pp. 69-70, 88-93, 100, 103, 106 (on life and practice); and Trotsky (on insurrection as a "continuation of politics," *pace* Clausewitz), *The History of the Russian Revolution* (New York: Doubleday, Anchor, 1959), Vol. III, Chap. 6, pp. 306, 310, 312, 315. For creation and rebirth in Maoism, see the provocative interpretation of R. J. Lifton, *Revolutionary Immortality* (New York: Vintage, 1968), especially pp. xvii, 66-71, 77-78,

80-85, and Chap. 4. On the ancient symbolic association of violence, especially fire, with destruction, purification, and creation, see M. J. Laski, "The Prometheans."

46. Abbie Hoffman ("Free"), *Revolution for the Hell of It* (New York: Dial Press, 1968), pp. 9-12, 186, 188.

47. Jerry Rubin, *Do It! A Scenario of the Revolution*, Social Education Foundation (New York: Simon & Schuster, 1970), pp. 37, 56, 87, 116, 125, 247, 251. On rock and roll, Telegraph Avenue, and the "head revolution," see pp. 17-19, 24, and 84; also see Rubin's "revolutionary scenario," with the two-page picture of "Apocalypse" (shades of Durer) and the echo of Marx in the penultimate sentence, pp. 253-256. The "rock and roll revolution" is originally the perception of Eldridge Cleaver, who associates it with a cosmogenic-social myth of his own: *Soul on Ice* (New York: Dell/Ramparts, 1968), pp. 176-190, and pp. 193, 195, 197-199, 202-204. The "end of history" thesis and its criticism (a curious inversion of Marx) is originally that of Mario Savio, "An End to History," reprinted in Hal Draper, ed., *Berkeley: The New Student Revolt* (New York: Grove Press, 1965), pp. 179-182.

48. From the collection of graffiti from "les évènements de mai," ed. J. Besançon, *Les Murs ont la parole: Journal mural, Mai 1968* (Paris: Ed. Claude Tchou, 1968), *passim*. Roughly Englished (much defies exact translation): "Dream is reality. . . . My desires are reality. . . . Be realists, demand the impossible. . . . The imagination seizes power. . . . Blow up your mind [sic] . . . . The Revolution is unbelievable because it is true. . . . Revolution is initiative. . . . Novelty is revolutionary. . . . Revolution, I love you." "The enemy of movement is skepticism. Everything which has been realized comes from dynamism, which springs from spontaneity. . . . There is no revolutionary thought. There are only revolutionary acts. . . . The Act is spontaneous. . . . Action shouldn't be a reaction but a creation. . . . Creativity, Spontaneity, Life. . . . Permanent, cultural vibration. . . . Here one acts spontaneously. . . . Frontiers = repression. . . . Don't insulate your acts!!! . . . Heraclitus returns. Down with Parmenides." Cf. *Posters from the Revolution* (Paris/Indianapolis: Atelier Populaire/Bobbs-Merrill, 1968-1969); also A. Willener, *The Action-Image of Society*, trans. A. M. Sheridan Smith (London: Tavistock, 1970), Chaps. 1 and 2 and Appendix III, for further examples. Willener's own treatment, unfortunately, is rather more ecstatic than analytic (see especially pp. 26-30, 64-68, 224-229, 273, 276-277).

49. Dieter Kunclemann, Berlin "Kommunard," quoted in *Encounter* (November 1970), p. 94; Hoffman, *Revolution*, pp. 27 and 61; Rubin, *Do It!* p. 85. Cf. Fritz Teufel, "Prophylactic Notes for the Self-Indictment of the Accused," in Tariq Ali, ed., *New Revolutionaries* (London: Peter Owen, 1969), especially p. 196; and Daniel and Gabriel Cohn-Bendit, *Obsolete Communism: The Left-Wing Alternative* (London: André Deutsch, 1968), pp. 13, 16, 17, 252-253. Varied examples of "birth/novelty/life/art/politics" can be found in the collection edited by P. Stansill and D. Z. Mairowitz, *BAMN: Outlaw Manifestos and Ephemera, 1965-70* (London: Penguin, 1971), especially pp. 71, 73, 78-79, 142, 145, 148-149, 152, 161, 165-166, 176, 219. See also M. Teodori, ed., *The New Left: A Documentary History* (New York: Bobbs-Merrill, 1969), especially pp. 364-365 and 380.

50. Rubin, *Do It!* pp. 113, 240, 250, (cf. p. 235, and on words, pp. 108-109, 249; on ideology, pp. 115, 246); Hoffman, *Revolution*, pp. 111 and 59 (on words, see pp. 15, 26, 29, 59, 68, 79; on ideology, pp. 36, 56, 61, 89); Besançon, *Les Murs, passim*. Of course, there are some fragmentary notions of post-revolutionary society, and some complete ideologues are evident in the the Paris happenings. But it is the extreme manifestations that concern us here. For similar tangles in relatively "straight" or "orthodox" offerings, see H. Zinn, "Marxism and the New Left," in P. Long, ed., *The New Left* (Boston: Porter Sargent, 1969), pp. 56, 58-59, 63-64, 67-68.

51. Malraux, interviewed in *Encounter* (January 1970), pp. 50-51.

52. Alain Touraine, *Le mouvement de mai ou le communisme utopique* (Paris: Ed. du Seuil, 1968), pp. 128, 202-203; Ronnie Davis, "Guerrilla Theatre: A Way of Life," in Teodori, *The New Left*, p. 397; Marx, letter to Arnold Ruge, in Loyd D. Easton and Kurt H. Guddat, *The Writings of the Young Marx on Philosophy and Society* (New York: Doubleday, Anchor, 1967), p. 204. Compare Kenneth Burke, *A Grammar of Motives* (Berkeley: University of California Press, 1969), "Introduction," Chap. 1, and pp. 59-61. Vague notions of theater/politics, invoked rather than explored, abound in recent activistic writing: see, for example, Hoffman, *Revolution, passim*, and the pieces by Domhoff, Lampe, and Allen Ginsberg in Teodori, *The New Left*. I stumbled on the quoted Marx passage only after completing this essay: its remarkable appropriateness (as will be seen) made its inclusion seem essential. Marx was later to return to the dramatic metaphor in the famous opening passage of *The 18th Brumaire*, where his stance is not unlike Malraux's, quoted previously.

53. Arendt, *The Human Condition* (New York: Doubleday, Anchor, 1959), pp. 9-14, 23-31, 72-76, 91, 125-126, 155-161, 221-222. On behavior, see pp. 10, 37-45, 55.

54. *Ibid.*, pp. 157-162, 167-173 (the last quotation is from p. 170). Arendt does note here (pp. 172-173) one way whereby an actor can determine the nature of his story and *self*-revelation—by making his revelation immediate and total, completing and summarizing his life in a single deed which culminates in his death, and thus allows him to withdraw from the tangled continuation of what he began. We can call this "The Achilles Gambit"; the modern example of Che Guevara immediately comes to mind. But Arendt herself stresses that this procedure is rare and highly "individualistic"; hence the alternative which she proceeds to offer.

55. *Ibid.*, p. 11. The similarities with Camus (and Malraux's *La Condition humaine*) are due to the links between existentialism and phenomenology. But the two strands also part, here notably over whether essence precedes existence, Camus affirming, Arendt and Malraux denying that proposition, all in unusual ways.

56. *Ibid.*, pp. 45-54, 175-179. On wall and laws, cf. pp. 317-318; on glory, also pp. 19, 21, 50-51, 160, 184-185.

57. Arendt's discussion here is intricately tied together: on continual willingness, see *ibid.*, pp. 177-180; on violence, pp. 25-26, 159, 181-182 (elaborated in her later book, *On Violence*); on labor and work (including legislation) as unpolitical, pp. 160-161, 168-169, 172-175, 185, 205-206; on action as an end in itself, also pp. 132-137. On the general "philosophical reversal," see also pp. 15-21, 34, 197-204, 277, and 287.

58. Arendt's criticism of Plato here is a familiar one. Indeed, Plato oddly resembles Marx in ways Arendt does not perceive, because of her own perspective. Both submerge or neglect political action—Plato by the static and nondiscursive nature of his Republic, Marx by his treatment of political action as epiphenomenal. The founder of the ideal polity is the "last actor" in Plato's scenario; the revolutionary proletariat, ushering in the withering of the state and the realization of philsosphy, plays a similar role (and a purely "social" one) in Marx's. But Aristotle's case is far more questionable: after all, he took pains to distinguish between making and doing and did so with explicit reference to the polis. See the *Nichomachean Ethics*, II and VI; and *Politics*, I.5-7, III.9-13, 17, IV.7-8, and *passim*. And Thucydides, to whom Arendt refers only indirectly, stressed the *common* and *constructive* nature of action, not just its supraeconomic links with immortal glory: see the *History*, I.1-3, 8, 10, 11, 16, and II.41-42.

59. *The Human Condition*, pp. 10-11 (my italics).

60. Compare *ibid.*, pp. 23 and 173-174, 176 (before action) with pp. 10 and 177 (after

the public space). The joint suggestion of pp. 10 and 23 is that action can be governmental organization—a view which roughly parallels Arendt's notion of foundation in *On Revolution* (pp. 44-51, 199-207, 214) but contradicts the general thesis of *The Human Condition*. Perhaps a slip, but a revealing one.

61. E. Goffman, *Encounters: Two Studies in the Sociology of Interaction* (Indianapolis: Bobbs-Merrill, 1961), pp. 10, 17-18, 26-27.

62. Note Arendt's reference to her public space as an audience (*The Human Condition*, p. 177, quoted previously); and cf. her comment on theater (*ibid.*, p. 167). My notion of innovation within a political public has obvious links with Weber's charismatic authority; but my suggestion ties up more closely with the watered-down or more mundane version of charisma outlined by S. Benn and R. Peters, *The Principles of Political Thought* (New York: Macmillan, Collier, 1964), pp. 20-22.

63. Goffman, *Encounters*, pp. 27-28. It should be obvious that rebellion is only one form of political action (just as action is only one form of political activity—but behavior, for all its importance, has been far overemphasized of late.) There can be innovation within or in terms of bureaucracies and established institutions. Arendt's foundation, in *On Revolution*, despite its flaws, is an obvious example. More generally, roles can emerge which are not yet normatively regulated (i.e., which have no centrally authorized or, alternatively, no generally and conventionally accepted, performance requirements and statuses); and actors can shift their tasks and their meanings (identities). Goffman devotes the second part of his book to this last possibility—both his terms and his focus tend to obscure the other one ("Role Distance," pp. 85-152). My focus in this essay, however, has been on the more obvious type of action as innovation, i.e., rebellion.

After completing this essay, I encountered another of Goffman's works, which seems to suggest some of the further analytic possibilities—but which also (despite its title) further confirms my contention that we have largely lost a serious and political sense of action. Goffman's usage is like Arendt's but seems much more confused. See the title essay in Goffman, *Where the Action Is* (London: Allen Lane, 1969), especially pp. 134-147, 180-181.

64. L. Kolakowski, *Toward a Marxist Humanism*, trans. J. Z. Peel (New York: Grove Press, 1969 [1968]). pp. 33-34.

65. My translation of the French text, given by E. Welsford in *The Court Masque* (New York: Russell & Russell, 1962), p. 377.

66. A. Nicoll, *Masks, Mimes and Miracles* (New York: Cooper Square, 1963), pp. 17-18.

67. J. Feibleman, *In Praise of Comedy: A Study of Its Theory and Practice* (New York: Russell & Russell, 1962), pp. 18-19, 101-102. On the fool and jester generally, also see W. Kaiser, *Praisers of Folly* (Cambridge: Harvard University Press, 1963), especially pp. 2-4, 6-13, 20-24, 267-273; A. Nicoll, *The Theory of Drama* (New York: Crowell, n.d.); E. K. Chambers, *The Medieval Stage* (Oxford: Oxford University Press, 1903) and *The English Folk-Play* (London: Russell & Russell, 1964); E. Welsford, *The Fool* (London: Russell & Russell, 1935).

68. *Henry IV, Part I*, I.2, lines 105-108.

69. Kolakowski, *Marxist Humanism*, p. 34.

70. Goffman, *Encounters*, p. 58 (his italics).

71. The play was "Le Retour de la foire de Bezons"; the incident is reported in Nicoll, *Masks, Mimes and Miracles*, pp. 281-282.

72. The play was "Love Rules All Dangers"; the incident is reported in T. Niklaus, *Harlequin Phoenix* (London: Bodley Head, 1956), pp. 153-154.

73. From "Arlequin Sauvage," quoted in Niklaus, *Harlequin Phoenix*, p. 112.

74. From "Arlequin Chevalier du Soleil," quoted in C. W. Beaumont, *The History of Harlequin* (New York: Blom, 1967), p. 78.

75. R. Courtney, *Play, Drama, and Thought* (London: Cassell, 1968), p. 121.

76. Welsford, *The Court Masque*, pp. 380-384, 387-388. On the *danse macabre*, see *ibid.*, pp. 77-78; and J. Huizinga, *The Waning of the Middle Ages*.

77. From Garrick's "Harlequin's Invasion" (1759), in E. Stein, ed. *Three Plays by David Garrick* (New York: Bey-Blom, 1967), pp. 25-26. On the origins and development of Harlequin, see Niklaus, *Harlequin Phoenix*, Chap. 1 and pp. 29-30; Beaumont, *History of Harlequin*, Chaps. 1 and 5; Nicoll, *Masks, Mimes, and Miracles*, especially pp. 267-282; Nicoll, *The World of Harlequin* (Cambridge: Cambridge University Press, 1963), *passim* — a superb characterization of Harlequin in his prime is on pp. 70-74; G. Oreglia, *The Commedia dell'arte*, trans. L. F. Edwards (London: Methuen, 1968), Chap. 4; D. C. McClelland, "The Harlequin Complex," in *The Roots of Consciousness* (Princeton: Van Nostrand, 1964). I am indebted to Charles Longley (Department of Psychology, Melbourne University) for drawing my attention to McClelland's piece and its emphasis on the symbolic link between Harlequin and death.

78. W. Kayser, *The Grotesque in Art and Literature*, trans. U. Weisstein (Bloomington: Indiana University Press, 1963), pp. 37-40, 54-55, 181-188.

79. B. Way, *Development Through Drama* (London: Longman's, 1967), p. 2 (his italics).

80. See for example A. R. Thompson, *The Anatomy of Drama* (Berkeley: University of California Press, 1964), pp. 4-9, 119-129, 154-157.

81. R. Schechner, *Public Domain* (Indianapolis: Bobbs-Merrill, 1969), pp. 213-214; J. Grotowski, *Towards a Poor Theatre* (New York: Simon & Schuster, 1969), pp. 22-23, 29-33.

82. See Bertold Brecht, in J. W. Willet's translation, *Brecht on Theatre* (London: Eyre Methuen, 1964), especially pp. 92, 188, 190, 192, and 205. Cf. Martin Esslin, *Brecht: The Man and His Work*, rev. ed. (New York: Doubleday, Anchor, 1960), Chap. 6, especially p. 150. R. Brustein, *The Theatre of Revolt* (London: Methuen, 1965), treats his subject in terms of Camus's "metaphysical rebellion" — and not surprisingly stresses that it is essentially unpolitical, concerned with pure vision and the impossible (pp. 8-9, 416-417). Even Martin Esslin's brilliant study, *The Theatre of the Absurd* (London: Eyre & Spottiswoode, 1964), faces a problem which seems identical with Camus's and equally insoluble in those terms: Esslin sees the absurd theater as producing Brecht's V-effect as Brecht never could but offering nothing "positive" and leaving each member of the audience to make his own, individual response (pp. 16-18, 291-304).

83. See Z. Barbu, "The Sociology of Drama", *New Society* (2 February, 1967), pp. 161-163.

84. Artaud, "Activities of the Surrealist Research Bureau," in *Collected Works*, trans. V. Corti (London: Calder & Boyers, 1968), Vol. I, p. 184. Cf. Artaud's "Le Theatre et son double," in *Oeuvres Completes* (Paris: Gallimard, 1956), Vol. V, especially pp. 272-273; and E. Sellin, *The Dramatic Concepts of Antonin Artaud* (Chicago: University of Chicago Press, 1968), p. 94. There are references to Artaud in Besançon and in Hoffman, *Revolution*.

85. See Part I of this essay; *The Rebel*, pp. 6, 8, 14, 269, 273, 290; and *Resistance, Rebellion and Death*, pp. 43-45, 70-74, 136.

86. *The Rebel*, p. 295.

IX. How People Change Themselves:
The Relationship between Critical Theory and Its Audience
Brian Fay

1. I wish to thank Don Moon, Barry Gruenberg, Phil Hallie, and Julie Schor for commenting on the manuscript and discussing it with me so thoroughly. Without their penetrating and yet supportive analyses, the paper would have been all the weaker. I also wish to acknowledge the inspiration of the deep little book by Allen Wheelis called *How People Change* (New York: Harper & Row, 1973), on which the title and content of the essay is, something of a gloss. Other works not cited in the text but important for the essay are: Isaiah Berlin, "Two Concepts of Liberty," in his *Four Essays on Liberty* (Oxford: Oxford University Press, 1969); Jürgen Habermas, *Theory and Practice* (Boston: Beacon Press, 1973); Alasdair MacIntyre, "Determinism," *Mind*, 66 (January 1957), pp. 23-41 (reprinted in B. Berofsky, ed., *Free Will and Determinism* [New York: Harper & Row, 1966]); MacIntyre, "Ideology, Social Science, and Revolution," *Comparative Politics*, 5, No. 3 (April 1973), pp. 321-342; MacIntyre, "Rationality and the Explanation of Action," in A. MacIntyre, *Against the Self Images of the Age* (London: Duckworth, 1971); John Plamenatz, *Ideology* (New York: Macmillan, 1971); Gary Watson, "Free Agency," *Journal of Philosophy* (April 1975), pp. 205-220; Max Weber, "Science as a Vocation," in H. Gerth and C. Wright Mills, eds., *From Max Weber* (London: Routledge & Kegan Paul, 1952); Albrecht Wellmer, *Critical Theory of Society* (New York: Herder & Herder, 1971).

The essay is meant to develop themes I only sketched in my *Social Theory and Political Practice* (London: Allen & Unwin, 1975; New York: Holmes & Meir, 1976), Chap. 5.

2. By putting the question in terms of reason guiding our actions, the underlying rationalism of the paper ought to be apparent. I mention this to indicate a basic commitment of the paper, for there are other views of theory and practice (those of Hegel and Oakeshott, for example) which are antithetical to this forward-looking rationalism.

3. For a philosophical account of why there is a conceptual connection between naturalist metatheories of social science and the instrumentalist model of theory and practice, see J. Habermas, *Knowledge and Human Interests* (Boston: Beacon Press, 1971), Chap. 6; and Fay, *Social Theory and Political Practice*, Chap. 2.

4. For an historical survey, see Nicholas Lobkowicz, *Theory and Practice: History of a Concept From Aristotle to Marx* (Notre Dame, Ind.: University of Notre Dame Press, 1967).

5. It is just such naiveté which makes so many critical analyses mere rhetoric whose sole use is a kind of empty preaching. It is this sort of pious and sentimental belief in the efficacy of theory which characterized the Left Hegelians and which Marx so brutally criticized in *The German Ideology* (in Loyd D. Easton and Kurt H. Guddat, eds., *Writings of the Young Marx on Philosophy and Society* [New York: Doubleday, Anchor, 1967]).

6. Of course, as is obvious from what I said earlier, this does not imply that people will always be able to say why they acted or even know why they did so. They may act but not know why they so acted, and this may be out of ignorance or self-deception; they may even act one way while claiming they are acting in another. (Indeed it is just this sort of unclarity which an educative theory seeks to remove.) When I say that actions are partly caused by self-understandings, I am not thereby saying that all actions are caused by consciously articulated self-understandings.

7. The relation of this to Marx's analysis of suffering in terms of alienation and its transcendence ought to be apparent here. For the alienated person is one who is a victim of processes that are in some sense creations of his own activity, and the first step in the process of de-alienation is the recognition of this fact.

8. In *Social Theory and Political Practice*, Chap. 5. It is important to note that in some circles the term critical theory does not refer to a particular *metatheoretical* conception of social science (as it does in this paper) but rather to the particular substantive *theories* of modern life associated with the Frankfurt school.

9. I adopt this term from G. H. von Wright, *Explanation and Understanding* (Ithaca: Cornell University Press, 1971), Chap. 4. Quasi-causal is meant to draw attention to the fact that in these sorts of condition-relationships consciousness functions as a mediator between the determining antecedent factors and the subsequent action. In other words, people act according to their interpretations of, and intentions toward, their external conditions, rather than being governed directly by them, and, therefore, these conditions must be understood not as causes but as warranting conditions that make a particular action appear reasonable or appropriate (given the beliefs and desires of the actors).

10. On this, see pages 217-221.

11. See J. Habermas, *Legitimation Crisis* (Boston: Beacon Press, 1975).

12. The clearest instance of this is in the writings of Saint-Simon.

13. It is also the only way to conceive of the instrumentalist model in a nonelitist manner, since the person is applying the social theory to himself.

14. Stuart Hampshire, *Freedom of the Individual* (London: Chatto & Windus, 1965).

15. Hampshire only says these things about feelings that he claims (mistakenly, but for reasons too complicated to go into here) are not "thought-dependent." For feelings that are "thought-dependent" he gives an account of theory and practice much like that of the educative model (*Freedom of the Individual*, p. 105). But he nowhere develops this account, nor does he distinguish it from his instrumentalism.

16. His belief in incompatabilism mars Wheelis's treatment of determinism and free will in psychotherapy (*How People Change*, Chap. 7). However, I think much of what he says there can be salvaged by purging it of this mistaken belief.

17. Freud, *The Future of an Illusion* (New York: Doubleday, 1961), p. 49.

18. For a discussion of these, see Fay, *Social Theory and Political Practice*, pp. 98-101.

19. See Georg Lukács, *History and Class Consciousness* (Cambridge, Mass: M.I.T. Press, 1971).

20. See Herbert Marcuse, *An Essay on Liberation* (Boston: Beacon Press, 1969), pp. 4-16.

21. At other places (pp. 80-84) he seems to think that revolution will occur when economic crises will lead to a "legitimation crisis" among vast numbers in industrial society. Why such a crisis would not lead to a New Fascism among people, given the "biological nature" that Marcuse says they have, he never even addresses.

22. For a discussion of the practices at Kingsley Hall, see Morton Schatzman, "Madness and Morals," in R. Boyers and R. Orrill, eds., *R. D. Laing and Anti-Psychiatry* (New York: Knopf, 1972), especially pp. 252-272.

23. Freire, in *Pedagogy of the Oppressed* (New York: Herder & Herder, 1972), develops a quite elaborate process (see especially pp. 101-108) in order to accomplish this. The interesting thing here is the amount of input that the students themselves provide in planning their own education—the process of conscientizaçao begins before the official teaching even commences.

24. See Rousseau, *Social Contract*, Book II, Chap. 10. Actually, the little that Rousseau does say about the process of establishing a free and just political order is at odds with the educative model I just outlined. He believed that people would be so attached to their unfree political order that there was little hope that they would or could make it free, and

he believed that even with a relatively undeveloped country, the emergence of such an order required the presence of a Legislator whose authority was ultimately based on "Divine Inspiration" (see Book II, Chap. 7). This is clearly an instrumentalist approach which anticipates Weber's charismatic type of authority.

25. On the Marxist conception of theory and practice as following the educative model, see his "Toward the Critique of Hegel's Philosophy of Law: Introduction" and the "Theses on Feuerbach," in Easton and Guddat, *Writings of the Young Marx*; and Shlomo Avineri, *The Social and Political Thought of Karl Marx* (London: Cambridge University Press, 1969), especially Chap. 5. For a criticism of Marx as being a utopian on the question of revolution, see M. Rubel, "Reflections on Utopia and Revolution," in E. Fromm, ed., *Socialist Humanism* (New York: Doubleday, Anchor, 1966).

26. In *Leninism or Marxism? (The Russian Revolution and Leninism or Marxism?* [Ann Arbor: University of Michigan Press, 1961]), Rosa Luxemburg does set out a conception of revolution in which "the activity of the party organization, the growth of the proletarian's awareness of the objective of the struggle and the struggle itself, are not different things separated chronologically and mechanically. They are only different aspects of the same process" (p. 88). In this conception, however—as Lukács so ably pointed out in his "Critical Observations on Rosa Luxemburg's 'Critique of the Russian Revolution'" (*History and Class Consciousness*, pp. 272-295)—Luxemburg never really developed in either her theoretical work or her practical political activity an analysis of how such a class consciousness could be achieved among a proletariat that had internalized the values of the bourgeoisie. Instead, she depended on the *spontaneous emergence* of proletarian class consciousness and thereby obviated the need for an analysis on her part of how to overcome resistance. Unfortunately, such a view is utopian, and, from the point of view of the educative model, a regressive step.

27. This is one of the reasons that Edgar Friedenberg in his book *R. D. Laing* (New York: Viking Press, 1974) claims Laing is an essentially antipolitical thinker (see pp. 84-86). Also, Avineri in his epilogue claims that the central weakness of Marx—and one that led to the instrumentalist misuse of his theory by totalitarian regimes—was partly a result of his inability to see the requirements of mass political action (the vulgarization of theory, an idolatrous attitude toward the founding fathers of Marxism, a hierarchically organized party) and of conspiratorial revolution (a tightly knit cadre organized on dictatorial lines). See *The Social and Political Thought of Karl Marx*, pp. 250-258.

28. Habermas makes this point in his essay "On Systematically Distorted Communication" in *Inquiry*, 13 (1970), p. 374; and Laing seems to be saying this in "The Study of Family and Social Contexts in Relation to 'Schizophrenia,'" *Politics of the Family and Other Essays* (New York: Random House, 1971), p. 48.

29. Another reason is their belief in the causal significance of people's beliefs in producing behavior. In this they differ from another instrumentalist thinker, B. F. Skinner, who, in blurring the distinction between action and movement and, therefore, in denying the causal efficacy of ideas, thinks it is unnecessary to engage in "consciousness raising" or "ideology-critique." Of course, one of the difficulties for Skinner—as critics have been quick to point out—is what effect he thought writing his book *Beyond Freedom and Dignity* (New York: Knopf, 1972), could possibly have, given the theory contained in it.

30. On Chinese techniques of brainwashing, cf. Robert J. Lifton, *Thought Reform and the Psychology of Totalism* (New York: Norton, 1961).

31. See E. Goffman, *Asylums* (New York: Doubleday, 1961).

32. Thus, it is only certain kinds of suffering that a critical theory can hope to eliminate, i.e., suffering which is both caused by other people and by the false-consciousness of the

sufferers. There are other sources of suffering—for example, suffering caused by others but not derived from the illusions and unwitting cooperation of the sufferers, existential suffering derived from the human condition, or physical suffering caused by injury—which a critical theory will not be able to eliminate. A critical theorist need not be committed to the possibility of creating heaven on earth (though some, like Marx, have been such utopians).

33. For a most interesting account of a drug clinic—Oddyssey House—which incorporates just the elements I have mentioned and which is an excellent case study of the educative model in action, see Judianne Densen-Gerber, *We Mainline Dreams* (Baltimore: Penguin, 1974).

34. For a justification along the lines of the educational model of the contemporary trend toward community cooperation of all sorts in the New Left's struggle to create a socialist society, see Gar Alperovitz, "Notes toward a Pluralist Commonwealth," in S. Lynd and G. Alperovitz, *Strategy and Program* (Boston: Beacon Press, 1973), especially pp. 89-96 and 103-106.

35. Another lesson it can teach is the mistake—usually developing out of the conspiratorial air generated by thinking that revolutions consist of a small group seizing power—of conceiving that social revolutions are conducted by a monolithic and homogeneous group controlled from the center following the correct ideological line.

36. Those who benefit may also suffer (the capitalists are also alienated; men suffer as a result of sexism, too), but because they do enjoy some benefit from this position, it is very unlikely that they will generally respond favorably to a critical analysis and to the consequent revolutionary activity that will lead to their own downfall.

37. Thus it is partly because of the difficulties to which this question points that Lenin justified an antidemocratic and elitist party which stands above its audience and acts in its name, i.e., an essentially instrumentalist conception of theory and practice. See *What Is To Be Done?* trans. J. Fineberg and G. Hanna (New York: International Publishers, 1969), Chap. 4, Sect. B. " 'Gonspiratorial' Organization and 'Democratism.' "